MODERN CHINESE

现代中文

TEXTBOOK 1B
SIMPLIFIED CHARACTERS

MODERN CHINESE 现代中文

Textbook Volume 1B

First Edition

Project Director:	James P. Lin
Editorial Consultant:	Li-Hsiang Yu Shen
Project Manager:	Angel Yeh
Assistant Editors:	Sue-Ann Ma and Christopher Peacock
Curriculum Advisors:	Norman Masuda and Rebecca Starr
Executive Publisher:	Chi-Kuo Shen
Illustrations:	Better World Ltd

© 2012 BETTER CHINESE LLC (a Better World LTD company)

Library of Congress Cataloging-in-Publication Data: To be Assigned

ISBN: 978-1-60603-484-2

1 2 3 XLA 14 13 12

For more information about our products, contact us at:

United States

640 Waverley Street

Palo Alto, CA 94301

Tel: 888-384-0902

Fax: 888-384-0901

Email: usa@betterchinese.com

Contents 目录

Modern Chinese has been several years in the making. Our company started this series because we believed there was a real need for a refreshing and relevant beginner-level college curriculum with engaging content, intuitive structure, and empowering technology.

The creation of *Modern Chinese* incorporated all of the pedagogical experiences that have allowed us to become one of the leading K-12 Chinese language publishers in the world. We began our journey by studying why our teachers and students love our existing curricula, which include the titles *My First Chinese Words*, *My First Chinese Reader*, *Discovering Chinese*, and *Magical Tour of China*. We then took our *Discovering Chinese* series to college professors, asking them to highlight what they liked about it and what they looked for in a college textbook. After years of research and writing, the result was *Modern Chinese*.

This program is revolutionary in many ways. The lessons appear in a complete story-based format that scaffolds vocabulary and grammar patterns from prior lessons to instill confidence in new learners. We took a new approach to the presentation of grammar, focusing on simple explanations and offering practical examples. In addition, we included enriching cultural spotlights to cultivate cultural awareness as well as a variety of exercises to encourage real-life communication. An accompanying website also offers supplemental learning tools such as lesson animations, audio recordings, and online practices.

Better Chinese is grateful to all those who have helped us with the creation of *Modern Chinese*. We would like to thank the authors of our K-12 curricula, which established the foundation for this series. Special thanks go to our Executive Publisher, Chi-Kuo Shen, for supporting this project; Chief Educator, Li-Hsiang Shen, for sharing her love of education and her inspirational attitude; Norman Masuda for sharing his years of classroom teaching experience and expertise in the area of language acquisition; Rebecca Starr for her invaluable insights as a linguist and providing a non-native learner's perspective; and some of the early team members who contributed to the research and pilot of the program, including Stephanie Puk, Sandra Tung, Chung Trung, and Hope Tammany. We would like to express our gratitude to the professors who provided feedback through various rounds of reviews: Wenhui Chen of Washington University in St. Louis; Hong Li of Emory University; Xianmin Liu of Vanderbilt University; Xuehong Lu of State University of New York at Buffalo; Christopher Lupke of Washington State University; Li Ma of Florida International University. We also wish to thank our advisory board members: Professor Yujie Ge of Santa Clara University, Professor Hong Jiang of Northwestern University, and Professor Cynthia Hsien Shen of University of Florida, each of whom provided invaluable and constructive feedback. Most importantly, Better Chinese would like to recognize the *Modern Chinese* team: Project Manager Angel Yeh for her creative story-telling abilities and critical eye in overseeing every detail of the *Modern Chinese* project; Joyce Fung, Sue-Ann Ma, and Christopher Peacock for their relentless pursuit of editorial perfection; and Roger Hsieh for his technical support.

Finally, on a personal note, I would like to thank my wife, Clarissa Shen, for her support, and my wonderful children, Maia and Lucas, for inspiring me to make this world a better place. I hope that by making *Modern Chinese* engaging, relevant, and effective, we will encourage more students to continue their studies of Chinese language and culture, empowering them to bring the world a little closer together.

James P. Lin
Project Director
February 2012

MODERN CHINESE 现代中文
Scope and Sequence

Units	Communication Goals	Structure Notes	Language Notes & Cultural Spotlights
中文 **Prelude: The Chinese Language**	• Learn the pinyin romanization system • Speak Chinese characters with standard tones and sentence inflection • Understand Chinese tonal changes (tone sandhi)	1. *Understand the 4 Chinese tones* 2. *Learn the Chinese phonetic system, pinyin* 3. *Understand the rules of Chinese stroke order*	• Understand the history of the Chinese language • Identify where the Chinese language is spoken today • Learn about the development of written Chinese, including simplified and traditional Chinese characters
我 **UNIT 1 Me**	• Greet and say goodbye to people • Introduce yourself and exchange names with others • Ask and answer questions pertaining to age and nationality • Count from 1 to 99	1. *Use an adjective phrase to describe a subject* 2. *Use 们 to convert a pronoun or noun (people only) to its plural form* 3. *Use 也 to express "also"* 4. *Use 吗 to turn a statement into a question* 5. *Use 呢 to ask "What about...?"* 6. *Use 叫 to state one's name* 7. *Use 什么 to ask "what?" questions* 8. *Use 多大 to ask about somone's age* 9. *Add 岁 after a number to state one's age* 10. *Use 是 to indicate equivalency* 11. *Use 哪国人 to ask about nationality and country + 人 to state nationality* 12. *Use 不 to negate a verb* 13. *Use Verb + 不 + Verb to form affirmative-negative questions* 14. *Use Verb or 不 + Verb to answer affirmative-negative questions*	• Understand how Chinese greet and address one another • Learn the structure of Chinese names • Learn about the Chinese diaspora • Learn how to ask for someone's age politely using the Chinese zodiac • Understand the rationale behind Chinese names for countries • Learn Chinese hand gestures for numbers 1 to 10 • Learn the connotations of the numbers 4 and 8 in Chinese culture • Learn about the Chinese Zodiac
家 **UNIT 2 Family**	• Identify family members and ask others about their families • Ask whether someone has pets • Ask and answer questions regarding quantity • Inquire about someone's occupation • Ask and answer questions about what languages one can speak	1. *Use 有 to express possession* 2. *Use 没有 to express "not have"* 3. *Use 有没有 to form a "have or not have" question* 4. *Use 有什么 to ask what one has* 5. *Use 的 to indicate possession* 6. *Use number + measure word to quantify a noun* 7. *Use 几 + measure word to ask how many and number + measure word to answer* 8. *Use 这 or 那 to express "this" or "that"* 9. *Use 谁 to ask "who?"* 10. *Use 还有 to express "also"* 11. *Use 会 to state what one knows how to do* 12. *Use 会不会 to ask whether or not one knows how to do something* 13. *Use 只 to express "only"*	• Learn how to address different family members in Chinese • Understand the evolution of the traditional Chinese family • Learn how people regard pets in China • Learn about the giant pandas in China • Understand the global response to studying Chinese as a world language • Learn about other varieties of spoken Chinese • Learn about the traditional professions of China

Units	Communication Goals	Structure Notes	Language Notes & Cultural Spotlights
时 **UNIT 3** **Time**	• State and ask the time • Talk about future events • Make appointments • Apologize for tardiness • Ask and answer questions about days of the week and months • State and ask for the date • Wish someone "happy birthday" and offer gifts	1. Use 会 to indicate the possibility of an action taking place in the future 2. Use 什么时候 to ask "when" 3. Use 星期几 to ask "what day of the week" and 星期 + number to state the day of the week 4. Use 几点 to discuss time 5. Use 差不多 to express "almost" 6. Use 还没(有) to express "not yet" or "still have not" 7. Use 吧 to make a suggestion 8. Use 几 to ask "what month" and "what day" 9. Use 都 to mean "both" or "all" 10. Use 了 to indicate a change of state or situation 11. Use the verb 送 in the context of gift giving 12. Use 的 to modify nouns	• Learn about auspicious dates in the Chinese calendar • Learn about how to tell time in Chinese • Compare the differences between the lunar and Western calendars • Look at the ways in which birthdays are celebrated in China • Understand the symbolism of certain gifts in China
食 **UNIT 4** **Food**	• Inquire and express preferences for food and drink • Express hunger • Order food and drinks at a restaurant • Discuss various dishes and their flavors • Offer to pay for a meal	1. Use 想 to indicate a desired action 2. Use 给 to mean "to give" 3. Use 喜欢 to express liking something or someone 4. Use Verb + 不 + Verb with two-character verbs to form affirmative-negtaive questions 5. Use 那(么) to mean "Well then" or "In that case" 6. Use 好 + Verb to form a compound adjective 7. Use 怎么样 to ask for an opinion of something 8. Use 太...了 to describe an exaggerated attribute 9. Use 要 to indicate desire 10. Use 为什么 and 因为 to ask questions and give explanations respectively 11. Use 一下 to express the brevity of an action	• Look at special pronouns in Mandarin Chinese and when to omit them • Learn about regional Chinese cuisines • Learn about symbolism in Chinese cuisine • Learn about Chinese uses of onomatopoeia • Learn about the Chinese equivalents of foreign names and locations • Learn about Chinese dining etiquette • Discover the art of tea
住 **UNIT 5** **Daily Lives**	• Make simple introductions of others • Be able to state where you or others live • Name buildings and facilities on campus • Be able to describe relative locations • Name furniture and rooms in a house • Use the appropriate expressions on the telephone	1. Use 在 to indicate location 2. Use 在 as a verb complement 3. Use 哪里 to ask "where" 4. Use 要 to talk about future events 5. Use 跟...一起 to express doing things together 6. Use 可以 to express permission 7. Use 在 with an action verb to indicate the location of an activity 8. Use 到 as a resultative complement to indicate completion of an action 9. Use 得 or 不 and a resultative complement to indicate whether it is possible or not possible to reach a result 10. Use 可能 to express likelihood	• Learn about introductions in Chinese • Learn about verb-object compounds • Learn about traditional Chinese architecture (Si He Yuan) • Discover some of the universities with study abroad opportunities in China • Review some spatial location words used in Chinese

Units	Communication Goals	Structure Notes	Language Notes & Cultural Spotlights
	• Ask and answer questions about relative locations	11. Use completion 了 to describe completed actions 12. Use 就 to indicate "right" or "precisely"	• Learn some of the contemporary slang used for texting • Learn about the art of Feng Shui and its modern applications
买 **UNIT 6** **Shopping**	• Ask about the availability and cost of different items or products in a store • Understand and use different denominations and amounts of money • Negotiate prices • Indicate that you wish to pay for an item with either cash or credit card • Use the correct expressions when paying with cash and receiving change	1. Use 有 to express existence rather than possession 2. Use 得 to express "must" 3. Use 给 as the preposition "to" 4. Use 多少 to ask "how many" or "how much" 5. Use Adjectives with (一)点(儿) to express "a little more" 6. Use 还是…吧 to express a suggested alternative 7. Use 再 to indicate a repeating action 8. Use 因为…所以… to express causal relationships 9. Use 不用 to say "need not" 10. Use 这么 or 那么 to intensify adjectives 11. Use Verb + 了 to describe specific completed actions 12. Use 已经 to express "already" 13. Use 要是…(的话)…就 to say "if… then…" 14. Use (是)…还是…to express either-or questions	• Learn how to bargain in Chinese markets • Learn about Silk Street • Learn about trade along the Silk Road • Learn about how Western chains have impacted China
行 **UNIT 7** **Travel &** **Navigation**	• Ask and answer questions about vacation plans • Give information about one's hometown and family background • Describe the attractions of China's capital • Express the distance between two places • Give and receive directions • Describe different modes of transportation	1. Use 的时候 to create "when" expressions 2. Use 才 to indicate an action occurring later than anticipated 3. Use 从 with a place word to indicate origin 4. Use 是…的 to emphasize the time, locale, or manner of a completed action 5. Use 送…去 to mean "take" 6. Use 离 to express location relative to a reference point 7. Use 到 with place words to indicate destination 8. Use 怎么 to ask how something is done 9. Use 往 to indicate directional movement 10. Use 先…, 再…, 然后 to indicate a sequence of events	• Learn the meaning of "hometown" in Chinese • Discover the relationship between seasons and how it classifies vacations • Learn about various modes of transportation in China • Discover activities done during China's "Golden Weeks" • Learn common direction expressions • Discover some of Beijing's historical hotspots

Units	Communication Goals	Structure Notes	Language Notes & Cultural Spotlights
学 **UNIT 8** **Academics**	• Discuss classes and school subjects • Express interest in something • Indicate levels of difficulty • Discuss exams, homework, and classroom situations • Ask to borrow something • Express subjective opinions	1. Use 懂 as a resultative complement to indicate ability to understand 2. Use 多 or 少 to express doing an activity more or less often 3. Use 只好 to indicate the best course of action among limited options 4. Use Verb + 完 to describe completed actions 5. Use 以后 to express "after doing something" 6. Use Verb + 了 to describe a sequence of events 7. Use 把 to indicate an action performed on a specific object 8. Use 怎么 to ask "how come" questions 9. Use 怎么这么/那么 to express incredulity or amazement regarding a situation 10. Use 一...就... to express "as soon as A, B" 11. Use 觉得 to express subjective opinions 12. Use 还是 with adjectives to compare qualities 13. Use 第 to express ordinal numbers 14. Use (正)在 ...(呢) to indicate ongoing actions	• Review previously learned radicals and learn about phono-semantic compounds • Learn about China's Four Great Inventions • Learn about homographs in the Chinese language • Learn about examinations in China • Learn about the Four Treasures of the Study
衣 **UNIT 9** **Fashion**	• Name different articles of clothing • Discuss and find appropriate sizes • Make comparisons and express sameness • List and express preferences for different colors • Make use of some basic loan words • Express superlatives	1. Use 或者 to express choices and options 2. Use 看/听 + 起来 to express a subjective impression 3. Use 比 to make comparisons 4. Use 更 to say "even more" 5. Use (一)点(儿) to describe small differences 6. Use 又...又... to express "both... and..." 7. Use 跟...一样 (adjective) to express sameness 8. Use Verb 一 Verb to describe casual or brief activities 9. Use 最 to express superlatives 10. Use reduplication to intensify adjectives or adverbs 11. Use Verb reduplication to describe casual or brief activities 12. Use 看 to mean "and see" 13. Use 有(一)点(儿) to express "somewhat" 14. Use 好 as an intensifier	• Review use of adjectives • Learn about color symbolism in Chinese • Learn about clothing terms • Explore Chinese fashion trends • Learn the history of foot-binding

Units	Communication Goals	Structure Notes	Language Notes & Cultural Spotlights
娱 **UNIT 10** **Hobbies & Activities**	• Inquire about what people like to do in their free time • Discuss sports and leisure activities • Express how often you like to do something • Discuss musical performances and instruments • Describe how well somebody does something • Indicate time periods and duration	1. Use 一边...一边 to describe simultaneous actions 2. Use 什么 to mean "any" 3. Use topic-comment sentences 4. Use 有的 to mean "some" 5. Use 对...有兴趣 to express interest in something 6. Use 常常 to express "often" 7. Use 能 to describe ability 8. Use name + 他们 to refer to a group of people 9. Use 得 to describe the manner of actions 10. Use 每...都... to express "every" 11. Use time periods to indicate duration 12. Use multiple numbers to estimate amounts 13. Use 不是...吗? to ask a rhetorical question 14. Use 对 as the preposition "to, towards"	• Learn about pictographs and ideographs in the evolution of Chinese characters • Learn about the culture of Karaoke or Chinese KTV • Learn about Mahjong • Learn about Chinese Martial Arts
情 **UNIT 11** **Relationships & People**	• Arrange to go on a date with someone • Describe a person's qualities and attributes • Discuss relationships, marriage, and break-ups • Describe your emotions • Refer to something using the passive voice • Talk about past experiences	1. Use 得 to indicate degree or result 2. Use 次 to express number of times 3. Use 让 to express to "let" or "make" someone do something 4. Use 记住 to describe keeping something in mind 5. Use 被 to form the passive voice 6. Use 一直 to express "constantly" 7. Use Verb + 过 to express a past experience	• Review loan words and associative compounds • Learn about Chinese Valentine's Day and the story of Qixi • Learn about China's Tallest Couple • Discuss relationship terms • Examine Chinese punctuation • Observe Chinese wedding traditions
医 **UNIT 12** **Medicine**	• Inquire after a person's health • Describe the symptoms of an illness • Talk about the weather and the seasons • Name illnesses and afflictions • Refer to different parts of the body • Describe some of the differences between Chinese and Western medicine	1. Use 最好 to make suggestions 2. Use 带 to express bringing objects or people 3. Use noun or measure word reduplication to express "every" 4. Use name/pronoun + 那儿 to talk about someone's location or home 5. Use 地 to express the manner in which an action is performed 6. Use 帮 to mean "for" 7. Use 好 as a resultative complement to describe a properly completed action 8. Use 又...了 to say "again"	• Review intensifiers used in the Chinese language • Learn about expressions used to discuss the weather • Learn about massages and Chinese Morning Exercises • Identify body parts in Chinese • Understand the difference between 等一会儿 and 一下 • Review different ways to talk about weeks • Learn about Western versus Eastern medicinal differences • Understand the importance of hot and cold foods in Chinese medical tradition

Units	Communication Goals	Structure Notes	Language Notes & Cultural Spotlights
商 **UNIT 13** **Business**	• Talk about your full- or part-time job • Offer words of encouragement • Indicate that something is unexpected • Discuss internships and working in China • Talk about your employment experience and resume • Discuss your post-graduation plans • Learn about the importance of *guanxi* or "connections"	1. Use 没想到 *to introduce an unexpected event* 2. Use 难怪 *to express "no wonder"* 3. Use 什么样 *to ask "what kind?"* 4. Use 不但... 而且... *to express "not only...but also..."* 5. Use 虽然... 但是... *to express "although...however..."* 6. Use 从...到... *to express length of time* 7. Use 想要 *to express a desire* 8. Use 极了 *as an intensifier* 9. Use 跟...有关 *to express relevance to a subject* 10. Use Noun + 这样/那样 *to say "this/ that type of..."*	• Identify different work titles • Learn about the concept of *guanxi*, or business relationships/networking in China • Review different professions • Examine basic characteristics of a Chinese resume • Learn about China's Special Economic Zones and find out the meaning of the term 'iron rice bowl'
节 **UNIT 14** **Festivals**	• Talk about the customs and traditions of Chinese New Year • Use the appropriate expressions to convey New Year's greetings and wishes • Indicate that something is an ongoing action • Compare and contrast various Chinese and Western holidays • Discuss the different foods that are eaten during Chinese holidays • Expand on a topic by providing examples	1. Use 用...来... *to describe the means of doing something* 2. Use 着 *to indicate an ongoing action* 3. Use 快要...了 *to say "be about to"* 4. Use 的时候 *to express "when the time comes"* 5. Use 像 *to express "resemble" or "is like"* 6. Use 越来越 *to mean "increasingly"* 7. Use 比方说 *to say "for example"* 8. Use 连...都 *to say "even..."*	• Observe greetings performed during Spring Festival • Learn about the use of idioms in the Chinese language • Learn about customs related to Tomb Sweeing Festival, the Dragon Boat Festival, and the Mid-Autumn Festival • Identify important foods related to Chinese holidays • Learn about the development of writing horizontal and vertical text in Chinese • Understand customs used during Chinese New Year and the Lantern Festival

Units	Communication Goals	Structure Notes	Language Notes & Cultural Spotlights
礼 **UNIT 15** **Chinese Ways**	• Politely ask someone to do something • Understand and follow Chinese social conventions • Use correct etiquette towards one's elders • Name some features of traditional Chinese culture • Express that one has "just" done something • Make basic comparisons between ancient and modern Chinese culture	1. Use 麻烦 to make requests 2. Use 来 before verbs to express commencing an activity 3. Use 要不然 to say "or else" or "otherwise" 4. Use 正好 to express "as it happens"; "happen to…" 5. Use 刚 or 刚刚 to express "just now" 6. Use nouns with 化 to form "-ize" verbs or "-ized" adjectives 7. Use 比如(说) to say "for instance" and give examples 8. Use double-了 to describe an action continuing up to the present	• Understand the Chinese concept of "face" • Compare the difference between 客气 and 礼貌 • Learn about Confucius and his teachings • Learn about the difference between classical and modern Chinese language usage • Learn about Daoism
@ **UNIT 16** **Technology & Modern China**	• Use expressions related to computers and the internet • Discuss city lifestyles • Understand and use the "besides" construction • Express that you will miss someone • Use terms for posting letters and packages as well as sending emails • Wish someone a safe trip	1. Use 除了…以外 to say "besides…" 2. Use question words with 都 to express "any" or "every" 3. Use 自己 to refer to oneself or another 4. Use 等 to express "at the point when/by the time" 5. Use Verb Phrase 给 Someone 看/听 to express doing something to show someone else 6. Use 陪 to express keeping someone company 7. Use 会…的 to stress that something will be the case 8. Use 死 to mean "extremely" or "to death"	• Learn about internet cafes • Review learned measure words • Explore Beijing's modern architecture • Learn about internet use in China • Review sentence-final particles • Learn about cell phone use in China • Learn more about the Maglev Train and China's high-speed rail

衣

Fashion

第九单元
UNIT 9

买衣服
Shopping for Clothes

欢迎光临！

你今天想买什么衣服？

máo yī
我想买毛衣、
chèn shān   qún zi
衬衫，还有裙子。

走吧，
我们去
máo yī
看毛衣。

jiàn máo yī
这件毛衣太大了，
chuān zhōng hào
你应该穿中号的
huò zhě xiǎo hào
或者小号的。

课 文 LESSON TEXT

LESSON TEXT 9.1

Shopping for Clothes 买衣服

Sun Mali and Zhang Anna are shopping for a sweater, shirt, and skirt for Sun Mali. After consdering different items, Sun Mali finds a sweater and matching skirt.

售货员：	欢迎光临！	Huānyíng guānglín!
王小美：	你今天想买什么衣服？	Nǐ jīntiān xiǎng mǎi shénme yīfu?
孙玛丽：	我想买毛衣、衬衫，还有裙子。走吧，我们去看毛衣。	Wǒ xiǎng mǎi máoyī, chènshān, háiyǒu qúnzi. Zǒu ba, wǒmen qù kàn máoyī.
张安娜：	这件毛衣太大了，你应该穿中号的或者小号的。	Zhèi jiàn máoyī tài dà le, nǐ yīnggāi chuān zhōnghào de huòzhě xiǎohào de.

孙玛丽：	这件很漂亮，你觉得呢？	Zhèi jiàn hěn piàoliang, nǐ juéde ne?
张安娜：	我觉得这件看起来比那件更大！	Wǒ juéde zhèi jiàn kànqilai bǐ nèi jiàn gèng dà!
孙玛丽：	可是这件比那件便宜一点。	Kěshì zhèi jiàn bǐ nèi jiàn piányi yì diǎn.
张安娜：	你看，这件红色的毛衣是中号的，又漂亮又便宜。	Nǐ kàn, zhèi jiàn hóngsè de máoyī shì zhōnghào de, yòu piàoliang yòu piányi.
孙玛丽：	不错啊！裙子呢？	Bú cuò a! Qúnzi ne?
张安娜：	这条裙子跟那件毛衣一样便宜，也很配。	Zhèi tiáo qúnzi gēn nèi jiàn máoyī yíyàng piányi, yě hěn pèi.

306 第九单元 ▪ 第一课 ▪ 衣

字 词 VOCABULARY

LESSON VOCABULARY 9.1

	SIMPLIFIED	TRADITIONAL	PINYIN	WORD CATEGORY	DEFINITION
1.	毛衣		máoyī	*n*	sweater
2.	衬衫	襯衫	chènshān	*n*	shirt
3.	裙子		qúnzi	*n*	skirt; dress
4.	件		jiàn	*mw*	(used for articles of clothing such as shirts, dresses, jackets and coats)
5.	穿		chuān	*v*	to wear
6.	中号	中號	zhōnghào	*adj*	medium size
	中		zhōng	*adj*	middle
	号	號	hào	*n*	size
7.	或者		huòzhě	*cj*	or
8.	小		xiǎo	*adj*	small; little
9.	漂亮		piàoliang	*adj*	pretty, beautiful
10.	看起来	看起來	kànqilai	*ie*	it appears, it seems
11.	比		bǐ	*prep*	compared to
12.	更		gèng	*adv*	even more
13.	红色	紅色	hóngsè	*n*	red
14.	又...又...		yòu...yòu...	*adv*	both ... and ...
15.	一样	一樣	yíyàng	*adj*	same
16.	配		pèi	*v, adj*	to match, suit

REQUIRED VOCABULARY 9.1

	SIMPLIFIED	TRADITIONAL	PINYIN	WORD CATEGORY	DEFINITION
WORDS RELATED TO CLOTHING					
17.	双	雙	shuāng	*adj, mw*	double, two; a pair
18.	鞋(子)		xié (zi)	*n*	shoes
19.	袜子	襪子	wàzi	*n*	socks
20.	戴		dài	*v*	to wear (for glasses and hats)
21.	帽子		màozi	*n*	hat
22.	眼镜	眼鏡	yǎnjìng	*n*	glasses
23.	墨镜	墨鏡	mòjìng	*n*	sunglasses

OPTIONAL VOCABULARY 9.1

	SIMPLIFIED	TRADITIONAL	PINYIN	WORD CATEGORY	DEFINITION
WORDS RELATED TO CLOTHING					
24.	顶	頂	dǐng	*mw*	(used for hats)
25.	外套		wàitào	*n*	coat, jacket
26.	大衣		dàyī	*n*	overcoat
27.	西装	西裝	xīzhuāng	*n*	suit
28.	T-恤衫		T-xùshān	*n*	T-shirt

ONLINE RESOURCES
Visit *http://college.betterchinese.com* for a list of other words related to clothing.

Review of Adjectives

In this lesson, adjectives are used to compare the qualities of two things. The following are some useful comparative adjectives which have appeared in the lessons so far.

好	hǎo	good
差	chà	poor
大	dà	big; old
小	xiǎo	small; young
贵	guì	expensive
便宜	piányi	cheap
漂亮	piàoliang	pretty
有意思	yǒu yìsi	interesting
难	nán	difficult
容易	róngyi	easy
近	jìn	close
远	yuǎn	far
好玩（儿）	hǎowán(r)	fun
简单	jiǎndān	simple
辣	là	spicy
好吃	hǎo chī	tasty

Remember that when an adjective is used in its regular form to describe something it is generally presented with a modifier such as 很, as in:

他做的饭很辣。

Tā zuò de fàn hěn là.

The food he made is spicy.

However, when adjectives are used in comparisons, they must appear either by themselves or with special modifying phrases used for comparisons:

他做的饭比你做的辣。

Tā zuò de fàn bǐ nǐ zuò de là.

The food he made is spicier than the food you made.

他做的饭比你做的辣一点。

Tā zuò de fàn bǐ nǐ zuò de là yì diǎn.

The food he made is a bit spicier than the food you made.

Use 或者 *to express choices and options*

In Structure Notes 6.14 and 8.12, 还是 was introduced as a way to ask either-or questions. However, this pattern cannot be used as an equivalent for "or" in other types of sentences. To express "or" in a statement as opposed to a question, one must use 或者 (huòzhě).

> Subject + Option A + 或者 + Option B

> Subject + Option A + 、 + Option B + 、 + 或者 + Option C

From the Lesson Text:　你应该穿中号的或者小号的。
Nǐ yīnggāi chuān zhōnghào de huòzhě xiǎohào de.
You should wear size medium or small.

Other examples:

我想去法国或者德国。
Wǒ xiǎng qù Fǎguó huòzhě Déguó.
I want to go to France or Germany.

你可以买毛衣、衬衫，或者裙子。
Nǐ kěyǐ mǎi máoyī, chènshān, huòzhě qúnzi.
You can buy a sweater, a shirt, or a skirt.

Practice: Create complete sentences with 或者 using the information provided below.

Example:　他 / 想 / 学 / 汉语 / 法语 → 他想学汉语或者法语。

1. 我 / 想 / 喝 / 茶 / 咖啡

   _____

2. 明天下午 / 我 / 想 / 去 / 健身房 / 图书馆

   _____

3. 今年 / 孙玛丽 / 打算 / 去 / 中国 / 加拿大

   _____

4. 我 / 要 / 去商店 / 买 / 毛衣 / 衬衫 / 鞋子

   _____

5. 我的书 / 可能 / 在桌子上 / 在沙发上

   _____

STRUCTURE NOTE 9.2

Use 看/听 + 起来 *to express a subjective impression*

To express that something seems to be a particular way, the phrases 看起来 *(kànqilai: "looks") and* 听起来 *(tīngqilai: "sounds") can be used.*

> Subject + 看/听 + 起来 + Adjective Phrase

From the Lesson Text:

我觉得这件看起来比那件更大！
Wǒ juéde zhèi jiàn kànqilai bǐ nèi jiàn gèng dà!
I think this one looks even bigger than that one!

Other examples:

那本书听起来很有意思。
Nèi běn shū tīngqilai hěn yǒu yìsi.
That book sounds very interesting.

他做的菜看起来不太好吃。
Tā zuò de cài kànqilai bú tài hǎo chī.
The food he made doesn't look very tasty.

NOTE: *Normally, the characters* 起来 *carry the tones qǐ and lái and mean "to rise" and "to come," respectively. When certain phrases like* 起来 *become part of fixed grammatical patterns, however, they lose their original meaning and they are pronounced with unstressed neutral tones.*

Practice: Transform the sentences below into Chinese using 看起来 or 听起来.

Example: That bowl of Hot and Sour Soup looks very spicy.
→ 那碗酸辣汤看起来很辣。

1. The grammar in lesson 14 looks very easy.
   _____

2. The sweater that you are talking about sounds very expensive.
   _____

3. That pair of black pants looks very big.
   _____

4. Beijing sounds like a lot of fun!
   _____

5. That new book that he has written looks interesting.
   _____

STRUCTURE NOTE 9.3
Use 比 to make comparisons

To express a comparison between two things that are of an unequal value, Chinese uses the character 比 (bǐ: "compared to"). In this pattern, 比 connects an item A that has more of some quality than item B, meaning "A is more (adjective) than B." To say "A is not more (adjective) than B," simply add 不 before 比.

A + 比 + B + Adjective

A + 不 + 比 + B + Adjective

From the Lesson Text:

我觉得这件看起来比那件更大！
Wǒ juéde zhèi jiàn kànqilai bǐ nèi jiàn gèng dà!
I think this one looks even bigger than that one!

Other examples:

我不比他大。
Wǒ bù bǐ tā dà.
I am not older than him. (i.e., I am as old as or younger than him)

这本书一定比那本书有意思。
Zhèi běn shū yídìng bǐ nèi běn shū yǒu yìsi.
This book is definitely more interesting than that book.

NOTE: *In a comparative sentence, the adjective appears either on its own or with certain special modifiers (see Structure Notes 9.4 and 9.5).* 很 *or other standard intensifiers may not be used with adjectives in a* 比 *sentence. As illustrated in the examples, optional modifying phrases such as* 看起来 *are located before* 比.

To express the idea "A is not as (adjective) as B," use 没有 *(那么).*

A + 没有 + B (+ 那么) + Adjective

Examples:

我没有他大。
Wǒ méiyǒu tā dà.
I am not as old as him.

这件毛衣没有那件那么贵。
Zhèi jiàn máoyī méiyǒu nèi jiàn nàme guì.
This sweater is not as expensive as that one.

Practice: Use 比, 不比, or 没有(那么) and the information provided below to create comparative sentences.

Example: 李中平/陈大东/大 → 李中平比陈大东大。

1. 音乐会/生日派对/好玩 _____
2. 生词/语法/难 _____
3. 青菜/醉鸡/好吃 _____
4. 袜子/鞋子/便宜 _____
5. 数学/历史/有意思 _____

STRUCTURE NOTE 9.4
Use 更 to say "even more"

更 (gèng) *is an adverb that modifies comparative adjectives. It is used to express that something is even more (adjective) than something else.*

Subject + 更 + Adjective

From the Lesson Text:

我觉得这件看起来比那件更大！
Wǒ juéde zhèi jiàn kànqilai bǐ nèi jiàn gèng dà!
I think this one looks even bigger than that one!

Other examples:

那只狗很小，可是这只狗更小。
Nèi zhī gǒu hěn xiǎo, kěshì zhèi zhī gǒu gèng xiǎo.
That dog is small, but this dog is even smaller.

我想找一本更有意思的书。
Wǒ xiǎng zhǎo yì běn gèng yǒu yìsi de shū.
I want to find an even more interesting book.

Practice: Turn the following statements into comparative sentences using 比 and 更, following the example provided.

Example: 茶很好喝。（咖啡）
→ 茶很好喝，可是咖啡比茶更好喝。

1. 这件衬衫很贵。（那件衬衫）

   _____

2. 我的英语很好。（汉语）

   _____

3. 波士顿很大。（北京）

   _____

4. 这杯茶很苦。（那杯茶）

   _____

5. 学校离我家很远。（博物馆）

   _____

STRUCTURE NOTE 9.5
Use （一）点（儿）to describe small differences

When describing to what extent two things are different in a comparative sentence, special modifying phrases are added after the adjective. This lesson features the modifying phrase （一）点（儿）, *which is used to express "A is a little more (adjective) than B."*

A + 比 + B + Adjective Phrase + （一）点（儿）

From the Lesson Text:

可是这件比那件便宜一点。
Kěshì zhèi jiàn bǐ nèi jiàn piányi yì diǎn.
But this one is a bit cheaper than that one.

Other examples:

我比他小点。
Wǒ bǐ tā xiǎo diǎn.
I am a bit younger than he is.

他写的字比我写的好一点儿。
Tā xiě de zì bǐ wǒ xiě de hǎo yì diǎnr.
The character he wrote was a bit better than the one I wrote.

Practice: Using the information given below, create comparative sentences with (一) 点 (儿).

Example: 醉鸡 / 饺子 / 好吃 → 醉鸡比饺子好吃一点。

1. 第九课 / 第八课 / 容易　　＿＿＿＿＿＿＿＿＿＿

2. 毛衣 / 衬衫 / 贵　　＿＿＿＿＿＿＿＿＿＿

3. 这条裙子 / 那条裙子 / 漂亮　　＿＿＿＿＿＿＿＿＿＿

4. 饭馆 / 商店 / 近　　＿＿＿＿＿＿＿＿＿＿

5. 哥哥 / 弟弟 / 大　　＿＿＿＿＿＿＿＿＿＿

STRUCTURE NOTE 9.6

Use 又...又... to express "both...and..."

In Chinese, 和 is generally used to join two nouns. To join related adjectives, the pattern 又... 又... (yòu... yòu...) can be used to express "both (adjective) and (adjective)."

Subject + 又 + Adjective + 又 + Adjective

From the Lesson Text:

这件红色的毛衣是中号的，又漂亮又便宜。
Zhèi jiàn hóngsè de máoyī shì zhōnghào de, yòu piàoliang yòu piányi.
This red sweater is a size medium. It's both pretty and cheap.

Other Examples:

她的房间听起来又大又漂亮。
Tā de fángjiān tīngqilai yòu dà yòu piàoliang.
It sounds like her room is large and also pretty.

我今天买的饭又便宜又好吃。
Wǒ jīntiān mǎi de fàn yòu piányi yòu hǎo chī.
The food I bought today was cheap and also delicious.

Practice: Construct sentences in Chinese using 又...又... and the information provided below.

Example: This cake is both sweet and delicious. → 这个蛋糕又甜又好吃。

1. After he finished class he was both tired and hungry.

   _____

2. The restaurant on campus is both large and cheap.

   _____

3. This Hot and Sour Soup is spicy and delicious.

   _____

4. Her cellphone looks new and expensive.

   _____

5. Let's go eat. I'm hungry and thirsty!

   _____

STRUCTURE NOTE 9.7
Use ...跟...一样 *(adjective) to express sameness*

So far this lesson has described a range of patterns that cover comparisons. The final pattern in this group is that which expresses sameness, or in other words, "A is as (adjective) as B." To create such a sentence, take the phrase "A is the same as B" (A 跟 B 一样) and add an an adjective to the end.

$$A + 跟 + B + 一样 + Adjective$$

From the Lesson Text:

这条裙子跟那件毛衣一样便宜。
Zhèi tiáo qúnzi gēn nèi jiàn máoyī yíyàng piányi.
This skirt is just as cheap as that sweater.

Other examples:

我跟他一样大。
Wǒ gēn tā yíyàng dà.
I am the same age as he is.

你觉得你们的老师跟我们的
一样好吗?
Nǐ juéde nǐmen de lǎoshī gēn wǒmen de
yíyàng hǎo ma?
Do you think your teacher is as good as ours?

Practice: Using the lists below, match the noun pairs with an appropriate adjective to form whole sentences.

红色毛衣跟黄色毛衣	难	Example: 醉鸡跟饺子一样好吃。
醉鸡跟饺子	便宜	
玛丽跟安娜	有意思	_____
这本书跟那本书	一样 好吃	_____
中文跟英文	漂亮	_____
那家饭馆跟那家餐厅	大	_____

PRACTICE 9.1

You go clothes shopping with your friend. Write the name of the product below the picture and choose the combination you want to buy. Ask your friend what he/she wants to buy.

Example:

A: 你今天想买什么？

B: 我想买毛衣和衬衫。你呢？

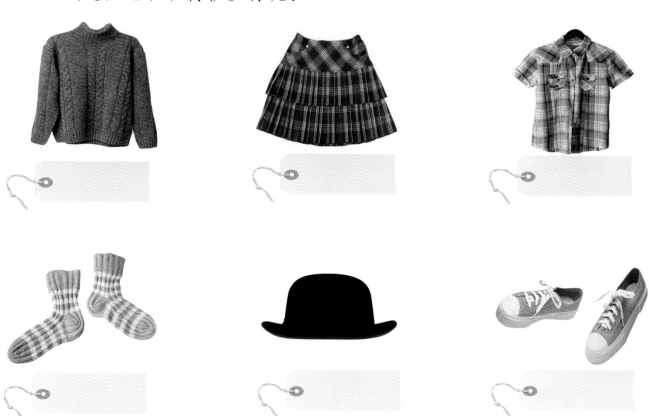

PRACTICE 9.2

You and your friend try on some clothes at a department store. Describe each item and comment on each other's clothes. Tell your friend which items you would like to buy and give the reason why. Talk about each of your preferences in terms of size, color, and price. Use the vocabulary you have learned as well as the words and patterns provided in the box below.

Example:

A: 这件毛衣很漂亮，你觉得呢？

B: 我觉得这件看起来比那件更大！

看起来　不错　很配　又...又...　应该　或者　比　更

✎ PRACTICE 9.3

	Radical	Stroke Order
比	比 bǐ compare	一 ヒ 比 比
号	口 kǒu mouth	' 口 口 号 号
样	木 mù wood	一 十 才 木 术 栏 栏 栏 栏 样
衣	衣 yī clothing	' 一 亠 亓 衣 衣
毛	毛 máo fur	' 二 三 毛
条	木 mù wood	ノ 夂 冬 冬 条 条 条
穿	穴 xué cave	' 八 宀 宀 宀 宀 空 穿 穿
件	亻(人) rén person	ノ 亻 亻 亻 件 件
漂	氵(水) shuǐ water	' 冫 氵 氵 氵 沪 沪 沪 沪 沪 沪 漂 漂 漂
亮	亠 tóu lid	' 亠 亠 亠 亠 亠 亠 亮
更	日 yuē say	一 一 一 一 百 更 更
红	纟(糸) sī silk	乚 纟 纟 纟 红 红
色	色 sè color	ノ 夕 色 色 色 色
配	酉 yǒu wine vessel	一 一 丁 丙 西 酉 酉 酉 配
又	又 yòu again	フ 又

🗨 PRACTICE 9.4

🎤 Make an audio recording and send it to your teacher. Discuss what you would wear if you were going to a formal party. Talk about what accessories and colors you would wear to make your outfit match.

PRACTICE 9.5

Type the following sentences on your computer.

1. 这件毛衣比那件便宜一点。
2. 你应该穿中号的或者小号的。
3. 我觉得这条裙子看起来比那条更漂亮。
4. 这件衬衫跟那条裙子很配。
5. 欢迎光临！

PRACTICE 9.6

Write the size of each sweater on the tag and create sentences to describe them.

Example:

这件红色的毛衣是中号的。

PRACTICE 9.7

我和安娜今天去百货公司。我想买一件红色的毛衣，可是红色的太大了。我问售货员有没有小号的，售货员说没有了，红色的都卖完了。安娜买了一条裙子，又漂亮又便宜。

Read Sun Mali's diary and answer the following questions.
1. Why couldn't Sun Mali buy her sweater?
2. What did Zhang Anna buy?

PRACTICE 9.8

售货员：欢迎光临！

李中平：我想买一件衬衫。

售货员：是你穿的吗？

李中平：是我穿的，有中号或小号的吗？

售货员：有，这件衬衫是中号的。

李中平：哦！看起来不错！请问多少钱？

售货员：十六块九毛九。

Read the dialogue and answer the following questions.
1. What does Li Zhongping want to buy?
2. Which size does the salesperson show Li Zhongping?

PRACTICE 9.9

Sender　玛丽

Subject　买衣服

小美：

我听大东说中国的衣服比美国的便宜，你这次去中国可不可以帮我去商店买衣服？我要一件小号的红色毛衣，还有一件衬衫，要比毛衣更小的。我还要一条大号的裙子，价钱不要太贵。你回来以后我会把钱还给你。谢谢！

Read Sun Mali's email and answer the following questions.
1. What color does Sun Mali want for her sweater?
2. What size does she want for her skirt?

Color Symbolism in Chinese

Red

The most prominent color in Chinese culture is red. Red represents celebration, good luck, and happiness. Traditionally, brides wore red clothing and veils for marriage ceremonies. Many still do, though it has also become popular to wear Western-style white dresses. Wedding ceremonies also involve the presentation of 红包 (hóngbāo: "red envelope"), a small packet filled with money. The positive associations with the color red have led to the meaning of the word 红 itself expanding to include success, popularity, and happiness.

White

In the West, black is typically identified as the color of funerals and mourning. In China, one conversely finds white objects and attire at funerals, as this color is associated with concepts such as pureness and immortality. Consequently, one should never send white flowers to a Chinese person, unless mourning a loss.

Yellow

Tradition has it that Chinese civilization began in the Yellow River basin. The Yellow River, China's second longest, is thought to have nurtured Chinese culture from the very beginning. The color also lent itself to the title of the Yellow Emperor, the legendary ruler of Chinese mythology who is said to be the ancestor of the Han race. From that period onward, many dynasties reserved yellow for the imperial house and forbade common people from using it.

Blue-Green

Blue and green are typically associated with nature, prosperity, and harmony. The usage of blue can symbolize immortality, with dark blue frequently used on somber occasions like funerals. A man should also take care never to wear a green hat or to present a man with a green hat as a gift because the Chinese expression 戴绿帽子 (dài lǜ màozi: "to wear a green hat") means that a man has been cuckolded.

售货员：	欢迎光临！	Welcome!
王小美：	你今天想买什么衣服？	What clothes do you want to buy today?
孙玛丽：	我想买毛衣、衬衫，还有裙子。走吧，我们去看毛衣。	I want to buy a sweater, a shirt, and a skirt. Come on, let's go look at sweaters.
张安娜：	这件毛衣太大了，你应该穿中号的或者小号的。	This sweater is too big. You should wear a medium or a small.

孙玛丽：	这件很漂亮，你觉得呢？	This one is very pretty. What do you think?
张安娜：	我觉得这件看起来比那件更大！	I think this one looks even bigger than that one!
孙玛丽：	可是这件比那件便宜一点。	But this one is a bit cheaper than that one.
张安娜：	你看，这件红色的毛衣是中号的，又漂亮又便宜。	Look, this red sweater is a medium; it's pretty and cheap too.
孙玛丽：	不错啊！裙子呢？	Not bad! What about the skirt?
张安娜：	这条裙子跟那件毛衣一样便宜，也很配。	This skirt is as cheap as that sweater and they match as well.

What Can You Do?

INTERPRETIVE
- I can distinguish between different articles of clothing and their appearances.
- I can understand comparisons and expressions of sameness.

INTERPERSONAL
- I can compare clothing sizes with others.
- I can discuss the relative merits of different items.

PRESENTATIONAL
- I can give a presentation of clothing which includes sizes, personal preferences, and specific comparisons.

你喜欢什么颜色?
What Colors do You Like?

嗨，祥安，
进来吧！

我看，你应该
买新裤子了。

不用啊，这条还
可以穿。我很喜欢
这条长裤 —

安娜，我先走了，祥安
需要帮忙，帮他找一找吧！

没问题！祥安，
你喜欢什么颜色？

课 文 LESSON TEXT

LESSON TEXT 9.2

What Colors Do You Like? 你喜欢什么颜色？

Sun Mali and Zhang Anna see Huang Xiang'an in a clothes store. Sun Mali enlists Zhang Anna's help to find a new pair of jeans for Huang Xiang'an, despite his reluctance.

孙玛丽：	嗨，祥安，进来吧！我看，你应该买新裤子了。	Hāi, Xiáng'ān, jìnlai ba! Wǒ kàn, nǐ yīnggāi mǎi xīn kùzi le.
黄祥安：	不用啊，这条还可以穿。我很喜欢这条长裤 —	Bú yòng a, zhèi tiáo hái kéyǐ chuān. Wǒ hěn xǐhuan zhèi tiáo chángkù –
孙玛丽：	安娜，我先走了，祥安需要帮忙，帮他找一找吧！	Ānnà, wǒ xiān zǒu le, Xiáng'ān xūyào bāng máng, bāng tā zhǎo yi zhǎo ba!
张安娜：	没问题！祥安，你喜欢什么颜色？	Méi wèntí! Xiáng'ān, nǐ xǐhuan shénme yánsè?

黄祥安：	我最喜欢蓝色。黑色，灰色或者黄色也可以。	Wǒ zuì xǐhuan lánsè. Hēisè, huīsè huòzhě huángsè yě kěyǐ.
张安娜：	明白了。这条黑黑的牛仔裤怎么样？大小合适吗？试试看！	Míngbai le. Zhèi tiáo hēihēi de niúzǎikù zěnmeyàng? Dàxiǎo héshì ma? Shìshi kàn!
黄祥安：	这条有一点儿短……	Zhèi tiáo yǒu yì diǎnr duǎn...
张安娜：	不短！我觉得很合适，你看起来好酷。	Bù duǎn! Wǒ juéde hěn héshì, nǐ kànqilai hǎo kù.
黄祥安：	哦—真的吗？好！就这条。	Ó – zhēnde ma? Hǎo! Jiù zhèi tiáo.

字 词 VOCABULARY

LESSON VOCABULARY 9.2

	SIMPLIFIED	TRADITIONAL	PINYIN	WORD CATEGORY	DEFINITION
1.	嗨		hāi	*ie*	hi
2.	进来	進來	jìnlai	*dc*	to come in
3.	裤子	褲子	kùzi	*n*	pants, trousers
4.	长裤	長褲	chángkù	*n*	pants, trousers (lit. "long pants")
5.	需要		xūyào	*v*	to need; to want
6.	帮忙	幫忙	bāng máng	*vo*	to help
7.	颜色	顏色	yánsè	*n*	color
8.	最		zuì	*adv*	most (used to describe superlative degree)
9.	蓝色	藍色	lánsè	*n*	blue
10.	黑色		hēisè	*n*	black
11.	灰色		huīsè	*n*	gray
12.	黄色		huángsè	*n*	yellow
13.	明白		míngbai	*v*	to understand
14.	牛仔裤	牛仔褲	niúzǎikù	*n*	jeans (lit. "cowboy pants")
15.	大小		dàxiǎo	*n*	size
16.	合适	合適	héshì	*adj*	suitable
17.	看		kàn	*v*	(after a reduplicated verb) try and see, do something and see
18.	短		duǎn	*adj*	short
19.	酷		kù	*adj*	cool
20.	真的		zhēnde	*adv, ie*	really

REQUIRED VOCABULARY 9.2

	SIMPLIFIED	TRADITIONAL	PINYIN	WORD CATEGORY	DEFINITION
COLORS					
21.	白色		báisè	n	white
22.	绿色	綠色	lùsè	n	green

OPTIONAL VOCABULARY 9.2

	SIMPLIFIED	TRADITIONAL	PINYIN	WORD CATEGORY	DEFINITION
COLORS					
23.	紫色		zǐsè	n	purple
24.	橙色		chéngsè	n	orange
25.	咖啡色		kāfēisè	n	coffee color; brown

 ONLINE RESOURCES

Visit *http://college.betterchinese.com* for a list of other words related to clothing.

Clothing Terms

帽子*
mǎozi

大衣
dàyī

裙子
qúnzi

眼镜*
yǎnjìng

西装
xīzhuāng

牛仔裤
niúzǎikù

衬衫
chènshān

T-恤衫
T-xùshān

袜子
wàzi

毛衣
máoyī

裤子
kùzi

鞋子
xiézi

外套
wàitào

Colors

红色
hóngsè

橙色
chéngsè

黄色
huángsè

绿色
lǜsè

蓝色
lánsè

紫色
zǐsè

黑色
hēisè

白色
báisè

咖啡色
kāfēisè

灰色
huīsè

Measure Words

Chinese	Pinyin	Used For
条	tiáo	裤子，裙子，牛仔裤
双	shuāng	鞋子，袜子
顶	dǐng	帽子
件	jiàn	衬衫，毛衣，外套，大衣，T-恤衫
套	tào	西装
副	fù	眼镜

* To talk about wearing hats and glasses, use the verb 戴 rather than 穿

STRUCTURE NOTE 9.8

Use Verb 一 Verb to describe casual or brief activities

When making suggestions or requests in Chinese, it is polite to soften the verb in order to suggest that the activity will be brief or casual. One way to do this is by inserting 一 between a repeated single-character verb. When the verb is part of a verb-object pair, the object is placed after the second verb.

> Subject + Verb + 一 + Verb (+ Object)

From the Lesson Text:
帮他找一找吧!
Bāng tā zhǎo yi zhǎo ba!
Why don't you help him look for a bit.

Other examples:
你试一试吧。
Nǐ shì yi shì ba.
Why don't you give it a try.

你看一看这件毛衣。
Nǐ kàn yi kàn zhèi jiàn máoyī.
Take a look at this sweater.

Practice: Use the verb 一 verb construction to soften the tone of the sentences below, following the example given.

Example: 你去跟朋友说。 → 你去跟朋友说一说吧。

1. 请读这本书。
   _____

2. 你进来坐吧。
   _____

3. 我想试这双鞋。
   _____

4. 我找不到钱包，你可以帮我找吗？
   _____

5. 有事吗？你跟我说。
   _____

STRUCTURE NOTE 9.9

Use 最 to express superlatives

最 (zuì) *means "the most" or "-est" and can be placed before adjectives or verbs like* 想, 喜欢, 要, 需要 *etc. to form superlatives.*

> Subject + 最 + Adjective / Verb Phrase

From the Lesson Text:	我最喜欢蓝色。 Wǒ zuì xǐhuan lánsè. I like blue the most.

Other examples:

哪件毛衣最便宜？
Něi jiàn máoyī zuì piányi?
Which of these sweaters is cheapest?

我最想去的地方就是北京。
Wǒ zuì xiǎng qù de dìfang jiùshì Běijīng.
The place that I want to go to the most is Beijing.

Practice: Express the following statements in Chinese using 最.

Example: I like dumplings the most. → 我最喜欢吃饺子。

1. Yellow is my favorite color.

   _____

2. This airport is the biggest one in China.

   _____

3. I want to take literature classes the most.

   _____

4. This is her favorite skirt.

   _____

5. This is the cheapest cellphone.

   _____

STRUCTURE NOTE 9.10
Use reduplication to intensify adjectives or adverbs

When an adjective is reduplicated, a more intense or emphatic effect is created. Monosyllabic adjectives are simply repeated, so 好, for example, becomes 好好. With disyllabic adjectives, the characters are doubled in an AABB pattern, so 漂亮 becomes 漂漂亮亮. Reduplicated adjectives have special tone patterns. If a single-character adjective is reduplicated, the second character generally switches to a first tone, as in 好好 (hǎohāo). Two-character adjectives with neutral tones, like 漂亮 (piàoliang), have their tones reinstated, as in 漂漂亮亮 (piàopiàoliàngliàng). Intensifiers such as 很 are not used when the adjective is reduplicated. Be aware that not all adjectives can be reduplicated.

> Character A + Character A (+ Character B + Character B)

From the Lesson Text: 这条黑黑的牛仔裤怎么样？
Zhèi tiáo hēihēi de niúzǎikù zěnmeyàng?
How about these black jeans? (lit. How about these really black jeans?)

Other examples:

我今天晚上要好好学习。
Wǒ jīntiān wǎnshang yào hǎohāo xuéxí.
I have to study really hard this evening.

我看到一个漂漂亮亮的女孩子。
Wǒ kàndào yí ge piàopiàoliàngliàng de nǚháizi.
I see a really pretty girl.

Practice: Complete the sentences below by adding the reduplicated form of the adjective in parentheses into the spaces provided.

Example: 这条（　　　）的裤子不合适。(短)

→ 这条短短的裤子不合适。

1. 今天的功课（　　　）的，你不需要人帮忙。(简单)
2. 这件毛衣（　　　）的，你觉得好吗？(大)
3. 今天的酸辣汤（　　　）的，很好喝。(酸，辣)
4. 这是一块（　　　）的蛋糕。(甜)
5. 今天是他的生日，你看他（　　　）的！(高兴)

STRUCTURE NOTE 9.11
Use Verb reduplication to describe casual or brief activities

In Structure Note 9.8, the pattern Verb + 一 + Verb was introduced as a way of describing casual or brief activities. An even more common way to express this same meaning is to reduplicate the verb. This pattern can also be used when making suggestions or requests. Unlike two-character adjective reduplication, where an AABB sequence is used, reduplicated verbs follow an ABAB structure, so 练习 is reduplicated as 练习练习. Be careful to only use this ABAB pattern for true two-character verbs. For verb-object compounds, repeat the verb only, as in 看看书.

Subject + Verb + Verb (+ Object)

From the Lesson Text:　试试看！
Shìshi kàn!
Try it on and see how it is!

Other examples:　跟我一起练习练习吧。　　晚上我喜欢看看书。
Gēn wǒ yìqǐ liànxi liànxi ba.　　Wǎnshang wǒ xǐhuan kànkan shū.
Why don't you practice a bit with　　In the evenings I like to do a bit of reading.
me.

Practice: Use the information given below to create sentences containing reduplicated verbs, following the example provided.

Example: 用筷子 / 简单 / 试 → 用筷子很简单，你来试试吧！

1. 今天的作业 / 难 / 帮忙 _____
2. 明天 / 小考 / 准备 _____
3. 今晚 / 听 / 音乐 _____
4. 跟 / 朋友 / 说话 _____
5. 进来 / 坐 / 吧 _____

STRUCTURE NOTE 9.12

Use 看 to mean "and see"

The verb 看 can be added after a reduplicated verb to add the meaning "... and see (how it is)." Essentially, this pattern means to see or find out by means of the preceding verb.

> Subject + Reduplicated Verb + 看 (+ Object)

From the Lesson Text:

试试看！
Shìshì kàn!
Try it on and see how it is!

Other Examples:

请帮我找找看。
Qǐng bāng wǒ zhǎozhǎo kàn.
Please help me look around and see.

老师想听听看我的中文怎么样。
Lǎoshī xiǎng tīngtīng kàn wǒ de Zhōngwén zěnmeyàng.
The teacher wants to have a listen and see how my Chinese is.

Practice: Answer the following questions in Chinese using reduplicated verbs and 看, in the manner of the example provided.

Example: 我的手机在哪里呢？（找）→ 不知道，我帮你找找看。

1. 这家饭馆怎么样？（试）

    _____

2. 第九课的录音容易懂吗？（听）

    _____

3. 你觉得那条裤子会太短吗？（试）

    _____

4. 这个沙发怎么样？（坐）

    _____

5. 你觉得这件毛衣好不好看？（穿）

    _____

STRUCTURE NOTE 9.13

Use 有(一)点(儿) to express "somewhat"

In Unit 2, Lesson 2, (一) 点 (儿) *was used before an object as a way to describe "a bit of something," as in* 喝一点咖啡, *"drink a bit of coffee." In this pattern,* 有（一）点（儿）*is placed before adjectives or verbs such as* 想 *and* 喜欢 *to mean "a little" or "somewhat."*

> Subject + 有（一）点（儿）+ Adjective / Verb Phrase

From the Lesson Text:

这条有一点儿短······
Zhèi tiáo yǒu yì diǎnr duǎn...
This pair (of pants) is a bit short...

Other examples:

我觉得他有点喜欢我。
Wǒ juéde tā yǒu diǎn xǐhuan wǒ.
I think he likes me a little.

我们的校园有点儿小。
Wǒmen de xiàoyuán yǒu diǎnr xiǎo.
Our campus is kind of small.

NOTE: *In Structure Note 9.5,* (一) 点 (儿) *was placed after the adjective to describe the degree to which something was different from something else, as in* 我比他大一点. *When this phrase is placed after an adjective, it has a comparative meaning of "a bit more." In this pattern,* 有（一）点（儿）*is placed before the adjective, and does not have a comparative meaning.*

Practice: Respond to the following questions using 有（一）点（儿）and the words provided in parentheses.

Example: 波士顿好玩吗？（小）→ 很好玩，可是有点小。

1. 你昨天买的茶好喝吗？（贵）

   _____

2. 她怎么在图书馆里睡觉呢？（累）

   _____

3. 那条黑色的牛仔裤怎么样？（大）

   _____

4. 你昨天晚上为什么没有去她家？（远）

   _____

5. 这个学期你选的课难吗？（难）

   _____

STRUCTURE NOTE 9.14

Use 好 as an intensifier

好 *can be interchangeable with* 很 *as an intensifier meaning "very." Different Chinese-speaking regions use* 好 *and* 很 *with different frequencies, and certain expressions are conventionally said using either one or the other. In general,* 好 *is a more casual intensifier than* 很.

> Subject + 好 + Adjective / Adverb / Verb

From the Lesson Text:

你看起来好酷。
Nǐ kànqilai hǎo kù.
You look very cool.

Other examples:

我好喜欢他。
Wǒ hǎo xǐhuan tā.
I like him a lot.

你的女朋友好漂亮啊！
Nǐ de nǚpéngyou hǎo piàoliang a!
Your girlfriend is very pretty!

Practice: Turn the following sentences into Chinese using 好 as an intensifier.

Example:　　　He really likes listening to music. → 他好喜欢听音乐。

1.　　Yesterday's homework was really easy.

　　　_____

2.　　I was very tired after I finished class yesterday.

　　　_____

3.　　The stationery in this shop is so cheap.

　　　_____

4.　　This rice is really salty; I don't want to eat anymore.

　　　_____

5.　　These medium-size pants are really short.

　　　_____

PRACTICE 9.10

Look around the classroom at the clothes your classmates are wearing. Identify as many of the different articles of clothing and their colors as you can.

Example: 陈大东今天穿红色的毛衣、黑色的裤子跟灰色的鞋子。

PRACTICE 9.11

You and your friends are reading a fashion magazine. Comment on the pictures you see below (e.g. price, color, size, length).

Example:

A: 你觉得这件怎么样?

B: 我觉得太短了。

$30.50 $5.50 $10.00 $39.99

$40.50 $29.99 $10.25 $250.50

$150.00 $50.00 $88.99 $12.00

PRACTICE 9.12

With a partner, practice words for colors by discussing which pairs of glasses below you would and wouldn't want to buy. Take turns to ask each other about each pair.

Example:

A: 你想买绿色的眼镜吗?

B: 我想买绿色的眼镜。/ 我不想买绿色的眼镜。

PRACTICE 9.13

Do a survey to determine what the most popular color in the class is. Record your findings below.

Color	Number of Students

PRACTICE 9.14

Type the following sentences on your computer and provide answers to the questions.

1. 你想买什么颜色的裤子?
2. 你觉得这条灰色的牛仔裤怎么样?
3. 他穿的那条牛仔裤看起来很酷!
4. 我想试试看这件中号的裙子。
5. 我觉得这件黄色的衬衫大小很合适。

PRACTICE 9.15

Make an audio recording and send it to your teacher. In the recording, talk about your favorite clothes and colors. On what occasion would you wear the kind of outfit you are describing?

	Radical	Stroke Order
帮	巾 jīn cloth	一　二　三　丰　邦　邦　帮　帮
忙	忄(心) xīn heart	丶　丷　忄　忄　忙　忙
进	辶 chuò walk	一　二　丰　井　`井　进
需	雨 yǔ rain	一　宀　宀　币　雨　雨　雫　雲　雲　雪　雫　需　需
颜	页 yè page	丶　亠　二　产　立　产　产　彦　彦　彦　颜　颜　颜
最	曰 yuē say	丶　冂　曰　曰　旦　旦　旱　旱　旱　最　最
蓝	艹 cǎo grass	一　十　艹　芐　芐　荘　荘　菥　菥　蓝　蓝　蓝
黑	黑 hēi black	丶　冂　口　四　四　甲　甲　里　黑　黑　黑
灰	火 huǒ fire	一　ナ　大　太　灰　灰
黄	黄 huáng yellow	一　十　艹　共　苹　昔　苗　黄　黄
或	戈 gē spear	一　一　口　口　豆　或　或　或
者	老 lǎo old	一　十　土　耂　者　者　者
合	口 kǒu mouth	丿　人　仝　仐　合　合
适	辶 chuò walk	丿　二　千　舌　舌　舌　适　适
短	矢 shǐ arrow	丿　丿　上　乍　矢　矢　知　知　短　短

336 第九单元 ▪ 第二课 ▪ 衣

PRACTICE 9.17

Sender 小美
Subject 颜色

玛丽：
昨天我在中国的一家商店买了一件小号的红色毛衣给你。可是我忘了你要什么颜色的衬衫和裙子。我看到了一件白色衬衫和一条灰色的裙子，你喜欢吗？

Sender 玛丽
Subject re: 颜色

小美：
我喜欢绿色，我要一条绿色或者白色的裙子。可是我不要绿色或者白色的衬衫，我觉得黑色的衬衫会跟红色的毛衣比较配。

Read the emails and answer the following questions.
1. What color does Sun Mali want for her skirt?
2. What color does Sun Mali want for her shirt?

PRACTICE 9.18

售货员：先生，需要帮忙吗？
陈大东：是的，可以帮我找一件中号的衬衫吗？
售货员：没问题！这件黄色的怎么样？
陈大东：我觉得这件看起来有一点儿小。
售货员：这件蓝色的比黄色的大一点，你试试看吧。
陈大东：不错！好！我就要这件蓝色的衬衫。

Read the dialogue and answer the following questions.
1. What size shirt does Chen Dadong initially want to buy?
2. What color is the shirt that he ends up buying?

PRACTICE 9.19

我很喜欢我的蓝色裤子，可是因为玛丽说那条裤子看起来有一点儿短，所以我们就去商店看一看别的长裤。商店有一条黑色的牛仔裤看起来很酷，跟我的T-恤衫很配。玛丽也说这条牛仔裤又好看又好配衣服，可是因为价钱太贵了，我没有买。

Read Li Zhongping's diary and answer the following questions.
1. Why did Li Zhongping decide to buy a new pair of pants?
2. Did he end up buying a new pair of pants? Why?

Chinese Fashion Trends

Like all fashions throughout the world, clothing trends in China have changed along with the times.

During the Qing Dynasty (1644 – 1912), the Manchu elite demanded that all males adopt the 长衫 (chángshān: "long gown") and a long braid known in English as a queue. Han women also adopted the Manchu 旗袍 (qípáo: "cheongsam"), the female equivalent of the male robe, commonly known in English by the Cantonese term "cheongsam."

After the Qing dynasty fell in 1912, Han men were ordered to sever their queues in order to symbolize a break with the past. Modernized men began to adopt a Western-style suit of jacket and trousers. For women, the old version of the cheongsam – a baggy, all-concealing garment – was discarded in favor of a more slender and form-fitting version that remains popular today as formal wear.

The rise of Communism saw yet another shift in China's fashions. The four-pocketed tunic worn by Mao Zedong, known in the West as the "Mao suit," became the standard for people all over the country, eventually becoming a sort of national uniform.

When China re-opened its doors to the world in the 1980s, Western fashions became influential once again. The situation in modern-day China is now much like that in the West, with popular trends from the West and Asia, along with domestic fashions, starting out in urban centers like Shanghai and spreading outwards.

Foot Binding

The practice of foot binding is one of the most well-known of imperial China's fashions. Tiny feet were considered beautiful on a woman, and thus a long process of shrinking a girl's feet was begun in infancy. A gruesome and excruciatingly painful procedure, foot binding entailed breaking the toes, curling them into the sole, and wrapping the feet in bandages until they were reduced to a miniature size.

By the Qing dynasty, foot binding had become widespread among all strata of society, but in the 20th Century it became a major political issue in the debates over China's modernization. Bound feet kept women at home and subservient to both men and their families, and so the practice became a magnet for criticism of misogyny in Chinese society. While the practice was formally banned under the Nationalist government, it was not until the foundation of the People's Republic that the policy was truly implemented and foot binding was made a thing of the past.

孙玛丽：	嗨，祥安，进来吧！我看，你应该买新裤子了。	Hi, Xiang'an, come in! It looks to me like you should buy a new pair of pants.
黄祥安：	不用啊，这条还可以穿。我很喜欢这条长裤 —	No need, this pair is still good. I like this pair of pants a lot –
孙玛丽：	安娜，我先走了，祥安需要帮忙，帮他找一找吧！	Anna, I have to leave. Xiang'an needs some help. Why don't you help him look around!
张安娜：	没问题！祥安，你喜欢什么颜色？	No problem. Xiang'an, what colors do you like?

———————————

黄祥安：	我最喜欢蓝色。黑色，灰色或者黄色也可以。	I like blue the most. Black, gray or yellow are okay too.
张安娜：	明白了。这条黑黑的牛仔裤怎么样？大小合适吗？试试看！	Got it. What do you think of this pair of black jeans? Does the size fit? Go try them on!
黄祥安：	这条有一点儿短……	This pair is a little short…
张安娜：	不短！我觉得很合适，你看起来好酷。	They're not short! I think they suit you well. You look really cool.
黄祥安：	哦 — 真的吗？好！就这条。	Oh – really? OK, then I'll buy this pair.

What Can You Do?

INTERPRETIVE
- I can understand a range of different colors.
- I can understand superlatives.

INTERPERSONAL
- I can use some basic colloquial loan words in conversation.
- I can complement someone on his or her appearance.

PRESENTATIONAL
- I can describe the colors of different items.
- I can present information about someone's appearance.

单元复习 UNIT REVIEW

ACT IT OUT

Working in groups, compose an original three-minute skit that utilizes the vocabulary and structures introduced in Unit 9. Each of you should assume a role and have a roughly equal number of lines in the skit. Be prepared to perform your skit in class. You can either come up with your own story or choose from one of the following situations:

A) You and a friend are at the mall. You discuss what stores you plan to go to and what you plan to buy there.
B) You and a group of friends are casually discussing campus fashion, including what's currently popular among the students.
C) You are trying on different articles of clothing and ask a sales associate for her opinion regarding style, size, color, and other features.

CHECK WHAT YOU CAN DO

RECOGNIZE

Adjectives
- 中
- 小
- 漂亮
- 一样
- 双
- 合适
- 短
- 酷

Adverbs
- 更
- 又…又…
- 最

Conjunctions
- 或者

Idiomatic Expressions
- 看起来
- 嗨
- 真的

Nouns
- 毛衣
- 衬衫
- 裙子
- 号
- 红色
- 鞋(子)
- 袜子
- 帽子
- 眼镜
- 墨镜
- 裤子
- 长裤

- 颜色
- 蓝色
- 黑色
- 灰色
- 黄色
- 牛仔裤
- 大小
- 白色
- 绿色

Prepositions
- 比

Verbs
- 穿
- 配
- 戴
- 进来
- 需要
- 帮忙
- 明白
- 看

WRITE
- 比
- 号
- 样
- 衣
- 毛
- 条
- 穿
- 件
- 漂亮
- 更
- 红色
- 配
- 又

- 帮忙
- 进
- 需
- 颜
- 最
- 蓝
- 黑
- 灰
- 黄
- 或者
- 合适
- 短

USE

- 或者 to express choices and options
- 看/听 + 起来 to express a subjective impression
- 比 to make comparisons
- 更 to say "even more"
- (一)点(儿) to describe small differences
- 又…又… to express "both…and…"
- …跟…一样 (adjective) to express sameness

- Verb 一 Verb to describe casual or brief activities
- 最 to express superlatives
- Reduplication to intensify adjectives or adverbs
- Verb reduplication to describe casual or brief activities
- 看 to mean "and see"
- 有(一)点(儿) to express "somewhat"
- 好 as an intensifier

340 第九单元 ▪ 第二课 ▪ 衣

Hobbies & Activities

第十单元
UNIT 10

UNIT 10
娱
LESSON 1

星期六的活动
Plans for Saturday

大家
都很忙，
máng
都没空！
kòng

看看
祥安在
不在。

喂，安娜！你好！

嗨，
祥安，
你在做
什么？

我一边吃饭
yì biān
一边跟你说
yì biān *shuō*
话啊！
huà

哈哈，我
是说，今天
是星期六，
你有什么
活动吗？
huó dòng

没什么活动。你呢？

玛丽他们呢？

他们有的去打球，有的去游泳，还有的去跑步，可是我对这些活动都没有兴趣。

那你喜欢做什么？

我常常去跳舞、唱歌、看电影……

是吗？我今天晚上八点要去看一部新的功夫电影。

你想跟我一起去吗？

哦！听起来很有意思。

好吧，你能不能七点五十分在电影院门口等我？

行，晚上见。

LESSON TEXT 10.1

Plans for Saturday 星期六的活动

Zhang Anna can't find anyone to go out with because they're all busy. She decides to call Huang Xiang'an to see what he's doing.

张安娜：	大家都很忙，都没空！看看祥安在不在。	Dàjiā dōu hěn máng, dōu méi kòng! Kànkan Xiáng'ān zài bu zài.
黄祥安：	喂，安娜！你好！	Wéi, Ānnà! Nǐ hǎo!
张安娜：	嗨，祥安，你在做什么？	Hāi, Xiáng'ān, nǐ zài zuò shénme?
黄祥安：	我一边吃饭一边跟你说话啊！	Wǒ yìbiān chī fàn yìbiān gēn nǐ shuō huà a!
张安娜：	哈哈，我是说，今天是星期六，你有什么活动吗？	Hāhā, wǒ shì shuō, jīntiān shì Xīngqī liù, nǐ yǒu shénme huódòng ma?
黄祥安：	没什么活动。你呢？玛丽他们呢？	Méi shénme huódòng. Nǐ ne? Mǎlì tāmen ne?
张安娜：	他们有的去打球，有的去游泳，还有的去跑步，可是我对这些活动都没有兴趣。	Tāmen yǒude qù dǎ qiú, yǒude qù yóu yǒng, hái yǒude qù pǎo bù, kěshì wǒ duì zhèxiē huódòng dōu méiyǒu xìngqu.

黄祥安：	那你喜欢做什么？	Nà nǐ xǐhuan zuò shénme?
张安娜：	我常常去跳舞、唱歌、看电影……	Wǒ chángcháng qù tiào wǔ, chàng gē, kàn diànyǐng...
黄祥安：	是吗？我今天晚上八点要去看一部新的功夫电影。你想跟我一起去吗？	Shì ma? Wǒ jīntiān wǎnshang bā diǎn yào qù kàn yí bù xīn de gōngfu diànyǐng. Nǐ xiǎng gēn wǒ yìqǐ qù ma?
张安娜：	哦！听起来很有意思。	Ò! Tīngqilai hěn yǒu yìsi.
黄祥安：	好吧，你能不能七点五十分在电影院门口等我？	Hǎo ba, nǐ néng bu néng qī diǎn wǔshí fēn zài diànyǐngyuàn ménkǒu děng wǒ?
张安娜：	行，晚上见。	Xíng, wǎnshang jiàn.

字 词 VOCABULARY

LESSON VOCABULARY 10.1

	SIMPLIFIED	TRADITIONAL	PINYIN	WORD CATEGORY	DEFINITION
1.	忙		máng	*adj*	busy
2.	有空		yǒu kòng	*vo*	to have free time
3.	一边	一邊	yìbiān	*conj*	on the one hand; at the same time
4.	说话	説話	shuō huà	*vo*	to talk
5.	活动	活動	huódòng	*n*	activity
6.	打球		dǎ qiú	*vo*	to play ball
7.	游泳		yóu yǒng	*vo*	to swim
8.	跑步		pǎo bù	*vo*	to jog
9.	对	對	duì	*prep*	at; toward
10.	这些	這些	zhèxiē	*n*	these
	些		xiē	*mw*	some
11.	兴趣	興趣	xìngqu	*n*	interest
12.	常常		chángcháng	*adv*	often
13.	跳舞		tiào wǔ	*vo*	to dance
14.	唱歌		chàng gē	*vo*	to sing
15.	电影	電影	diànyǐng	*n*	movie
16.	部		bù	*mw*	(used for movies)
17.	功夫		gōngfu	*n*	Kung Fu
18.	听起来	聽起來	tīngqilai	*ie*	to sound like
19.	能		néng	*av*	can; be able to
20.	电影院	電影院	diànyǐngyuàn	*n*	cinema, movie theater
21.	门口	門口	ménkǒu	*n*	entrance
22.	等		děng	*v*	to wait
23.	行		xíng	*adj*	OK, all right

REQUIRED VOCABULARY 10.1

	SIMPLIFIED	TRADITIONAL	PINYIN	WORD CATEGORY	DEFINITION
OTHER					
24.	玩		wán	*v*	to play
25.	游戏	遊戲	yóuxì	*n*	game
26.	很少		hěnshǎo	*adv*	very infrequently; rarely

OPTIONAL VOCABULARY 10.2

	SIMPLIFIED	TRADITIONAL	PINYIN	WORD CATEGORY	DEFINITION
MOVIE GENRES					
27.	喜剧	喜劇	xǐjù	*n*	comedy
28.	悲剧	悲劇	bēijù	*n*	tragedy
29.	恐怖片		kǒngbù piàn	*n*	horror movie
HOBBIES & ACTIVITIES					
30.	乒乓球		pīngpāngqiú	*n*	ping pong
31.	羽毛球		yǔmáoqiú	*n*	badminton
32.	骑马	騎馬	qí mǎ	*vo*	to ride a horse
33.	高尔夫球	高爾夫球	gāo'ěrfūqiú	*n*	golf
34.	排球		páiqiú	*n*	volleyball
35.	踢		tī	*v*	to kick
OTHER					
36.	不常		bùcháng	*adv*	not often; seldom

ONLINE RESOURCES

Visit *http://college.betterchinese.com* for a list of other words related to hobbies and activities.

Pictographs

Most Chinese characters are 'phono-semantic compounds,' meaning that they are comprised of a radical, which relates to the character's meaning, and a phonetic component, which hints at its pronunciation. Some characters, however, are structured differently. Pictographs are characters that originated as actual graphic representations of the things they signify. The modern forms of these characters don't always have a strong visual link to their subject, but we can still trace their development and perceive the resemblance. The following are some examples of pictographs starting from their origin in bone script, to seal script, and then to their modern day forms.

	Bone Script	Seal Script	Modern Script		Bone Script	Seal Script	Modern Script
mù: "eye"			目	yuè: "moon"			月
rén: "person"			人	shuǐ: "water"			水
rì: "sun"			日	shān: "mountain"			山

Ideographs

Another category of Chinese characters, and one that is also comparatively rare, is the ideograph. Unlike pictographs, ideographs are an abstract representation of the concept that they signify. The following are some examples of ideographs.

Character		Meaning	Derivation
一	yī	one	a single stroke
二	èr	two	two strokes
三	sān	three	three strokes
上	shàng	above	above a horizontal line
下	xià	below	below a horizontal line
中	zhōng	center	a line through the center
凸	tū	convex	a protruding component
凹	āo	concave	a sunken component

STRUCTURE NOTE 10.1
Use 一边...一边... to describe simultaneous actions

To indicate that someone is doing one action at the same time as doing another, add 一边 *(yìbiān: "at the same time") before each of the actions that is occurring simultaneously. In English, this pattern is usually translated as "while" or "at the same time as," or even simply as "and."*

> Subject + 一边 + Verb Phrase A + 一边 + Verb Phrase B

From the Lesson Text:

我一边吃饭一边跟你说话啊。
Wǒ yìbiān chī fàn yìbiān gēn nǐ shuō huà a.
I'm talking to you while eating.

Other examples:

我常常一边看电视一边吃饭。
Wǒ chángcháng yìbiān kàn diànshì yìbiān chī fàn.
I often watch television and eat at the same time.

他不能一边跳舞一边唱歌。
Tā bù néng yìbiān tiào wǔ yìbiān chàng gē.
He can't dance and sing at the same time.

Practice: Use the 一边...一边... construction and the verb phrases provided to create complete sentences in Chinese.

Example: 大东 / 上课 / 说话 → 大东一边上课一边说话。

1. 你 / 开车 / 打电话 _____
2. 弟弟 / 做功课 / 唱歌 _____
3. 他 / 看书 / 听音乐 _____
4. 我 / 工作 / 喝咖啡 _____
5. 我们 / 运动 / 看电视 _____

STRUCTURE NOTE 10.2
Use 什么 to mean "any"

什么 *has already been introduced as a question word meaning "what," but it can also be used before nouns to mean "some" or "any." When it is negated, this pattern means "not much/not many" or "none/nothing in particular."*

> 什么 + Object

From the Lesson Text:

今天是星期六，你有什么活动吗?
Jīntiān shì Xīngqī liù, nǐ yǒu shénme huódòng ma?
Today is Saturday, do you have any plans?

没什么活动。你呢?
Méi shénme huódòng. Nǐ ne?
None in particular. What about you?

Other examples:

他说他要去买什么东西。
Tā shuō tā yào qù mǎi shénme dōngxi.
He said he had to go buy something or other.

这里没什么人。
Zhèli méi shénme rén.
There aren't many people here.

NOTE: *Look out for the use of* 吗 *in questions in which* 什么 *appears. In questions in which* 什么 *is used to mean "any,"* 吗 *is used to turn the statement into a question, while in questions where* 什么 *means "what,"* 吗 *cannot be used.*

Examples:

你今天有什么活动？
Nǐ jīntiān yǒu shénme huódòng?
What plans do you have today?

你今天有什么活动吗？
Nǐ jīntiān yǒu shénme huódòng ma?
Do you have any plans today?

Practice: Respond to the following questions in the negative using 什么, following the example shown below.

Example: 这里有好玩的活动吗？ → 这里没什么好玩的活动。

1. 你今天有时间吗？ _____
2. 那边有很多人吗？ _____
3. 我可以借点钱吗？ _____
4. 有事吗？ _____
5. 你对数学有兴趣吗？ _____

STRUCTURE NOTE 10.3
Use topic-comment sentences

Chinese is characterized by linguists as a topic-comment language. This means that, although the basic sentence structure is subject-verb-object, many sentences have an alternative structure in which the topic of the sentence is put first, followed by a comment that says something about that topic. There is a pattern in English that is similar to this, although it is rarely used: "Bagels, I like. Muffins, not so much." The topic is generally a definite noun phrase that would have been the object in a regular sentence pattern.

Topic + Comment

From the Lesson Text: 他们有的去打球，有的去游泳，还有的去跑步。
Tāmen yǒude qù dǎ qiú, yǒude qù yóu yǒng, hái yǒude qù pǎo bù.
Some of them went to play sports, some went swimming, and some went running.

Other examples:

那本书我很喜欢。
Nèi běn shū wǒ hěn xǐhuan.
I really like that book.

汉字他觉得很难写。
Hànzì tā juéde hěn nán xiě.
He thinks that Chinese characters are difficult to write.

Practice: Rewrite the following sentences as topic-comment sentences, following the example provided.

Example:　　我很喜欢吃中国菜。　→ 中国菜我很喜欢吃。

1.　我很想去中国。

    _____

2.　中平有的时候听不懂你的录音。

    _____

3.　我不懂你说的话。

    _____

4.　我今天早上就做中文作业了。

    _____

5.　她最喜欢的活动就是唱歌。

    _____

STRUCTURE NOTE 10.4
Use 有的 to mean "some"

In Unit 2, Lesson 1, 有 *was introduced as the verb "to have" or "there is/are." In this lesson,* 有的 *is introduced as a means to say "some." In this construction, the subject normally appears following* 有的*, as in* 有的 人 *("some people"). However, if the subject of conversation is already clear, the* 有的 *can appear on its own. In the example from the Lesson Text, the subject has been topicalized (see Structure Note 10.3), so it is not repeated.*

有的 (+ Subject) + Verb Phrase

From the Lesson Text:　他们有的去打球，有的去游泳，还有的去跑步。
Tāmen yǒude qù dǎ qiú, yǒude qù yóu yǒng, hái yǒude qù pǎo bù.
Some of them went to play sports, some went swimming, and some went running.

Other examples:　有的人喜欢吃肉，有的人不喜欢吃。
Yǒude rén xǐhuan chī ròu, yǒude rén bù xǐhuan chī.
Some people like to eat meat, and some people don't.

学生们有的学中文，有的学英语，还有的学法语。
Xuéshēngmen yǒude xué Zhōngwén, yǒude xué Yīngyǔ, hái yǒude xué Fǎyǔ.
Some of the students study Chinese, some study English, and some study French.

Practice: Use the following sets of words and 有的 to create complete sentences in Chinese.

Example: 人／打球／游泳／跳舞

→有的人喜欢打球，有的人喜欢游泳，还有的人喜欢跳舞。

1. 人／吃肉／吃素

_____

2. 小孩子／蓝色／黄色

_____

3. 女孩子／裙子／裤子／牛仔裤

_____

4. 人／开车／ 火车／公共汽车

_____

5. 这些人／美国人／加拿大人

_____

STRUCTURE NOTE 10.5
Use 对...有兴趣 to express interest in something

The phrase 有意思 *(yǒu yìsi), though ostensibly a verb and an object ("to have interest"), is actually used as an adjective meaning "interesting." The word* 兴趣 *(xìngqu), however, does mean "interest," and is paired with* 有 *only as part of a set pattern to indicate something that one is interested in. To express that someone is (or isn't) interested in something,* 对 *is placed before the object, and* 有兴趣 *follows.*

> Subject + 对 + Object + 有 / 没(有) + 兴趣

From the Lesson Text:　可是我对这些活动都没有兴趣。
Kěshì wǒ duì zhèxiē huódòng dōu méiyǒu xìngqu.
But I'm not interested in any of these activities.

Other examples:　他对功夫很有兴趣。　　你对法文有没有兴趣？
Tā duì gōngfu hěn yǒu xìngqu.　　Nǐ duì Fǎwén yǒu méiyǒu xìngqu?
He is very interested in Kung Fu.　　Are you interested in French?

Practice: Change the following sentences into Chinese. Pay particular attention to when you should use 有兴趣 and when you should use 有意思.

Example:	I'm very interested in languages. →	我对语言很有兴趣。
1.	This book isn't very interesting.	_____
2.	Xiang'an is interested in soccer.	_____
3.	Are you interested in cooking?	_____
4.	Do you think she's interested in me?	_____
5.	They have no interest in movies.	_____

STRUCTURE NOTE 10.6
Use 常(常) to express "often"

Adverbial expressions of frequency, like 常常 *(chángcháng), are placed between the subject and the verb phrase. While the reduplicated form* 常常 *is used more frequently, the expression can also be abbreviated to the single character* 常*. Other useful expressions of frequency are* 不常 *(bùcháng: "not often") and* 很少 *(hěnshǎo: "very infrequently").*

> Subject + 常(常) + Verb Phrase

From the Lesson Text:

我常常去跳舞、唱歌。
Wǒ chángcháng qù tiào wǔ, chàng gē.
I often go dancing and singing.

Other examples:

我常常跟朋友一起去看电影。
Wǒ chángcháng gēn péngyou yìqǐ qù kàn diànyǐng.
I often go see movies with my friends.

你常给爸爸妈妈打电话吗?
Nǐ cháng gěi bàba māma dǎ diànhuà ma?
Do you call your parents often?

Practice: Use the information below to create sentences with 常(常), 不常, or 很少.

Example: 中平 / 下课以后 / 去图书馆
→ 中平下课以后常常去图书馆。

1.	爸爸 / 去饭馆 / 喝酸辣汤	_____
2.	妹妹 / 早上 / 运动	_____
3.	我 / 上课的时候 / 睡觉	_____
4.	他 / 周末 / 去听音乐会	_____
5.	姐姐 / 看电影 / 读书	_____

STRUCTURE NOTE 10.7

Use 能 to describe ability

能 (néng) *means "can," describing physical ability to do something. Just as in English, where "can" is often used to mean "may," in Chinese* 能 *and* 可以 *can often be used interchangeably, although* 能 *corresponds more closely to "can" and* 可以 *corresponds more to "may."*

Subject + 能 + Verb Phrase

From the Lesson Text:

你能不能七点五十分在电影院门口等我？
Nǐ néng bu néng qī diǎn wǔshí fēn zài diànyǐngyuàn ménkǒu děng wǒ?
Can you wait for me at the entrance to the theater at 7:50?

Other examples:

她今天不能跟我们一起去跳舞。
Tā jīntiān bù néng gēn wǒmen yìqǐ qù tiào wǔ.
She can't go dancing with us today.

现在太晚了，我不能再等了。
Xiànzài tài wǎn le, wǒ bù néng zài děng le.
It's too late now; I can't wait anymore.

NOTE: 能 *can sometimes be confused with* 会. *In English, we can say "Can you speak English?" or "Do you know how to speak English?" but in Chinese, this is usually expressed with* 会, *not with* 能. *A good rule to keep in mind is that* 会 *refers to general knowledge of how to do something, while* 能 *refers to ability to do something in a specific instance.*

Practice: Use 能, 会, or 可以 to fill in the gaps in the sentences below.

Example: 你 __ 跳舞吗？ → 你会跳舞吗？

1. 我太累了，不 __ 做作业了。 _____
2. 服务员，我们 __ 点菜吗？ _____
3. 你 __ 说中文吗？ _____
4. 她们 __ 吃辣吗？ _____
5. 这么贵的东西我不 __ 买。 _____

STRUCTURE NOTE 10.8

Use name + 他们 *to refer to a group of people*

When a plural pronoun (most often 他们) is added after a name it indicates that the speaker is referring to a particular person and the people associated with him or her. This is similar to English expressions such as "Mali and the others," and "Mali and the rest of them."

Name + Plural Pronoun

From the Lesson Text:

玛丽他们呢？
Mǎlì tāmen ne?
What about Mali and the others?

Other examples:

安娜她们都喜欢跳舞。
Ānnà tāmen dōu xǐhuan tiào wǔ.
Anna and the rest of them all like dancing.

我不知道大东他们在哪里。
Wǒ bù zhīdào Dàdōng tāmen zài nǎli.
I don't know where Dadong and the others are.

Practice: Express the following sentences in Chinese using the name + 他们 pattern.

Example: Xiang'an and the others have all gone to the library.
→ 祥安他们都去图书馆了。

1. What do Dadong and the rest of them have for lunch?

   _____

2. Do Mali and the others like soccer?

   _____

3. Anna and the others will wait for you at school.

   _____

4. Zhongping and the others have an important test next week.

   _____

5. Xiang'an and the rest all went swimming.

   _____

✏ PRACTICE 10.1

In the spaces provided, write the activity that matches the picture.

💬 PRACTICE 10.2

Working with a partner, use the information in the table below to engage in a dialogue about what each of the characters did last weekend and what their plans for this weekend are.

Example:

A: 陈大东上个周末有什么活动?

B: 大东上个星期去打球了。

A: 他这个星期六有什么计划?

B: 他要跟玛丽吃晚饭。

名字	上个周末	这个星期六
1. 陈大东	打球	跟玛丽吃晚饭
2. 李中平	在图书馆看书	打功夫
3. 王小美	画画儿	画画儿
4. 黄祥安	看足球比赛	看功夫电影
5. 孙玛丽	做中文功课	跟大东吃饭
6. 张安娜	买东西	给祥安打电话

Unit 10 ▪ Lesson 1 ▪ Hobbies & Activities **355**

PRACTICE 10.3

Working with a partner, practice the following conversation in which you make a phone call to your friend to invite him/her to go to a movie with you.

Example:

A: 喂？你这个周末有空吗？

B: 有什么事吗？

A: 星期天我想去看电影。你想跟我一起去吗？

B: 你想看什么电影？

A: 我想看功夫电影。

B: 好啊。电影几点开始？

A: 电影下午三点开始。

B: 好。那，我下午两点三刻在电影院门口等你。

PRACTICE 10.4

Interview your classmates about their hobbies and fill out the chart below. What are their favorite things to do? What did they do last weekend? Did they enjoy it?

Example:

A: 你上个周末有什么活动？

B: 我上个星期六去看电影了。

A: 电影怎么样？

B: 很有意思。

名字	喜欢什么活动？	上个周末做什么了？	怎么样？

PRACTICE 10.5

Do a survey of the class to find out what weekend activity is most common among your classmates. Record the most popular answer below.

Activity	Number of Students

PRACTICE 10.6

	Radical	Stroke Order
说	讠(言) yán speech	、 讠 讠 讠 讠 讠 讠 说
打	扌(手) shǒu hand	一 扌 扌 扌 打
球	玉 yù jade	一 二 干 王 玎 玎 玎 球 球 球
口	口 kǒu mouth	丨 口 口
空	穴 xué cave	、 丷 宀 宀 穴 空 空 空
边	辶 chuò walk	刁 力 力 边 边
活	氵(水) shuǐ water	、 冫 氵 汗 汗 汗 活 活
画	田 tián field	一 厂 厅 百 雨 面 画 画
些	二 èr two	丨 卜 止 止 此 此 些
常	巾 jīn cloth	丨 丷 丷 丷 尚 尚 常 常 常
部	阝 yì city	、 二 立 立 音 音 音 部 部
夫	大 dà big	一 二 夫 夫
影	彡 shān hair	丶 口 曰 日 旦 早 昌 景 景 景 景 影 影 影
院	阝 fù hill	了 阝 阝 阝 阼 阼 阼 院 院
等	竹(竹) zhú bamboo	丿 卜 卜 松 竹 竹 竿 竿 竿 笟 等 等

PRACTICE 10.7

Make an audio recording and send it to your teacher. In the recording, talk about your plans for the coming weekend.

PRACTICE 10.8

Type the following sentences on your computer and provide answers to the questions.

1. 他一边吃饭一边看电视。
2. 这个周末你有什么活动吗？
3. 我对这些活动都没什么兴趣。
4. 你想跟我一起去看一部新的功夫电影吗？
5. 明天晚上八点十五分我在电影院门口等你。

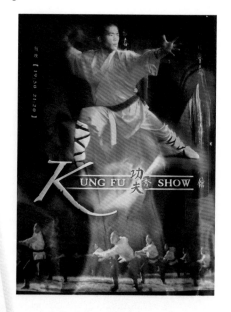

PRACTICE 10.9

今天我想找朋友一起去听音乐会，可是大家都很忙，有的准备考试，有的做作业，只有祥安有空，他今天没什么活动。晚上七点十五分，祥安会在图书馆门口等我，然后我们会去听音乐会。

Read Zhang Anna's diary and answer the following questions.
1. Why can't Zhang Anna's friends go to the concert with her?
2. Where will Huang Xiang'an meet Zhang Anna?

PRACTICE 10.10

李中平：你喜欢做什么活动？

孙玛丽：我喜欢游泳，每天早上我都去游泳。

李中平：我对游泳没兴趣，可是我喜欢打球。

孙玛丽：周末我还喜欢和朋友一起吃饭、跳舞、看电影。

李中平：是吗？那我们这个星期六中午一起去中国饭馆吃饭，怎么样？

孙玛丽：行，吃完午饭后，我请你去看电影。

李中平：看什么电影？

孙玛丽：一部新的中国电影。

李中平：听起来很有意思。

Read the dialogue and answer the following questions.
1. What activity does Li Zhongping like doing?
2. What will Li Zhongping and Sun Mali do after having lunch?

Karaoke or Chinese KTV

Karaoke or 卡拉OK (kǎlā-OK) might be known throughout the world, but this entertainment sensation from Japan is especially popular in contemporary China. While many Westerners view the experience as an embarrassing public display of talent (or lack thereof), in China karaoke has developed into a more serious social activity. The interactive sing-a-long game first emerged on China's social scene via upscale hotels in Hong Kong, Beijing, and Shanghai in the late 1980s. The appellation KTV (short for "karaoke television") was later adopted to denote the Chinese version of karaoke. In their early years, the first KTV bars acquired a bad reputation as somewhat seedy places. However, the widespread expansion of KTV in the 1990s gradually built a legitimate reputation for the pastime, establishing it as one of China's most widespread and popular social activities.

Mahjong

There is much debate over the exact origins of the Chinese game 麻将 (májiàng: "Mahjong"). One of the most popular myths suggests that the game was invented by the Chinese philosopher Confucius in around 500 BC. As the story goes, Confucius was fond of birds, hence the game's original name of 麻雀 (máquè: "sparrow").

Mahjong consists of a set of 144 tiles based on Chinese characters and symbols and typically involves four players. The game is a favorite pastime in China as well as in Chinese-speaking communities around the world. Today, when strolling about narrow alleys in any part of China, one can often hear clacking tiles and catch a glimpse of four competitors seated around a square table playing this time-honored game.

Chinese Martial Arts

According to legend, the genesis of Chinese 武术 (wǔshù: "martial arts") dates back more than 4,000 years to when the Yellow Emperor introduced the earliest fighting systems to China. Legend also has it that he was a great general who wrote lengthy treatises on ancient forms of martial arts. Later, the subject began to crop up in famed texts such as 庄子 (Zhuāngzǐ: "Zhuangzi"), 道德经 (Dàodéjīng: "The Daodejing"), and 孙子兵法 (Sūnzǐ Bīngfǎ: "The Art of War"), all of which refer to martial arts being more than merely a sport or a means of physical combat. These works define the discipline as a philosophy, an art, and a means to cultivate the unity of body, soul, and universe. The true goal of martial arts is thus not to inflict pain on others, but to attain spiritual enlightenment for oneself through the strict physical and mental discipline that it demands. It is still a significant aspect of China's cultural heritage, and hundreds of forms of martial arts – some of which are referred to as 功夫 (gōngfu: "kung fu"), others as 武术 – continue to be practiced both in China and throughout the rest of the world.

张安娜：	大家都很忙，都没空！看看祥安在不在。	Everyone is busy, no one has any free time! Let's see if Xiang'an is around.
黄祥安：	喂，安娜！你好！	Hello Anna!
张安娜：	嗨，祥安，你在做什么？	Hi Xiang'an, what are you doing?
黄祥安：	我一边吃饭一边跟你说话啊！	I'm talking to you while eating.
张安娜：	哈哈，我是说，今天是星期六，你有什么活动吗？	Haha, I mean, today is Saturday, do you have any plans?
黄祥安：	没什么活动。你呢？玛丽他们呢？	Not really. And you? What about Mali and the others?
张安娜：	他们有的去打球，有的去游泳，还有的去跑步，可是我对这些活动都没有兴趣。	Some went to play sports, some went swimming, and others went running, but I'm not interested in any of those activities.

黄祥安：	那你喜欢做什么？	Then what do you like to do?
张安娜：	我常常去跳舞、唱歌、看电影……	I often go dancing, singing, or to see movies.
黄祥安：	是吗？我今天晚上八点要去看一部新的功夫电影。你想跟我一起去吗？	Oh really? Tonight at 8 o'clock I'm going to see a new kung fu movie. Would you like to go with me?
张安娜：	哦！听起来很有意思。	Oh! Sounds interesting.
黄祥安：	好吧，你能不能七点五十分在电影院门口等我？	OK, Can you wait for me at the entrance to the movie theatre at 7:50?
张安娜：	行，晚上见。	Sure, see you tonight.

What Can You Do?

INTERPRETIVE
- I can understand different terms for sports, hobbies, and leisure activities.

INTERPERSONAL
- I can discuss leisure activities with others.
- I can make arrangements to play sports or go to the movies with someone.

PRESENTATIONAL
- I can give a basic presentation about my hobbies.
- I can express how frequently I do something.

在音乐会
At a Concert

大东，中平，你们下个周末有空吗？

有什么
tè bié
特别的
事吗？

星期六小美会在音
biǎo yǎn
乐会表演，我们一起
去看，好不好？

哇，小美真
tiān cái
是个天才！

niàn shū niàn de   wǎng qiú   de   huà huàr
念书念得好，网球打得好，画画儿
huà de   yīn yuè jiā   ya
也画得好，还是个音乐家呀！

她今天
biǎo yǎn
表演什
么呢？

tán jí tā　　zuì jìn měi
她要弹吉他。她最近每天都
xiǎo shí　　rèn zhēn
练习五六个小时，很认真！

玛丽，你不是
lā xiǎo tí qín
会拉小提琴吗？
tiān cái
你也是个天才！

nǎ lǐ　　nǎ lǐ　　　lā de
哪里，哪里！大东拉得比我更好！

chū lai
小美出来了！

xiào　　　　kāi xīn
你们看，她笑得这么开心。

喂，大东，为什么
xiào
小美只对你笑呢？

LESSON TEXT 10.2

At a Concert 在音乐会

Sun Mali, Li Zhongping, and Chen Dadong make plans to go to Wang Xiaomei's concert the following Saturday. They attend, then chat about hobbies and music.

孙玛丽：	大东，中平，你们下个周末有空吗？	Dàdōng, Zhōngpíng, nǐmen xià ge zhōumò yǒu kòng ma?
李中平：	有什么特别的事吗？	Yǒu shénme tèbié de shì ma?
孙玛丽：	星期六小美会在音乐会表演，我们一起去看，好不好？	Xīngqī liù Xiǎoměi huì zài yīnyuèhuì biǎoyǎn, wǒmen yìqǐ qù kàn, hǎo bu hǎo?

陈大东：	哇，小美真是个天才！念书念得好，网球打得好，画画儿也画得好，还是个音乐家呀！	Wā, Xiǎoměi zhēn shì ge tiāncái! Niàn shū niàn de hǎo, wǎngqiú dǎ de hǎo, huà huàr yě huà de hǎo, hái shì ge yīnyuèjiā ya!
李中平：	她今天表演什么呢？	Tā jīntiān biǎoyǎn shénme ne?
孙玛丽：	她要弹吉他。她最近每天都练习五六个小时，很认真！	Tā yào tán jítā. Tā zuìjìn měi tiān dōu liànxí wǔ liù ge xiǎoshí, hěn rènzhēn!
李中平：	玛丽，你不是会拉小提琴吗？你也是个天才！	Mǎlì, nǐ bú shì huì lā xiǎotíqín ma? Nǐ yě shì ge tiāncái!
孙玛丽：	哪里，哪里！大东拉得比我更好！	Nǎlǐ, nǎlǐ! Dàdōng lā de bǐ wǒ gèng hǎo!
孙玛丽：	小美出来了！你们看，她笑得这么开心。	Xiǎoměi chūlai le! Nǐmen kàn, tā xiào de zhème kāixīn.
李中平：	喂，大东，为什么小美只对你笑呢？	Wèi, Dàdōng, wèishénme Xiǎoměi zhǐ duì nǐ xiào ne?

字词 VOCABULARY

LESSON VOCABULARY 10.2

	SIMPLIFIED	TRADITIONAL	PINYIN	WORD CATEGORY	DEFINITION
1.	特别	特别	tèbié	adj	special
2.	表演		biǎoyǎn	v, n	to perform; performance
3.	天才		tiāncái	n	genius; talent
4.	念书	念書	niàn shū	vo	to study; to read
5.	网球	網球	wǎngqiú	n	tennis
6.	画画(儿)	畫畫(兒)	huà huà(r)	vo	to paint; to draw
	画儿	畫兒	huàr	n	painting; drawing
7.	音乐家	音樂家	yīnyuèjiā	n	musician
8.	呀		ya	p	(used to express surprise like 啊 but follows vowels)
9.	弹	彈	tán	v	to play (a musical instrument); to pluck
10.	吉他		jítā	n	guitar
11.	最近		zuìjìn	adv	recently
12.	每		měi	pr	every, each
13.	小时	小時	xiǎoshí	n	hour
14.	认真	認真	rènzhēn	adj	serious; conscientious; diligent
15.	拉		lā	v	to play (an instrument with a bow); to pull
16.	小提琴		xiǎotíqín	n	violin
17.	哪里哪里	哪裏哪裏	nǎlǐ nǎlǐ	ie	not at all (a polite reply to a compliment)
18.	出来	出來	chūlai	dc	to emerge; come out
19.	笑		xiào	v	to smile; to laugh
20.	开心	開心	kāixīn	adj	happy

REQUIRED VOCABULARY 10.2

Simplified	Traditional	Pinyin	Word Category	Definition
Musical Instruments				
21. 乐器	樂器	yuèqì	*n*	musical instrument
22. 打鼓		dǎ gǔ	*vo*	to play the drums
23. 钢琴	鋼琴	gāngqín	*n*	piano
24. 大提琴		dàtíqín	*n*	cello
Adjectives				
25. 快		kuài	*adj*	fast
26. 慢		màn	*adj*	slow

OPTIONAL VOCABULARY 10.2

Simplified	Traditional	Pinyin	Word Category	Definition
Musical Genres				
27. 好听	好聽	hǎo tīng	*adj*	lovely; pleasant (to the ear)
28. 摇滚乐	摇滚樂	yáogǔnyuè	*n*	rock music
29. 古典音乐	古典音樂	gǔdiǎn yīnyuè	*n*	classical music
30. 流行音乐	流行音樂	liúxíng yīnyuè	*n*	pop music

 ONLINE RESOURCES
Visit *http://college.betterchinese.com* for a list of other words related to music.

Verbs for Hobbies and Activities

In English, the verb "to play" is used with most hobbies (tennis, basketball, soccer, cards, video games, etc.). In Chinese, the verb 打 (dǎ: "to hit; to do; to play") covers much of the same ground. In particular, 打 is used when referring to sports played with the hands. However, there are some activities that require specific verbs. Below is a list of some of the common pairings.

The Verb 打

	篮球	lánqiú	basketball
	乒乓球	pīngpāngqiú	ping-pong
	高尔夫球	gāo'ěrfūqiú	golf
	羽毛球	yǔmáoqiú	badminton
	网球	wǎngqiú	tennis
打	排球	páiqiú	volleyball
	橄榄球	gǎnlǎnqiú	rugby; football (American)
	麻将	májiàng	mahjong
	功夫	gōngfu	Kung Fu
	太极拳	tàijíquán	Tai Chi
	鼓	gǔ	drums

Other Activity Verbs

踢	tī	kick	足球，毽子	zúqiú, jiànzi	soccer, hacky sack
玩	wán	play	（电子）游戏	(diànzǐ) yóuxì	(video) games
看	kàn	watch, read	书，电影，电视	shū, diànyǐng, diànshì	books, movies, television
骑	qí	ride	马，自行车	mǎ, zìxíngchē	horses, bikes
弹	tán	play (lit. "pluck")	吉他，琴，钢琴	jítā, qín, gāngqín	guitar, harp, piano
拉	lā	play (lit. "pull")	小提琴，大提琴	xiǎotíqín, dàtíqín	violin, cello
唱	chàng	sing; recite	歌，诗	gē, shī	songs, poetry
画	huà	draw, paint	画儿	huàr	drawings, paintings
跑	pǎo	run	步，马拉松	bù, mǎlāsōng	jogging, marathons

STRUCTURE NOTE 10.9
Use 得 *to describe the manner of actions*

There are several patterns that can be used to describe the manner in which something is done. The most common way to do this is to add 得 *(de, pronounced the same as* 的*) to the verb followed by an adverb. Sentences that describe the manner of an action may contain modifiers such as* 很 *and* 太 *as well as comparative phrases, but they may not use* 了*. Note also that negation comes before the adverb, not the verb.*

> Subject + Verb + 得 + Adverb

From the Lesson Text:

你们看，她笑得这么开心。
Nǐmen kàn, tā xiào de zhème kāixīn.
Look, she's smiling so happily.

大东拉得比我更好！
Dàdōng lā de bǐ wǒ gèng hǎo!
Dadong plays even better than me!

Other examples:

他练习得不太认真。
Tā liànxí de bú tài rènzhēn.
He didn't practice that diligently.

说得好！
Shuō de hǎo!
Well said!

Most verbs phrases in Chinese consist of a verb-object pair. When an object is introduced into the equation, the basic rule is that 得 *must directly follow the verb. This is achieved by using the whole verb-object phrase followed by a repetition of the verb. If the object in the verb-object pair is a noun that commonly appears on its own (e.g.,* 篮球*), the verb can optionally be deleted before the object (*他篮球打得很好*). Some verb-object pairs are equivalent to intransitive verbs in English (e.g.,* 说话 *"to talk words" – "to talk"), so it is important to remember which two-character verb phrases are verb-object pairs, and which are two-character verbs.*

> Subject (+ Verb) + Object + Verb + 得 + Adverb

From the Lesson Text:

念书念得好，网球打得好，画画儿也画得好，
还是个音乐家呀！
Niàn shū niàn de hǎo, wǎngqiú dǎ de hǎo, huà huàr yě huà de hǎo, hái shì ge yīnyuèjiā ya!
She studies well, plays tennis well, draws well, and she's a musician too!

Other examples:

他车开得很小心。
Tā chē kāi de hěn xiǎoxīn.
He drives very carefully.

她弹吉他弹得很好。
Tā tán jítā tán de hěn hǎo.
She plays the guitar very well.

368 第十单元 ▪ 第二课 ▪ 娱

Practice: Create statements with 得 that comment on the manner of an action using the information given below.

Example:　说中文 / 好 → 他说中文说得很好。

1.　写字 / 大　　_____

2.　打球 / 不好　_____

3.　复习 / 认真　_____

4.　考试 / 差　　_____

5.　做菜 / 好吃　_____

STRUCTURE NOTE 10.10

Use 每...都... to express "every"

The 每...都... (měi...dōu) *pattern expresses that something is true for each item in a category. The* 每 *can be applied to the subject of the sentence, or to a unit of time to create a time expression. Place a measure word between* 每 *and nouns that normally use measure words; none is required for* 年, 天 *etc.*

> 每 (+ Measure Word) + Noun Phrase + 都 + Verb Phrase

From the Lesson Text:

她最近每天都练习五六个小时。
Tā zuìjìn měi tiān dōu liànxí wǔ liù ge xiǎoshí.
Recently she's been practicing for five or six hours every day.

Other examples:

每个人都有一张纸。
Měi ge rén dōu yǒu yì zhāng zhǐ.
Everyone has a sheet of paper.

我每个星期三都去中国饭馆。
Wǒ měi ge Xīngqī sān dōu qù Zhōngguó fànguǎn.
I go to a Chinese restaurant every Wednesday.

Practice: Write the following sentences in Chinese using the 每...都... pattern.

Example:　He has a test every week. → 他每个星期都有考试。

1.　Every year he goes back to China to see his family.

　　_____

2.　Every student in the school likes Teacher Zhang.

　　_____

3.　Every one of my classmates thinks that test was hard.

　　_____

4.　I go to the gym every two days.

　　_____

5.　Every item of clothing in this shop is really pretty.

　　_____

STRUCTURE NOTE 10.11
Use time periods to indicate duration

In expressions that indicate how long someone does something for, the duration follows the verb.

If the verb has an object, there are two methods that can be used. The first is to use the whole verb-object phrase

---

Subject + Verb (+ 了) + Duration

---

and then repeat the verb. The second is to move the object to the end of the statement and attach it to the expression of duration with 的. 了 *can also be added after the verb in order to establish that the action took place in the past.*

Subject + Verb + Object + Verb (+ 了) + Duration

Subject + Verb (+ 了) + Duration + 的 + Object

From the Lesson Text:
她最近每天都练习五六个小时。
Tā zuìjìn měi tiān dōu liànxí wǔ liù ge xiǎoshí.
Recently she's been practicing for five or six hours every day.

Other examples:
她昨天跑步跑了两个小时。
Tā zuótiān pǎo bù pǎo le liǎng ge xiǎoshí.
She went running for two hours yesterday.

我的同学上个星期学了十二个小时的中文。
Wǒ de tóngxué shàng ge xīngqī xué le shí èr ge xiǎoshí de Zhōngwén.
My classmate studied Chinese for twelve hours last week.

Practice: Create complete sentences with the following information. Use one of the three patterns given above, as appropriate.

Example: 我 / 写 / 汉字 / 一个小时
→ 我每天都写一个小时的汉字。

1. 妹妹 / 弹 / 钢琴 / 三个小时

   _____

2. 我 / 睡 / 觉 / 六个小时

   _____

3. 朋友 / 打 / 网球 / 四十分钟

   _____

4. 同学 / 复习 / 一个小时

   _____

5. 他 / 开 / 车 / 一天

   _____

STRUCTURE NOTE 10.12
Use multiple numbers to estimate amounts

An estimate that lists two possible amounts, such as "three or four" in English, can be expressed in Chinese by simply listing two numbers consecutively. For estimates over 20, the first part of the number (the number 1 – 9) is repeated, but the unit (十, 百, 千, etc.) is not.

> Number + Number + Measure Word + Noun

From the Lesson Text:

她最近每天都练习五六个小时。
Tā zuìjìn měi tiān dōu liànxí wǔ liù ge xiǎoshí.
Recently she's been practicing for five or six hours every day.

Other examples:

我一共会写五六十个汉字。
Wǒ yígòng huì xiě wǔ liù shí ge Hànzì.
I can write fifty or sixty Chinese characters in total.

那个手机的价钱是四五百块。
Nèi ge shǒujī de jiàqián shì sì wǔ bǎi kuài.
The price of that cellphone is four or five hundred dollars.

Practice: Insert or substitute estimates that list two possible amounts into the appropriate places in the sentences below.

Example:　　我昨天学了很多生词。
　　　　　　→ 我昨天学了五六十个生词。

1.　　我今天晚上打算弹几个小时的吉他。

　　　　_____

2.　　学校要我选课。

　　　　_____

3.　　他在商店买了很多衣服。

　　　　_____

4.　　我的朋友每天都跑几个小时的步。

　　　　_____

5.　　我今天花了很多钱。

　　　　_____

STRUCTURE NOTE 10.13
Use 不是…吗？ *to ask a rhetorical question*

In English, the question "Don't you know how to play the violin?" can imply that the speaker thinks that the listener does indeed know how to play the violin. In Chinese, the pattern 不是…吗？ *is used in the same way in order to ask rhetorical questions.*

Subject + 不是 + Verb Phrase + 吗 ?

From the Lesson Text:

你不是会拉小提琴吗？
Nǐ bú shì huì lā xiǎotíqín ma?
Don't you know how to play the violin?

Other Examples:

你爸爸不是中国人吗？
Nǐ bàba bú shì Zhōngguó rén ma?
Isn't your dad Chinese?

你不是说他西班牙语说得很好吗？
Nǐ bú shì shuō tā Xībānyáyǔ shuō de hěn hǎo ma?
Didn't you say that he speaks Spanish really well?

Practice: Turn the following statements into rhetorical questions using the 不是…吗？ pattern.

Example:　他说他没有钱了。→ 他不是说他没有钱了吗？

1. 她喜欢看电视。

   _____

2. 你说她是个天才。

   _____

3. 你哥哥弹吉他弹得很好。

   _____

4. 他觉得这门课很难。

   _____

5. 大东的朋友是个音乐家。

   _____

STRUCTURE NOTE 10.14
Use 对 *as the preposition "to, towards"*

对 (dùi) *is a preposition meaning "towards" that is used in many common sentence patterns, as in the pattern* 对 ... 有兴趣. *Like most prepositional phrases in Chinese,* 对 *phrases are placed before the main verb phrase.*

> Subject + 对 + Object + Verb Phrase

From the Lesson Text:

为什么小美只对你笑呢？
Wèishénme Xiǎoměi zhǐ duì nǐ xiào ne?
Why is Xiaomei only smiling at you?

Other examples:

你对我太好了。
Nǐ duì wǒ tài hǎo le.
You are too good to me.

他对我说生日快乐。
Tā duì wǒ shuō shēngrì kuàilè.
He said happy birthday to me.

Practice: Transform the following sentences into Chinese using 对 .

Example: You should say sorry to her. → 你应该对她说对不起。

1. She's very good to her friends.

   _____

2. That student said thanks to the teacher.

   _____

3. The teacher spoke to the boy.

   _____

4. The girl is singing to me.

   _____

5. He's very diligent when it comes to studying.

   _____

练习 PRACTICE

💬 PRACTICE 10.11

✏️ Write the appropriate noun and verb pairing next to the image to describe the activity depicted. Then, with a partner, practice the dialogue shown below.

弹钢琴

Example:
A: 他会做什么？
B: 他会弹钢琴。

💬 PRACTICE 10.12

Working with a partner, ask and answer questions based on the activity schedule shown below.

Example:
A: 你什么时候练习钢琴？练习几个小时？
B: 我每个星期一和星期三练习五个小时的钢琴。

星期/时间	日	一	二	三	四	五	六
07:00 - 12:00		钢琴		钢琴	画画		画画
13:30 - 15:00			网球		网球		
16:00 - 20:00	大提琴					大提琴	
21:00 - 22:00	篮球	篮球	篮球	篮球	篮球	篮球	篮球

PRACTICE 10.13

Working in groups, ask your classmates what they can do well and what they can't do well. Choose someone from your group to report your findings to your class.

Example: 李中平篮球打得好，可是钢琴弹得不好。

名字	什么活动做得好?	什么活动做得不好?

PRACTICE 10.14

Do a survey to determine which musical instrument the most students in the class can play. Record your findings below.

Musical Instrument	Number of Students

PRACTICE 10.15

Type the following sentences on your computer and provide answers to the questions.

1. 你明天晚上有空吗?
2. 我们一起去看小美的表演，好不好?
3. 他弟弟真是个天才!
4. 我最近每天练习四五个小时的钢琴。
5. 他弹吉他弹得比我好。

PRACTICE 10.16

Make an audio recording and send it to your teacher. In the recording, talk about what hobbies you have and how much time you spend doing them.

	Radical	Stroke Order
哪	口 kǒu mouth	丶 丷 口 叮 叼 叼 哪 哪ˀ 哪
特	牜(牛) niú cow	丿 丿 牛 牛 牛 牛 牪 特 特 特
别	刂(刀) dāo knife	丶 口 口 弓 另 别 别
才	手 shǒu hand	一 十 才
表	衣 yī clothes	一 二 耂 丰 耒 耒 表 表
演	氵(水) shuǐ water	丶 丶 氵 汃 汃 沪 沪 沪 沪 渖 渖 演 演
网	网 wǎng net	丨 冂 冂 冈 网 网
近	辶 chuò walk	丿 广 斤 斤 沂 近 近
每	毋 wú not	丿 丿 匚 勹 每 每 每
弹	弓 gōng bow	丶 勹 弓 弓 弓 弓 弹 弹 弹 弹
吉	口 kǒu mouth	一 十 士 吉 吉 吉
拉	扌(手) shǒu hand	一 十 扌 扌 扩 扩 拉 拉
提	扌(手) shǒu hand	一 十 扌 扌 护 护 押 押 捍 捍 提
琴	玉 yù jade	一 二 于 王 玉 玕 玗 玨 珡 琴 琴 琴
笑	竹(竹) zhú bamboo	丿 丿 𥫗 竹 竹 竹 竿 竿 笑 笑

PRACTICE 10.18

孙玛丽：你下个周末有空吗？
李中平：有。有什么特别的事吗？
孙玛丽：我会在学校的音乐会表演，你能来吗？
李中平：好啊！你会表演什么乐器？
孙玛丽：我会拉小提琴。最近我每天都练习六七个小时。
李中平：哇！你真认真！那我一定得去听听。
孙玛丽：太好了！音乐会是下星期六下午三点，不要忘哦！
李中平：行！

Read the dialogue and answer the following questions.
1. What musical instrument is Sun Mali going to play?
2. When is the performance?

PRACTICE 10.19

小美今天在学校打网球，她网球打得真不错！小美还会画画儿、弹吉他、拉小提琴，她真是个天才！小美说她常常练习，星期一和星期三练习两个小时的吉他，星期二和星期四练习一个小时的小提琴，星期五画画儿，周末就打网球。

Read Chen Dadong's diary and answer the following questions.
1. On what days does Xiaomei practice guitar? How long does she practice for?
2. What does she do on the weekend?

PRACTICE 10.20

Sender 祥安
Subject 音乐会

中平：你上个星期的西班牙文考试考得怎么样？明天晚上七点半有个音乐会，张安娜会拉大提琴，我们一起去听，好不好？

Read the emails and answer the following questions.
1. Who will perform in the concert?
2. Why doesn't Li Zhongping want to go to the concert?

Sender 中平
Subject re: 音乐会

祥安：我的西班牙文考试考得不好，明天早上要再考一次。晚上我要和我的同学打篮球。因为下个星期有篮球比赛，所以我们得多练习。我对音乐没什么兴趣，所以我不会去听音乐会了。

Peking Opera

Among the many of forms of opera that exist in China, 京剧 (Jīngjù: "Beijing Opera" or "Peking Opera") is undoubtedly the most well known, both in China and abroad. Beijing Opera is a form of traditional Chinese theater that incorporates diverse elements of drama, music, vocal performance, costume, make-up, dance, and acrobatics. It presents dramatic plays and figures mainly by infusing four artistic methods: singing, dialogue, dancing, and martial arts.

At first, only men were permitted to perform in Beijing Opera. This trend slowly began to change towards the end of the 19th century, and today the many diverse roles of Beijing opera are played by both men and women. Among these various roles, there are four main character types: 生 (shēng), 旦 (dàn), 净 (jìng), and 丑 (chǒu):

生	leading male actors who might appear as decent, middle-aged men 老生 (lǎo shēng), acrobats who play military figures 武生 (wǔ shēng), young men 小生 (xiǎo shēng), or kids 娃娃生 (wáwa shēng)
旦	female characters comprising old ladies 老旦 (lǎo dàn), women skilled in martial arts 武旦 (wǔ dàn), strong-minded, middle-aged women of elegance 正旦 (zhèng dàn), and lively young girls from the lower class 花旦 (huā dàn)
净	males covered by elaborate face-paint to depict the unique appearances or personalities of warriors, heroes, statesmen, adventurers, and demons
丑	Comical characters distinguished by a white patch on the nose. Most of the time, these clowns are witty characters who keep the audience laughing and the mood light

Performers adhere to a variety of stylistic conventions and musical genres to help audiences navigate the plot. Certain costumes, make-up, and stage props help to identify roles within the opera. Beijing Opera is also famous for the many symbolic and suggestive gestures that are to be found in its performances. Simple footwork, hand gestures, and various kinds of body movements can all contribute to the portrayal of actions such as opening a door, climbing a hill, going upstairs, or rowing a boat.

Beijing Opera does not limit itself in space or time. The art allows audiences to enjoy vivid performances involving dynamic acrobatic fights, elaborate face paintings, and colorful costumes, all while peering into a narrative window of China's rich past.

孙玛丽：	大东，中平，你们下个周末有空吗？	Dadong, Zhongping, are you free next weekend?
李中平：	有什么特别的事吗？	Is there something special going on?
孙玛丽：	星期六小美会在音乐会表演，我们一起去看，好不好？	Xiaomei is performing at a concert on Saturday. Let's go see her play, OK?

陈大东：	哇，小美真是个天才！念书念得好，网球打得好，画画儿也画得好，还是个音乐家呀！	Wow, Xiaomei is so talented! She's good at her studies, tennis, and painting, and on top of that she's a musician!
李中平：	她今天表演什么呢？	What is she performing today?
孙玛丽：	她要弹吉他。她最近每天都练习五六个小时，很认真！	She will be playing the guitar. Recently, she's been practicing for five to six hours a day, she's very diligent!
李中平：	玛丽，你不是会拉小提琴吗？你也是个天才！	Mali, don't you play the violin? You're talented too!
孙玛丽：	哪里，哪里！大东拉得比我更好！	No, no, not at all! Dadong plays even better than I do!
孙玛丽：	小美出来了！你们看，她笑得这么开心。	Xiaomei's coming on to the stage! Look, she's smiling so happily.
李中平：	喂，大东，为什么小美只对你笑呢？	Hey, Dadong, why is Xiaomei only smiling at you?

What Can You Do?

INTERPRETIVE
- I can understand the terms for different kinds of musical instruments.
- I can understand terms for time periods and duration.

INTERPERSONAL
- I can discuss my musical preferences and abilities with others.
- I can invite people to attend concerts and receive replies.

PRESENTATIONAL
- I can present information about what instruments I play and what kind of music I like.
- I can comment upon how well someone performs an action.

ACT IT OUT

Working in groups, compose an original three-minute skit that utilizes the vocabulary and structures introduced in Unit 10. Each of you should assume a role and have a roughly equal number of lines in the skit. Be prepared to perform your skit in class. You can either come up with your own story or choose from one of the following situations:

A) You are on vacation with some friends and can't decide what to do.
B) You and your younger brother went to see a movie and both have different opinions about it.
C) You go to a concert with a friend and afterwards discuss the performance of each of the musicians.

CHECK WHAT YOU CAN DO

RECOGNIZE						WRITE	
Adjectives □ 忙 □ 特别 □ 认真 □ 开心 □ 快 □ 慢 *Conjunctions* □ 一边 *Adverbs* □ 一边 □ 常常 □ 很少 □ 最近	*Measure Words* □ 部 *Idiomatic Expressions* □ 听起来 □ 行 □ 哪里哪里 *Nouns* □ 活动 □ 这些 □ 兴趣 □ 功夫 □ 电影 □ 电影院	□ 门口 □ 游戏 □ 天才 □ 网球 □ 音乐家 □ 吉他 □ 小时 □ 小提琴 □ 乐器 □ 钢琴 □ 大提琴 *Particles* □ 呀	*Prepositions* □ 对 *Prepositions* □ 每 *Verbs* □ 有空 □ 说话 □ 打球 □ 游泳 □ 跑步 □ 跳舞 □ 唱歌 □ 等 □ 玩	□ 表演 □ 念书 □ 画画(儿) □ 弹 □ 拉 □ 出来 □ 笑 □ 打鼓		□ 说 □ 打 □ 球 □ 口 □ 空 □ 边 □ 活 □ 画 □ 些 □ 常 □ 部 □ 夫 □ 影 □ 院 □ 等	□ 哪 □ 特 □ 别 □ 才 □ 表 □ 演 □ 网 □ 近 □ 每 □ 弹 □ 吉 □ 拉 □ 提 □ 琴 □ 笑

USE

□ 一边…一边… to describe simultaneous actions

□ 什么 to mean "any"

□ Topic-comment sentences

□ 有的 to mean "some"

□ 对…有兴趣 to express interest in something

□ 常(常) to express "often"

□ 能 to describe ability

□ Name + 他们 to refer to a group of people

□ 得 to describe the manner of actions

□ 每…都… to express "every"

□ Time periods to indicate duration

□ Multiple numbers to estimate amounts

□ 不是…吗？ to ask a rhetorical question

□ 对 as the preposition "to, towards"

情

Relationships & People

第十一单元
UNIT 11

Communication Goals

Lesson 1: 约会 A Date
- Arrange to go on a date with someone
- Describe a person's qualities and attributes

Lesson 2: 分手 A Break Up
- Discuss relationships, marriage, and break-ups
- Describe your emotions
- Refer to something using the passive voice
- Talk about past experiences

约会
A Date

小美，你的表演
bàng
真棒！我可以请
你去吃晚饭吗？

好啊！玛丽、
中平他们也
一起去吗？

xiǎng
我想就只有
我和你……

哦……好的！

wǎn diǎnr
我晚点儿跟你
jiàn miàn
说在哪儿见面。

好，你再打电
gào su
话告诉我吧！

jǐn zhāng　　bù dé liǎo
我真的紧张得不得了。这是
cì　　　　　yuē huì
我第一次跟小美约会。

你喜欢小美的哪一点？

她很聪明，善良，也很可爱。

女孩子都希望听别人说她美。你不要忘记对她说喔。

什么，我会记不住！

你还要让她知道，你对她的感情是真的！

祥安！不要闹了，你还有什么建议吗？

吃完饭，你可以跟她去公园散散步，再约她下次出去玩。

嗨！

你今天真漂亮……

课 文 LESSON TEXT

LESSON TEXT 11.1

A Date 约会

A couple of days after the concert, Chen Dadong asks Wang Xiaomei to dinner. The day of the date, Chen Dadong confesses to Huang Xiang'an that he is extremely nervous, and Huang Xiang'an offers him some advice.

陈大东：	小美，你的表演真棒！我可以请你去吃晚饭吗？	Xiǎoměi, nǐ de biǎoyǎn zhēn bàng! Wǒ kěyǐ qǐng nǐ qù chī wǎnfàn ma?
王小美：	好啊！玛丽、中平他们也一起去吗？	Hǎo a! Mǎlì, Zhōngpíng tāmen yě yìqǐ qù ma?
陈大东：	我想就只有我和你……	Wǒ xiǎng jiù zhǐ yǒu wǒ hé nǐ...
王小美：	哦……好的！	Ò... hǎo de!
陈大东：	我晚点儿跟你说在哪儿见面。	Wǒ wǎndiǎnr gēn nǐ shuō zài nǎr jiàn miàn.
王小美：	好，你再打电话告诉我吧！	Hǎo, nǐ zài dǎ diànhuà gàosu wǒ ba!

陈大东：	我真的紧张得不得了。这是我第一次跟小美约会。	Wǒ zhēnde jǐnzhāng de bùdéliǎo. Zhè shì wǒ dì yī cì gēn Xiǎoměi yuēhuì.
黄祥安：	你喜欢小美的哪一点？	Nǐ xǐhuan Xiǎoměi de nǎ yì diǎn?
陈大东：	她很聪明、善良，也很可爱。	Tā hěn cōngmíng, shànliáng, yě hěn kě'ài.
黄祥安：	女孩子都希望听别人说她美。你不要忘记对她说喔。	Nǚháizi dōu xīwàng tīng biérén shuō tā měi. Nǐ bú yào wàngjì duì tā shuō o.
陈大东：	什么？我会记不住！	Shénme, wǒ huì jì bu zhù!
黄祥安：	你还要让她知道，你对她的感情是真的！	Nǐ hái yào ràng tā zhīdào, nǐ duì tā de gǎnqíng shì zhēn de!
陈大东：	祥安！不要闹了，你还有什么建议吗？	Xiáng'ān! Bú yào nào le, nǐ hái yǒu shénme jiànyì ma?

384 第十一单元 · 第一课 · 情

字词 VOCABULARY

黄祥安:	吃完饭，你可以跟她去公园散散步，再约她下次出去玩。	Chī wán fàn, nǐ kěyǐ gēn tā qù gōngyuán sànsan bù, zài yuē tā xià cì chūqu wán.

王小美:	嗨！	Hāi!
陈大东:	你今天真漂亮……	Nǐ jīntiān zhēn piàoliang…

LESSON VOCABULARY 11.1

	SIMPLIFIED	TRADITIONAL	PINYIN	WORD CATEGORY	DEFINITION
1.	棒		bàng	adj	great; wonderful
2.	想		xiǎng	v	to think
3.	晚点	晚點	wǎndiǎn	adv	(a bit) later
4.	见面	見面	jiàn miàn	vo	to meet
5.	告诉	告訴	gàosu	v	to tell
6.	紧张	緊張	jǐnzhāng	adj	nervous
7.	不得了		bùdéliǎo	adv	(to a degree)
8.	次		cì	mw	(used to describe the frequency of an action)
9.	约会	約會	yuē huì	vo, n	to go on a date; date
	约	約	yuē	v	to arrange; to make an appointment
10.	点	點	diǎn	n	point, characteristic
11.	聪明	聰明	cōngmíng	adj	smart, intelligent
12.	善良		shànliáng	adj	nice, kind, kind-hearted
13.	可爱	可愛	kě'ài	adj	cute
14.	希望		xīwàng	v, n	to hope; hope
15.	别人	別人	biérén	n	other people
16.	美		měi	adj	beautiful
17.	不要		bú yào	adv	don't
18.	忘记	忘記	wàngjì	rv	to forget

LESSON VOCABULARY 11.1 (continued)

	SIMPLIFIED	TRADITIONAL	PINYIN	WORD CATEGORY	DEFINITION
19.	喔		o	*interj*	(used to indicate a reminder, admonition, or warning)
20.	记不住	記不住	jì bu zhù	*rv*	to be unable to remember
21.	让	讓	ràng	*v*	to allow or cause (somebody to do something)
22.	感情		gǎnqíng	*n*	feeling, emotion
23.	不要闹了	不要鬧了	bú yào nào le	*ie*	stop it! (used when others are not being serious, poking fun at someone)
	闹	鬧	nào	*v*	to stir up trouble; to make noise
24.	建议	建議	jiànyì	*v, n*	to suggest; suggestion, advice
25.	公园	公園	gōngyuán	*n*	park
26.	散步		sàn bù	*vo*	to go for a stroll
27.	下次		xiàcì	*n*	next time
28.	出去玩(儿)	出去玩(兒)	chūqu wán(r)	*ie*	to go out and play, have a good time
	出去		chūqu	*dc*	to go outside

REQUIRED VOCABULARY 11.1

ADJECTIVES

29.	好看		hǎokàn	*adj*	pretty; good-looking
30.	帅	帥	shuài	*adj*	handsome

OPTIONAL VOCABULARY 11.1

RELATED TO RELATIONSHIPS

31.	玫瑰花		méiguīhuā	*n*	rose
32.	送花		sòng huā	*vo*	to give flowers
33.	吻		wěn	*v, n*	to kiss; kiss

OTHER

34.	上次		shàngcì	*n*	last time

386 第十一单元 ▪ 第一课 ▪ 情

Loan Words

A loan word is a word that one language borrows from another. English has an abundance of such words; from French phrases like "déjà vu," "faux pas," and "souvenir," to "kindergarten" from German and "guerilla" from Spanish.

As China's contact with the world has increased, so too has the amount of loan words in the Chinese language. Chinese has taken many loan words from English, but there are also a number from other languages. In Taiwan, a common example is 便当 (biàndāng), meaning "boxed meal," which is taken from the Japanese "bento," while both Taiwan and Mainland China use 榻榻米 (tàtàmǐ) as the word for "tatami."

Loan words in Chinese are absorbed in two primary ways. Some words are translated in conceptual terms, for example 电脑 (diànnǎo: "electric brain" – "computer"), while others are simply a phonetic representation of the original word. The following is a list of the main phonetic loan words that have been introduced so far. Note that some of the words combine phonetic components with existing Chinese terms.

Term	Pinyin	Meaning
咖啡	kāfēi	coffee
派对	pàiduì	party
沙发	shāfā	sofa
摩托车	mótuōchē	motorcycle

Term	Pinyin	Meaning
T-恤衫	T-xùshān	T-Shirt
酷	kù	cool
高尔夫球	gāo'ěrfūqiú	golf
吉他	jítā	guitar

English is not without its share of words borrowed from Chinese, either. "Kung Fu" 功夫 (gōngfu), "feng shui" 风水 (fēngshuǐ), "typhoon" 台风 (táifēng), and "gung-ho" 工合 (gōnghé) are just some of the diverse words and phrases that have entered into English from Chinese.

Online Resources

Visit *http://college.betterchinese.com* for a list of other loan words.

Associative Compounds

As has been seen in previous lessons, Chinese characters can be classified as phono-semantic compounds, pictographs, and ideographs. Another classification that is relatively common is the associative compound (会意 huìyì). With associative compounds, different elements are joined into a single character, the meaning of which is suggested by the combination of its components. Below are some examples of associative compounds.

Compound	Components
好 (hǎo: "good")	女 (nǚ: "woman")
	子 (zǐ: "son")
男 (nán: "male")	田 (tián: "field")
	力 (lì: "strength")
明 (míng: "bright")	日 (rì: "sun")
	月 (yuè: "moon")

Compound	Components
安 (ān: "peaceful; safe")	女 (nǚ: "woman")
	宀 (mián: "roof")
家 (jiā: "home; family")	豕 (shǐ: "pig")
	宀 (mián: "roof")

STRUCTURE NOTE 11.1

Use 得 to indicate degree or result

In Structure Note 10.8, 得 was used to describe the manner in which something is done. With this pattern, it is also possible to place a complement of degree after the adjective instead of using the standard adverbial modifiers before it. 很 and 不得了 (bùdéliǎo) are the most common of these, both of which mean "very" or "extremely" in English. However, when a whole phrase follows 得, it is equivalent to "so much that…" or "to the extent that…" in English.

Subject + Adjective + 得 + 很

Subject + Adjective + 得 + 不得了

Subject + Adjective + 得 + Clause

From the Lesson Text:
我真的紧张得不得了。
Wǒ zhēnde jǐnzhāng de bùdéliǎo.
I am really incredibly nervous. (Literally, "I am really nervous to a great extent.")

Other examples:
他的女儿聪明得很。
Tā de nǚér cōngmíng de hěn.
His daughter is really smart.

我高兴得想跳舞了!
Wǒ gāoxìng de xiǎng tiào wǔ le!
I'm so happy that I want to dance!

Practice: Transform the following sentences into Chinese using 得 and a complement of degree.

Example: Their kids are really cute. → 他们的小孩子可爱得很。

1. This park is really beautiful.

   _____

2. I'm so tired that I can't get out of bed.

   _____

3. After he finished the test, he was incredibly happy.

   _____

4. It's extremely quiet in this library.

   _____

5. He's so busy that he doesn't have time to meet his friends.

   _____

STRUCTURE NOTE 11.2

Use 次 *to express number of times*

次 (cì) *is a special type of measure word called a verbal measure word. Instead of measuring quantities of a noun, like* 两个人, *verbal measure words measure events. Just as different types of objects use different measure words, different types of events have different verbal measure words.*

次 *is used in a way similar to the English word "times," as in "I have been to China three times." To express that someone does or has done something a certain number of times, the* 次 *phrase is most commonly located between the verb and the object. Questions are formed by placing* 几 *or* 多少 *before* 次. 次 *can also be combined with ordinal numbers (using* 第 *) to make phrases like* 第一次 *(the first time), and with* 上 *and* 下 *to make* 上次 *(last time) and* 下次 *(next time).*

Subject + Verb + Frequency Phrase (+ Object)

From the Lesson Text:
这是我第一次跟小美约会。
Zhè shì wǒ dì yī cì gēn Xiǎoměi yuē huì.
This is the first time I've gone on a date with Xiaomei.

Examples:

我去了两次北京。
Wǒ qù le liǎng cì Běijīng.
I went to Beijing twice.

你这个星期给爸爸妈妈打了几次电话？
Nǐ zhèi ge xīngqī gěi bàba māma dǎ le jǐ cì diànhuà?
How many times did you call your parents this week?

Practice: Form complete sentences using the information below, following the example given.

Example: 二零零八年 / 波士顿(三次)
→ 二零零八年，我去了三次波士顿。

1. 昨天 / 打 / 网球(第一次)

   _____

2. 今天 / 看 / 课文(两次)

   _____

3. 昨天 / 去 / 图书馆(三次)

   _____

4. 今天 / 拉 / 小提琴(一次)

   _____

5. 最近 / 回 / 家(几次)

   _____

STRUCTURE NOTE 11.3

Use 让 *to express to "let" or "make" someone do something*

The verb 让 *(ràng) has several distinct meanings. It can mean, among other things, to allow someone to do something or to make someone do something. These meanings are expressed using the same sentence structure, so be careful to check the context of the statement to figure out the specific meaning of* 让 *in each instance.*

> Subject + 让 + Someone + Verb Phrase

From the Lesson Text:

你还要让她知道，你对她的感情是真的！
Nǐ hái yào ràng tā zhīdào, nǐ duì tā de gǎnqíng shì zhēn de!
You also have to let her know that your feelings for her are true!

Other examples:

我哥哥常常让我送他
去看他的女朋友。
Wǒ gēge chángcháng ràng wǒ
sòng tā qù kàn tā de nǚpéngyou.
My older brother often makes me
take him to see his girlfriend.

她爸爸妈妈不会让她来
我们的派对。
Tā bàba māma bú huì ràng tā lái
wǒmen de pàiduì.
Her parents aren't going to let her
come to our party.

Practice: Change the following Chinese sentences into English. Remember to pay attention to the meaning of 让 in different contexts.

Example: 她不喜欢让别人弹她爸爸的吉他。

→ She doesn't like to let other people play her dad's guitar.

1. 妈妈让我给弟弟做晚饭。

   _____

2. 他不让我开他新买的车子。

   _____

3. 老师让同学帮我做作业。

   _____

4. 这家商店不让人刷卡，你得付现金。

   _____

5. 你应该让她知道你对他有兴趣。

   _____

STRUCTURE NOTE 11.4

Use 记住 *to describe keeping something in mind*

The character 记 *(jì) on its own means "to remember," but in Chinese this meaning is usually expressed with one of several two-character expressions. In this lesson,* 记 *is combined with the resultative complement* 住 *(zhù) to describe keeping something in mind. As with all resultative complement patterns,* 得 *or* 不 *can be inserted between the verb and its complement to express that someone is or is not able to keep something in mind.*

> Subject + 记 + (得 / 不) + 住

From the Lesson Text:

我会记不住！
Wǒ huì jì bu zhù!
I won't remember!

Other examples:

记住，明天一定要给
我打电话！
Jìzhù, míngtiān yídìng yào gěi
wǒ dǎ diànhuà!
Remember, you must call me
tomorrow!

这么难的生词，你记得
住吗？
Zhème nán de shēngcí, nǐ jì de zhù
ma?
Will you be able to remember such difficult vocabulary?

Practice: Turn the following fragments into complete sentences using 记住, 记得住, or 记不住 as directed.

Example: 明天有考试 → 同学们，你们明天有考试，你们一
定要记住啊！

1. 这么容易的语法 (记住)

   _____

2. 到图书馆怎么走 (记不住)

   _____

3. 老师给你的建议 (记得住)

   _____

4. 给他生日礼物 (记住)

   _____

5. 小美星期六要表演 (记住)

   _____

练习 PRACTICE

PRACTICE 11.1

Working with a partner, use the images and numbers below to act out dialogues in which you ask each other how many times you have done the activities shown before.

Example:
A: 这是你第几次去北京?
B: 这是我第三次去北京。

PRACTICE 11.2

With a partner, create a short dialogue based on the following scenario.
1. You want to ask someone to go out.
2. You try to coordinate schedules to meet but his or her schedule keeps conflicting.
3. Discuss where to go, where to meet, and what to do.
4. After a date is settled, write the final decision in the table.

Where are you going?	What are you doing?	Where are you meeting?	When are you going?

PRACTICE 11.3

Write a letter to someone you like using the vocabulary and sentence patterns that you have learned. An example is given for you.

小美：
第一次跟你约会，我真的紧张得不得了！
我觉得你很聪明、善良，也很可爱。
可以再约你下次出去玩吗？
大东

PRACTICE 11.4

Make an audio recording and send it to your teacher. In the recording, describe some of the positive or admirable qualities of someone you know.

	Radical	Stroke Order
美	羊 yáng sheep	丶 丷 丷 쓰 芏 兰 羊 美 美
告	口 kǒu mouth	丿 ㇒ 牛 生 牛 告 告
诉	讠(言) yán speech	丶 讠 订 讠 诉 诉 诉 诉
紧	纟(糸) sī silk	丨 刂 刂ㄱ 刂又 刂又 竖 竖 竖 紧
约	纟(糸) sī silk	乙 纟 纟 纟 约 约
聪	耳 ěr ear	一 丆 丌 丌 耳 耳 耵 耵 耴 耵 耵 耵 聪 聪 聪
希	巾 jīn cloth	丿 乂 兰 产 齐 希 希
望	月 yuè moon	丶 亠 亡 切 圽 叨 钥 铒 望 望
让	讠(言) yán speech	丶 讠 计 让 让
感	忄(心) xīn heart	一 厂 厂 厉 咸 咸 咸 咸 咸 感 感 感
情	忄(心) xīn heart	丶 丷 忄 忄 忄 忴 情 情 情 情
建	廴 yǐn stride	乛 ㇕ 彐 彐 彐 聿 建 建
议	讠(言) yán speech	丶 讠 讠 议 议
公	八 bā eight	丿 八 公 公
散	攵(攴) pū knock	一 十 卄 芣 艹 苩 昔 菁 昔 散 散

394 第十一单元 ▪ 第一课 ▪ 情

PRACTICE 11.6

Type the following sentences on your computer and provide answers to the questions.

1. 你今晚的表演真棒！
2. 我晚点儿再打电话告诉你在哪儿见面。
3. 这是我第一次约会，真的紧张得不得了。
4. 我的女朋友又聪明又善良。
5. 你对我的感情是真的吗？

PRACTICE 11.7

明天我要跟小美约会。因为这是我第一次约会，所以我紧张得不得了！我不知道应该对她说什么。祥安说我要对小美说她很漂亮，也很可爱。还要让她知道，我很喜欢她，我对她的感情是真的。祥安还建议吃完晚饭以后带小美去公园散散步，再约她下次见面。

Read Chen Dadong's diary and answer the following questions.
1. How does Chen Dadong feel about his upcoming date?
2. What does Huang Xiang'an suggest that Chen Dadong should do after dinner?

PRACTICE 11.8

黄祥安：我可以请你吃晚饭吗？
张安娜：好啊！你还请了哪些人？
黄祥安：我只请你一个人。
张安娜：哦……好的！我们在哪儿见面？
黄祥安：我五点半在你宿舍的门口等你。
张安娜：行，我们去哪儿吃饭？
黄祥安：你喜欢吃法国菜吗？
张安娜：法国菜太贵了，我们还是吃便宜一点的吧！
黄祥安：你真是个好女孩！

Read the dialogue and answer the following questions.
1. Where are Huang Xiang'an and Zhang Anna going to meet?
2. Are they going to have French food? Why?

Sender　玛丽
Subject　约会

大东：
你跟小美第一次约会怎么样？小美约会回来以后高兴得不得了！你们去哪里玩了？她喜欢吃中国菜，你跟她去中国饭馆吃晚饭了吗？

Sender　大东
Subject　re: 约会

玛丽：
上个星期六我跟小美约会很开心。我跟她去听钢琴音乐会，然后我们还去了中国饭馆吃她喜欢的醉鸡。我下个月要回加拿大去，我打算问小美要不要跟我一起去那儿玩。

Read the e-mails and answer the following questions.
1. Where did Chen Dadong take Wang Xiaomei for their date?
2. What does he plan to ask her to do next?

Chinese Valentine's Day: The Story of the Cowherd and Weaver Girl

The story of the cowherd and the weaver girl is a well-known romantic folk tale in China. Although there are many versions of the tale, the basic story goes something like this:

One day, 牛郎 (niúláng: "the cowherd") encountered seven immortal fairy sisters. The cowherd fell in love with the youngest fairy, 织女 (zhīnǚ: "the weaver girl"), the most beautiful of the sisters and a skilled seamstress. The pair was soon happily wed with two children. Everything was going well until the Goddess of Heaven found out about the forbidden marriage between the mortal and the fairy. Enraged, she forced the weaver girl to return to the skies.

One of the cowherd's oxen saw how distraught his master was and suddenly began to speak. The ox told the cowherd that if he killed him and put on his hide, the cowherd would be able to ascend to Heaven in search of his wife. The cowherd followed the ox's instructions and rose to the sky carrying his two children. After discovering this, the wrathful Goddess of Heaven used her hairpin to create a wide river in the sky separating the two lovers forever. From then on, the weaver girl lived on one side of the river crafting embroidery, while the cowherd lived on the other side taking care of their two children. But, once every year, magpies take to the sky to form a bridge across the river so that the cowherd and the weaver girl can be together again for one night.

On 七夕 (Qīxī: "the seventh night of the seventh lunar month"), the stars which represent the cowherd and the weaver girl appear to be moving closer together, and thus this day became the Qixi Festival, a time to celebrate romance and relationships.

China's Tallest Couple

At 7'6" and 6'3", 姚明 (Yáo Míng) and 叶莉 (Yè Lì) are certainly the tallest celebrity couple in China! Yao Ming, an international basketball superstar who has played for the NBA's Houston Rockets, is a huge source of national pride in China. Arguably the most influential athlete in Chinese history, Yao was the number one NBA draft pick in 2002 and made the All-Star team in his rookie year. But he is not the first in his family to excel at the sport—Yao's father was a professional basketball player, and his mother a captain of the women's Chinese national team.

His wife, the only woman he has ever dated, is also a former basketball player. She played professionally in China and was also a captain of the national team. Initially, Ye was not interested in dating Yao. However, she began to reconsider after Yao gave her the team pins he had collected during the Olympic Games in Sydney. After eight years of dating, Yao and Ye married in Shanghai in August 2007. The couple is praised not only for their athletic talent, but also for their numerous contributions to charity. Yao has been active in environmental protection campaigns and has served as a global ambassador for the Special Olympics. In addition, he created the Yao Ming Foundation, an organization dedicated to rebuilding schools destroyed by the 2008 earthquake in Sichuan and helping those affected by Hurricane Ike in Houston.

陈大东：小美，你的表演真棒！我可以请你去吃晚饭吗？

Xiaomei, your performance was great! May I treat you to dinner?

王小美：好啊！玛丽、中平他们也一起去吗？

Sure! Will Mali, Zhongping and the others be going too?

陈大东：我想就只有我和你……

I was thinking just me and you...

王小美：哦……好的！

Oh...OK!

陈大东：我晚点儿跟你说在哪儿见面。

I'll tell you later where we should meet.

王小美：好，你再打电话告诉我吧！

Sure, just call me.

陈大东：我真的紧张得不得了。这是我第一次跟小美约会。

I'm so nervous. This is my first date with Xiaomei.

黄祥安：你喜欢小美的哪一点？

What do you like about Xiaomei?

陈大东：她很聪明、善良，也很可爱。

She's smart, kind-hearted, and also very cute.

黄祥安：女孩子都希望听别人说她美。你不要忘记对她说喔。

Girls all want to be told that they're beautiful. Don't forget to tell her, OK?

陈大东：什么？我会记不住！

What? I won't remember!

黄祥安：你还要让她知道，你对她的感情是真的！

You also have to let her know that your feelings for her are true!

黄祥安：祥安！不要闹了，你还有什么建议吗？

Stop it Xiang'an! Do you have any other suggestions?

王小美：吃完饭，你可以跟她去公园散散步，再约她下次出去玩。

After dinner, you can take her for a stroll in the park, and then ask her out on another date.

王小美：嗨！

Hi!

陈大东：你今天真漂亮……

You look so pretty today...

What Can You Do?

INTERPRETIVE
- I can understand different terms for personal characteristics and features.

INTERPERSONAL
- I can arrange to go on a date with someone.
- I can offer suggestions to someone and receive them in return.

PRESENTATIONAL
- I can give a basic presentation about a person's qualities and attributes.

分手
A Break Up

安娜，你<ruby>怎么了<rt>zěn me le</rt></ruby>？<ruby>发生<rt>fā shēng</rt></ruby>了什么事？可以跟我说说吗？

我……跟我的<ruby>男朋友分手<rt>nán péng you fēn shǒu</rt></ruby>了。

哦，别<ruby>难过<rt>nán guò</rt></ruby>了！

我不是<ruby>难过<rt>nán guò</rt></ruby>，我是<ruby>非常生气<rt>fēi cháng shēng qì</rt></ruby>。

他做什么了？

我<ruby>被<rt>bèi</rt></ruby>他<ruby>骗<rt>piàn</rt></ruby>了。他跟我<ruby>交往<rt>jiāo wǎng</rt></ruby>的时侯，还<ruby>一直<rt>yì zhí</rt></ruby>跟他在俄罗斯的<ruby>女朋友<rt>nǚ péng you</rt></ruby>有<ruby>联络<rt>lián luò</rt></ruby>。

真的吗？怎么会这样？

tán guo jié hūn
我们还谈过结婚的事，可是现在……

ài　　　kū
唉，别哭了。就忘了他吧。

可是我做不到，
cóng lái
我从来没有这么
ài guo
爱过一个人。

nán péng you
你会找到一个更好的男朋友。

LESSON TEXT 11.2

A Break Up 分手

Sun Mali sees that Zhang Anna is upset and asks her what is wrong. Zhang Anna reveals that she has broken up with her boyfriend.

孙玛丽：	安娜，你怎么了？发生了什么事？可以跟我说说吗？	Ānnà, nǐ zěnme le? Fāshēng le shénme shì? Kěyǐ gēn wǒ shuōshuo ma?
张安娜：	我……跟我的男朋友分手了。	Wǒ... gēn wǒ de nánpéngyou fēn shǒu le.
孙玛丽：	哦，别难过了！	Ò, bié nánguò le!
张安娜：	我不是难过，我是非常生气。	Wǒ bú shì nánguò, wǒ shì fēicháng shēngqì.
孙玛丽：	他做什么了？	Tā zuò shénme le?
张安娜：	我被他骗了。他跟我交往的时候，还一直跟他在俄罗斯的女朋友有联络。	Wǒ bèi tā piàn le. Tā gēn wǒ jiāowǎng de shíhou, hái yìzhí gēn tā zài Éluósī de nǚpéngyou yǒu liánluò.

孙玛丽：	真的吗？怎么会这样？	Zhēnde ma? Zěnme huì zhèyàng?
张安娜：	我们还谈过结婚的事，可是现在……	Wǒmen hái tán guo jié hūn de shì, kěshì xiànzài...
孙玛丽：	唉，别哭了。就忘了他吧。	Ài, bié kū le. Jiù wàng le tā ba.
张安娜：	可是我做不到，我从来没有这么爱过一个人。	Kěshì wǒ zuò bu dào, wǒ cónglái méiyǒu zhème ài guo yí ge rén.
孙玛丽：	你会找到一个更好的男朋友。	Nǐ huì zhǎo dào yí ge gèng hǎo de nánpéngyou.

LESSON VOCABULARY 11.2

	SIMPLIFIED	TRADITIONAL	PINYIN	WORD CATEGORY	DEFINITION
1.	怎么了	怎麼了	zěnme le	*qph*	what's wrong; what's the matter
2.	发生	發生	fāshēng	*v*	to happen
3.	男朋友		nánpéngyou	*n*	boyfriend
4.	分手		fēn shǒu	*vo*	to break up
5.	难过	難過	nánguò	*adj*	sad
6.	非常		fēicháng	*adv*	very, extremely
7.	生气	生氣	shēngqì	*adj*	mad, angry
8.	被		bèi	*prep*	by (passive)
9.	骗	騙	piàn	*v*	to trick, to fool, to cheat
10.	交往		jiāowǎng	*v*	to be in a relationship; to associate (with); to contact
11.	一直		yìzhí	*adv*	straight; continuously; all along
12.	女朋友		nǚpéngyou	*n*	girlfriend
13.	联络	聯絡	liánluò	*v*	to contact; to have contact
14.	谈	談	tán	*v*	to talk, discuss
15.	过	過	guo	*p*	(used after a verb to indicate a past experience)
16.	结婚	結婚	jié hūn	*vo*	to get married
17.	唉		ài	*interj*	(expresses sadness, sympathy, disappointment etc.)
18.	哭		kū	*v*	to cry
19.	从来	從來	cónglái	*adv*	always, all along; never (when used in the negative)
20.	爱	愛	ài	*v*	to love

REQUIRED VOCABULARY 11.2

	SIMPLIFIED	TRADITIONAL	PINYIN	WORD CATEGORY	DEFINITION
	RELATED TO RELATIONSHIPS				
21.	相信		xiāngxìn	*v*	to believe
22.	心		xīn	*n*	heart

OPTIONAL VOCABULARY 11.2

	SIMPLIFIED	TRADITIONAL	PINYIN	WORD CATEGORY	DEFINITION
	RELATED TO RELATIONSHIPS				
23.	眼泪	眼淚	yǎnlèi	*n*	tears
24.	情人		qíngrén	*n*	lover; sweetheart
25.	离婚	離婚	lí hūn	*vo*	to divorce
26.	坏	壞	huài	*adj*	bad
27.	吵架		chǎo jià	*vo*	to quarrel; to fight

Relationship Terms

Just as in other languages, terms for relationships and dating change in Chinese as customs change and trends come and go. Below are some common relationship terms that one may come across.

Term	Pinyin	Meaning	Example	Meaning
交往	jiāowǎng	to date	我跟他交往。	I am dating him.
分手	fēn shǒu	to break up	我跟他分手了。	I broke up with him.
吹	chuī	to break up (slang)	我跟他吹了。	I broke up with him.
对象	duìxiàng	boyfriend/girlfriend; partner	她有没有对象？	Does she have a partner?
情人	qíngrén	lover (either illicit or not)	她有没有情人？	Does she have a lover?
宝贝	bǎobèi	treasure, darling, baby	宝贝，我爱你。	Baby, I love you.

Chinese Punctuation

By now, you may have noticed that Chinese punctuation is not always identical to punctuation in English. While Chinese has borrowed the question mark, exclamation mark, and comma, among other things, it also has a number of punctuation marks of its own. We have already encountered one of these in the form of the enumeration comma (、). The following are some of the other punctuation marks used in modern Chinese.

Punctuation Mark	Name	Usage
。	句号 jùhào	Period – used in the same way as its English equivalent.
《 》	双书名号 shuāng shūmínghào	Title marks – used for the title of a book or film, e.g., 《三国演义》
·	间隔号 jiàngéhào	Middle dot – sometimes used to separate foreign names, e.g., 文森特·梵·高 (Wénsēntè·Fàn·Gāo: Vincent Van Gogh)
「 」	引号 yǐnhào	Quotation marks – Simplified Chinese uses the same quotation marks as English when written horizontally. Traditional Chinese indicates single quotation marks with 「…」 and double quotation marks with 『…』
——	破折号 pòzhéhào	Dash – The dash in Chinese is longer than its English counterpart in order to distinguish it from the character 一.
___	专名号 zhuānmínghào	In some texts, proper nouns are underscored with a straight line, e.g., 陈大东
···	着重号 zhuózhònghào	Chinese does not commonly use italics. Instead, a single dot is written underneath every character that one wishes to emphasize.
……	省略号 shěnglüèhào	The Chinese ellipsis consists of six dots, unlike the English equivalent which is made up of three (...).

STRUCTURE NOTE 11.5

Use 被 to form the passive voice

The passive voice is used when the subject is acted upon by something else. In English, "he was hit" and "he was hit by a car" are both examples of passive statements. The first example is called an "agentless passive," because the person or thing responsible for the action is not specified, while in the second statement the agent is clearly specified. In Chinese, there are similar patterns for passive statements with and without agents. One way to form these is with the passive marker 被 (bèi). As is the case with 把, sentences with passive markers require that the verb take a suff or complement.

In general, Chinese uses the passive voice less frequently than English. It is usually used in situations where something unpleasant has happened, such as getting hit by a car or being tricked. In neutral or positive situations, one should therefore avoid using 被.

Subject + 被 + Agent + Verb Phrase

Subject + 被 + Verb Phrase

From the Lesson Text:
我被他骗了。
Wǒ bèi tā piàn le.
I was tricked by him.

Other examples:

不好意思，那本书被人借走了。
Bù hǎo yìsi, nà běn shū bèi rén jiè zǒu le.
I'm sorry, that book has been taken out by someone.

真的，我的作业被狗吃了！
Zhēn de, wǒ de zuòyè bèi gǒu chī le!
Honestly, my homework was eaten by the dog!

NOTE: 被 *is the most frequent passive marker in the written language, but* 让, 给, *and* 叫 *can also be used for the same purpose.* 叫 *and* 让 *are not used without an agent.*

Practice: Use 被 to rewrite the following statements as passive expressions.

Example:　他打了我三次。→ 我被他打了三次。

1.　哎呀！那个售货员骗我了。

_____

2.　有人吃我们的米饭了。

_____

3.　儿子考试考得不好了，爸爸就打了他。

_____

4.　服务员，看起来这双筷子有人用过。

_____

5.　小狗把我做的蛋糕都吃了！

_____

STRUCTURE NOTE 11.6
Use 一直 to express "constantly"

There are a few ways in Chinese to express that something has repeatedly or continuously been going on over a period of time. The term 一直 *(yìzhí) literally means "straight," but it is also used figuratively to mean "always" or "the whole time." This is appropriate to use for a state or situation that has been consistent over a given period. In this pattern,* 都 *can also be added after* 一直 *for emphasis.*

Subject + 一直 (+ 都) + Verb Phrase

From the Lesson Text: 他跟我交往的时候，还一直跟他在俄罗斯的女朋友有联络。

Tā gēn wǒ jiāowǎng de shíhou, hái yìzhí gēn tā zài Éluósī de nǚpéngyou yǒu liánluò.

While he was dating me, he was still in contact with his girlfriend from Russia the whole time.

Other examples: 我在他家的时候，他一直都在看功夫电影。

Wǒ zài tā jiā de shíhou, tā yìzhí dōu zài kàn gōngfu diànyǐng.

When I was at his house he was watching Kung Fu movies the whole time.

我一直都希望可以找到一个爱我的人。

Wǒ yìzhí dōu xīwàng kěyǐ zhǎo dào yí ge ài wǒ de rén.

I have always hoped to be able to find a person to love me.

Practice: Use 一直 to change the following sentences into Chinese, following the example provided.

Example: I've always liked that teacher. → 我一直都喜欢那位老师。

1. She has always been good to her friends.

   _____

2. My girlfriend has always been a vegetarian.

   _____

3. Last Saturday he was watching TV all day long.

   _____

4. Those two girls are always singing and dancing at parties.

   _____

5. When we had exams, he was always in the library reading.

   _____

STRUCTURE NOTE 11.7
Use Verb + 过 *to express a past experience*

To express that one has done something before, as in "I have been to Beijing before," the suffix 过 *(guo) is used. This is distinct from the* 了 *described in Structure Notes 5.11 and 6.11, which marks an action that was completed at a certain point in the past. As opposed to the relative specificity of* 了, *the* 过 *suffix refers to a more general or undefined time period, and is often used to ask people about things they have or have not done in their lifetime.* 过 *must always immediately follow the verb; any object, including in a verb-object construction, comes afterwards.*

> Subject + Verb + 过 (+ Object)

From the Lesson Text:

我们还谈过结婚的事，可是现在……
Wǒmen hái tán guo jié hūn de shì, kěshì xiànzài…
We talked about getting married, too, but now…

Other examples:

他去过加州。
Tā qù guo Jiāzhōu.
He has been to California.

我哥哥吃过醉鸡。
Wǒ gēge chī guo Zuìjī.
My older brother has eaten Drunken Chicken before.

Like 了, *the suffix* 过 *is negated by* 没(有). *Unlike* 了, *however,* 过 *is preserved in negative sentences rather than omitted. To give added emphasis to a negative* 过 *sentence,* 从来 *(cónglái) may be added in front of* 没有 *to express "never (before)."*

> Subject + 从来没(有) + Verb + 过 (+ Object)

From the Lesson Text:

我从来没有这么爱过一个人。
Wǒ cónglái méiyǒu zhème ài guo yí ge rén.
I never loved anyone so much before.

Other examples:

我从来没有去过日本。
Wǒ cónglái méiyǒu qù guo Rìběn.
I've never been to Japan in my life.

醉鸡，我没吃过。
Zuìjī, wǒ méi chī guo.
I've never had Drunken Chicken before.

Practice: Create affirmative or negative sentences using 过 or (从来)没(有)…过 in conjunction with the verbs, objects, and verb-object pairs given below.

Example: 我 / 去 / 北京 → 我从来没有去过北京。
1. 你们 / 打 / 网球 _____
2. 他 / 看 / 功夫电影 _____
3. 我哥哥 / 结婚 _____
4. 我朋友 / 表演 _____
5. 她 / 学 / 中文 _____

PRACTICE 11.10

Working with a partner, use the passive voice to ask and answer questions about the situations below.

Example:
A: 你被谁骗了？
B: 我被男朋友骗了。

男朋友骗我了。

朋友说她不漂亮。

她吃完了这盘饺子。

陈先生和陈太太买了那个手机。

小狗吃我的作业了。

姐姐喝完我的咖啡了。

有人用过这个盘子。

💬 PRACTICE 11.11

Working with a partner, use the information below to ask each other what you have and have not done before.

钢琴

Example:
A: 我学过钢琴，你学过钢琴吗？
B: 我也学过。／我从来没有学过。

英国

宿舍

车

筷子

✏️ PRACTICE 11.12

Using the words in the box, write the correct emotion or feeling for each picture in the space provided.

难过　紧张　高兴　累　生气

	Radical	Stroke Order
男	田 tián field	丶 冂 日 曱 田 罗 男
女	女 nǚ woman	乀 夕 女
朋	月 yuè moon	丿 刀 月 月 朋 朋 朋 朋
友	又 yòu again	一 ナ 方 友
难	隹 zhuī short-tailed bird	乛 又 叉 刄 对 好 难 难 难
过	辶 chuò walk	一 寸 寸 寸 讨 过
分	刂(刀) dāo knife	丿 八 分 分
非	非 fēi wrong	丨 刂 丮 刲 非 非 非
被	衤(衣) yī clothes	丶 ㇇ 衤 衤 衤 衤 衤 衤 被 被
交	亠 tóu roof	丶 亠 六 六 夯 交
直	目 mù eye	一 十 亠 古 声 直 直 直
联	耳 ěr ear	一 厂 ㄇ 刂 月 耳 耴 耴 联 联 联
谈	讠(言) yán speech	丶 讠 讠 讧 谈 谈 谈 谈 谈
结	纟(糸) sī silk	乁 纟 纟 纟 纠 纣 结 结
婚	女 nǚ woman	乀 夕 女 妁 妌 妎 婚 婚 婚 婚 婚

🎤 PRACTICE 11.14

Make an audio recording and send it to your teacher. In the recording, use the verb + 过 pattern to describe places that you have been to and experiences that you have had.

▨ PRACTICE 11.15

Type the following sentences on your computer and provide answers to the questions.

1. 发生了什么事？可以告诉我吗？
2. 我跟我的女朋友分手了。
3. 我不是生气，我是非常难过。
4. 我从来没有这么爱过一个人。
5. 他跟我交往的时候，还跟别的女孩约会。

📖 PRACTICE 11.16

Sender　中平

Subject　女朋友

大东：
我昨天听到我的女朋友在房间里打电话，我问她打电话给谁，她说她跟她以前的男朋友一直还有联络。现在我应该怎么办呢？我也不知道我是生气还是难过。你觉得她是个很好的女朋友吗？

Sender　大东

Subject　re: 女朋友

中平：
我觉得她没有骗你啊！她是个好女孩吧！你应该找时间跟她谈谈，多跟她约会，这样你们的感情才会好。

Read the emails and answer the following questions.
1. Is Li Zhongping angry or sad?
2. What does Chen Dadong say that Li Zhongping should do?

国粹传情

王小美：喂，安娜，你在做什么？
张安娜：没做什么，你有什么特别的事吗？
王小美：我想找你去看电影。
张安娜：对不起，我不想去。
王小美：你不是最爱看电影的吗？你怎么了？
张安娜：我很难过，昨天跟男朋友分手了。
王小美：别难过了！那我们去喝杯咖啡，谈一谈！
张安娜：好吧，我也希望听听你的建议。

Read the dialogue and answer the following questions.
1. Why doesn't Zhang Anna want to go to see a movie?
2. What do they decide to do instead?

昨天我跟大东去看电影的时候，我很紧张，因为我很喜欢他。我一直在等他问我可不可以跟他交往，可是他还没有问我。我不想跟大东只做好朋友，因为我觉得他是会跟我谈结婚的人。如果我这样告诉大东的话，不知道他会觉得怎么样。

Read Wang Xiaomei's diary and answer the following questions.
1. What is Wang Xiaomei waiting for Chen Dadong to ask her?
2. What does Wang Xiaomei think about Chen Dadong?

Chinese Wedding Traditions

Historically, Chinese marriages were arranged by the couple's parents and matchmakers. The couple would also consult a Chinese fortune-teller who would examine their birth dates and determine their compatibility. Many Chinese couples continue to follow a belief in lucky calendar dates today to pick the most auspicious day to wed.

Modern-day Chinese weddings have many unique conventions that are based on old customs, and many that were created in the modern era. Below are some of the typical features of a Chinese wedding.

Wedding Portraits

Many couples take their formal wedding portraits well before the ceremony itself, sometimes so early that they are even included with the invitations. These photo-shoots are often very elaborate and expensive. The bride and groom will model different outfits and take pictures in a variety of fairytale studio backgrounds, as well as idyllic natural settings and famous locations.

Fetching the Bride

Another unique element of a Chinese wedding is a playful game where the bride's parents and friends officially "give away" the bride to the groom. Nowadays, this game is usually held at the bride's family home, where the bride is hidden inside a room. The groom, accompanied by his best men, attempts to coax the bride out by persuading her friends that he is worthy of her. To test his sincerity, he may have to answer questions about the bride, sing love songs, recite poetry, or even demonstrate his physical strength. Finally, after the groom has satisfied the demands of the bride's friends, she emerges and her friends and family wish the couple well as they depart.

Lavish Ceremonies

Because many Chinese families only have one child, the parents will often pay for a highly lavish ceremony. Wealthier families typically rent luxury cars adorned with special decorations for the couple and their motorcade. Chinese brides usually wear at least three dresses: a white, western style gown during the wedding ceremony; an elegant, traditional red cheongsam for the reception; and another ballroom dress to be worn at the end of the reception as guests leave.

Wedding Banquet

Wedding ceremonies are typically followed by a large banquet where guests enjoy food and entertainment. Following the Chinese belief that red is a lucky color, red foods such as lobster, Peking duck, and red bean soup are served. It is common to serve a total of eight courses, eight being a lucky number in Chinese culture. However, the couple does not typically eat with everyone else—instead, they visit each table, toasting their guests and thanking them for attending.

孙玛丽：	安娜，你怎么了？发生了什么事？可以跟我说说吗？	Anna, what's wrong? What happened? Can you tell me?
张安娜：	我……跟我的男朋友分手了。	I…broke up with my boyfriend.
孙玛丽：	哦，别难过了！	Oh, don't be sad!
张安娜：	我不是难过，我是非常生气。	I'm not sad, I'm extremely angry.
孙玛丽：	他做什么了？	What did he do?
张安娜：	我被他骗了。他在跟我交往的时候，还一直跟他在俄罗斯的女朋友有联络。	He cheated on me. While we were dating, he was still in touch with his girlfriend in Russia.

孙玛丽：	真的吗？怎么会这样？	Really? How can that be?
张安娜：	我们还谈过结婚的事，可是现在……	We even talked about getting married, but now…
孙玛丽：	唉，别哭了。就忘了他吧。	There there, don't cry. Just forget about him.
张安娜：	可是我做不到，我从来没有这么爱过一个人。	But I can't. I never loved anyone this much.
孙玛丽：	你会找到一个更好的男朋友。	You will find a much better boyfriend.

What Can You Do?

INTERPRETIVE
- I can understand expressions in the passive voice.
- I can understand when someone is referring to a past experience.

INTERPERSONAL
- I can discuss issues relating to interpersonal relationships.
- I can talk about my emotions with someone.

PRESENTATIONAL
- I can give an account of a relationship between two people.
- I can give a description of how someone is feeling.

ACT IT OUT

Working in groups, compose an original three-minute skit that utilizes the vocabulary and structures introduced in Unit 11. Each of you should assume a role and have a roughly equal number of lines in the skit. Be prepared to perform your skit in class. You can either come up with your own story or choose from one of the following situations:

A) Your friend is planning a date with his new girlfriend and asks you for suggestions on what to do.

B) You come across two of your close friends arguing, and you help resolve the conflict.

C) Your friend is thinking of breaking up with her boyfriend. She explains to you why and you offer advice.

CHECK WHAT YOU CAN DO

RECOGNIZE

Adjectives
- ☐ 棒
- ☐ 紧张
- ☐ 聪明
- ☐ 善良
- ☐ 可爱
- ☐ 美
- ☐ 安静
- ☐ 好看
- ☐ 帅
- ☐ 难过
- ☐ 生气

Adverbs
- ☐ 晚点
- ☐ 非常
- ☐ 一直
- ☐ 从来
- ☐ 不得了

Idiomatic Expressions
- ☐ 不要闹了
- ☐ 出去玩（儿）

Interjections
- ☐ 喔
- ☐ 唉

Measure Words
- ☐ 次

Nouns
- ☐ 点
- ☐ 别人
- ☐ 感情
- ☐ 建议
- ☐ 公园
- ☐ 下次
- ☐ 男朋友
- ☐ 女朋友
- ☐ 心

Particles
- ☐ 过

Prepositions
- ☐ 被

Question Phrases
- ☐ 怎么了

Verbs
- ☐ 想
- ☐ 见面
- ☐ 告诉
- ☐ 约会
- ☐ 希望
- ☐ 忘记
- ☐ 记不住
- ☐ 让

- ☐ 散步
- ☐ 发生
- ☐ 分手
- ☐ 骗
- ☐ 出去玩
- ☐ 交往
- ☐ 联络
- ☐ 谈
- ☐ 结婚
- ☐ 哭
- ☐ 爱
- ☐ 相信

WRITE
- ☐ 美
- ☐ 告诉
- ☐ 紧约
- ☐ 聪希
- ☐ 望让
- ☐ 感情
- ☐ 建议
- ☐ 公散

- ☐ 男女
- ☐ 朋友
- ☐ 难过
- ☐ 分非
- ☐ 被交
- ☐ 直联
- ☐ 谈结
- ☐ 婚

USE
- ☐ 得 to indicate degree or result
- ☐ 次 to express number of times
- ☐ 让 to express to "let" or "make" someone do something
- ☐ 记住 to describe keeping something in mind

- ☐ 被 to form the passive voice
- ☐ 一直 to express "constantly"
- ☐ Verb + 过 to express a past experience

Medicine
第十二单元
UNIT 12

Communication Goals

Lesson 1: 生病了 **Getting Sick**
- Inquire after a person's health
- Describe the symptoms of an illness
- Talk about the weather and the seasons

Lesson 2: 看病 **At the Doctor's**
- Name illnesses and afflictions
- Refer to different parts of the body
- Describe some of the differences between Chinese and Western medicine

生病了
Getting Sick

安娜，你还好吗？你看起来不舒服，你生病了吗？

我想是吧。我跟男朋友分手了以后，天天睡不着。

我肚子疼，头也很疼。

最近天气冷得很，你要注意身体啊！你的眼睛和鼻子都红了，你最好去看病。

可是现在下雨了，我不想出去......

我可以送你去啊！你在这儿等我，我马上回来。

好吧，谢谢！

我认识一个很好的中医。我带你去他那儿看看好不好？

中医？为什么不去看西医？

他真的很不错。

好，试试吧。

LESSON TEXT 12.1

Getting Sick 生病了

Huang Xiang'an visits Zhang Anna and finds out that she is not feeling well. They decide to see a doctor of Traditional Chinese Medicine.

黄祥安：安娜，你还好吗？你看起来不舒服，你生病了吗？

Ānnà, nǐ hái hǎo ma? Nǐ kànqilai bù shūfu, nǐ shēng bìng le ma?

张安娜：我想是吧。我跟男朋友分手了以后，天天睡不着。我肚子疼，头也很疼。

Wǒ xiǎng shì ba. Wǒ gēn nánpéngyou fēn shǒu le yǐhòu, tiāntiān shuì bu zháo. Wǒ dùzi téng, tóu yě hěn téng.

黄祥安：最近天气冷得很，你要注意身体啊！你的眼睛和鼻子都红了，你最好去看病。

Zuìjìn tiānqì lěng de hěn, nǐ yào zhùyì shēntǐ a! Nǐ de yǎnjing hé bízi dōu hóng le, nǐ zuìhǎo qù kàn bìng.

张安娜：可是现在下雨了，我不想出去……

Kěshì xiànzài xià yǔ le, wǒ bù xiǎng chūqu....

黄祥安：我可以送你去啊！你在这儿等我，我马上回来。

Wǒ kěyǐ sòng nǐ qù a! Nǐ zài zhèr děng wǒ, wǒ mǎshàng huílai.

张安娜：好吧，谢谢！

Hǎo ba, xièxie!

黄祥安：我认识一个很好的中医。我带你去他那儿看看好不好？

Wǒ rènshi yí ge hěn hǎo de zhōngyī. Wǒ dài nǐ qù tā nàr kànkan hǎo bu hǎo?

张安娜：中医？为什么不去看西医？

Zhōngyī? Wèishénme bú qù kàn xīyī?

黄祥安：他真的很不错。

Tā zhēn de hěn bú cuò.

张安娜：好，试试吧。

Hǎo, shìshi ba.

字词 VOCABULARY

LESSON VOCABULARY 12.1

	SIMPLIFIED	TRADITIONAL	PINYIN	WORD CATEGORY	DEFINITION
1.	还好	還好	háihǎo	*adj*	not bad; OK; so-so
2.	舒服		shūfu	*adj*	comfortable; feeling well
3.	生病		shēng bìng	*vo*	to get sick
4.	天天		tiāntiān	*adv*	every day
5.	睡不着		shuì bu zháo	*rv*	to be unable to sleep
6.	肚子		dùzi	*n*	stomach
7.	疼		téng	*adj*	painful; sore
8.	头	頭	tóu	*n*	head
9.	天气	天氣	tiānqì	*n*	weather
10.	冷		lěng	*adj*	cold
11.	注意		zhùyì	*v*	to be careful; to pay attention to
12.	身体	身體	shēntǐ	*n*	body
13.	眼睛		yǎnjing	*n*	eyes
14.	鼻子		bízi	*n*	nose
15.	最好		zuìhǎo	*adv*	had better
16.	看病		kàn bìng	*vo*	to see a doctor
17.	下雨		xià yǔ	*vo*	to rain
18.	中医	中醫	zhōngyī	*n*	(doctor of) Traditional Chinese Medicine
19.	带	帶	dài	*v*	to bring
20.	西医	西醫	xīyī	*n*	(doctor of) Western medicine

REQUIRED VOCABULARY 12.1

SIMPLIFIED	TRADITIONAL	PINYIN	WORD CATEGORY	DEFINITION
BODY PARTS				
21. 手		shǒu	*n*	hand
22. 脚	腳	jiǎo	*n*	foot
SEASONS				
23. 春天		chūntiān	*n*	spring
24. 夏天		xiàtiān	*n*	summer
25. 秋天		qiūtiān	*n*	autumn
26. 冬天		dōngtiān	*n*	winter
OTHER				
27. 痛		tòng	*adj*	painful
28. 下雪		xià xuě	*vo*	to snow
29. 热	熱	rè	*adj*	hot (as in temperature)

OPTIONAL VOCABULARY 12.1

SIMPLIFIED	TRADITIONAL	PINYIN	WORD CATEGORY	DEFINITION
WEATHER				
30. 晴天		qíngtiān	*n*	clear day, sunny day
31. 阴天	陰天	yīntiān	*n*	cloudy day

Review of Intensifiers

Chinese includes a wide variety of intensifiers (adverbs that increase the degree of an adjective). Here are the intensifiers that have appeared in the lessons so far.

Intensifier	Meaning
还 + ADJ	Quite
很 + ADJ	Very
好 + ADJ	Very
真的 + ADV + ADJ	Really (真的 is usually followed by another intensifier, such as "真的很漂亮")
太 + ADJ + 了	So very
非常 + ADJ	Extremely
ADJ + 得很	Extremely
ADJ + 得不得了	Extremely

Weather Vocabulary

There are innumerable set expressions regarding weather and the seasons in Chinese. Many of these are four-character phrases that have their origins in classical poetry or fiction. Some are used in everyday speech and some have a more ornate feel, but it is nevertheless common to send poetic seasonal greetings to friends, particularly in the spring. Below are some examples of set expressions relating to different types of weather.

Expressions	Pinyin	Literal Meaning	Describes
滴水成冰	dīshuǐchéngbīng	dripping water becomes ice	freezing weather
骄阳似火	jiāoyángsìhuǒ	a harsh sun like fire	very hot weather
风和日丽	fēnghérìlì	wind gentle, sun beautiful	warm and sunny weather
万里无云	wànlǐwúyún	10,000 *li* no clouds	clear and sunny weather

STRUCTURE NOTE 12.1
Use 最好 *to make suggestions*

The expression 最好 *(zuìhǎo) is similar to* 只好*, which was introduced in Structure Note 8.3 as a means to express "the only thing to do is..."* 最好 *is likewise used to suggest the best course of action in a given situation, and is similar in meaning to "it would be best to..." It differs slightly in emphasis from* 只好*, which lays stress on the fact that one is being somewhat forced to do something.*

Subject + 最好 + Verb Phrase

From the Lesson Text:

你最好去看病。
Nǐ zuìhǎo qù kàn bìng.
You'd better go see a doctor.

Other examples:

你最好别再来这里。
Nǐ zuìhǎo bié zài lái zhèli.
You shouldn't come here anymore.

下次他最好跑得快一点儿。
Xiàcì tā zuìhǎo pǎo de kuài yìdiǎnr.
Next time he should run a bit faster.

Practice: Using 最好, suggest a course of action that could be taken in the following situations, following the example provided.

Example: 大东生病了。→ 你最好送他去看病。

1. 你看，外面下雨了。

   _____

2. 西医我已经看了，还是不舒服。

   _____

3. 他说他昨天晚上睡不着。

   _____

4. 我真爱他！

   _____

5. 我不爱他了。

   _____

STRUCTURE NOTE 12.2
Use 带 *to express bringing objects or people*

带 *(dài) means "to bring/take an item/person to a destination." In some cases,* 带 *is equivalent to* 送*. However, while* 送 *means to escort or transport someone somewhere,* 带 *is more frequently employed when taking some-one along to a shared destination, or to a destination where the subject was heading anyway.*

Subject + 带 + Something / Someone (+ Verb Phrase)

From the Lesson Text:	我带你去他那儿看看好不好？
	Wǒ dài nǐ qù tā nàr kànkan hǎo bu hǎo?
	I'll take you to go see him, okay?

Other examples:

我忘了带我的本子。
Wǒ wàng le dài wǒ de běnzi.
I forgot to bring my notebook.

他没有带他妹妹来。
Tā méiyǒu dài tā mèimei lái.
He didn't bring his younger sister.

Practice: Complete the sentences below using expressions containing 带, as in the example given.

Example: 去上课的时候... → 不应该带手机。
1. 明天是她的生日... _____
2. 我们明天在音乐会表演... _____
3. 去商店买东西的时候... _____
4. 学校离这里不远... _____
5. 外面冷了... _____

STRUCTURE NOTE 12.3
Use noun or measure word reduplication to express "every"

When nouns and measure words are reduplicated, it creates the meaning "every," as in "every book." Only certain words are capable of reduplication. Among these, 人, 天, 年, 个, and 本 are some of the most common. Such expressions are often augmented with the use of 都, which follows the reduplicated noun or measure word.

> Noun + Noun (+ 都) + Verb Phrase/Adjective

> Measure Word + Measure Word (+ 都) + Verb Phrase/Adjective

From the Lesson Text: 我跟男朋友分手了以后，我天天睡不着。
Wǒ gēn nánpéngyou fēn shǒu le yǐhòu, wǒ tiāntiān shuì bu zháo.
Ever since I broke up with my boyfriend, I haven't been able to sleep.

Other examples:

人人都会生病。
Rénrén dōu huì shēng bìng.
Everyone gets sick.

他写的书本本都有意思。
Tā xiě de shū běnběn dōu yǒu yìsi.
All of the books that he writes are interesting.

Practice: Change the following sentences into "every" sentences using noun or measure word reduplication.

Example:　这里的天气 / 天 / 热 → 这里的天气天天都很热。

1.　不是 / 家 / 有宠物　　　＿＿＿＿＿＿＿＿＿＿

2.　这本课本 / 课 / 难　　　＿＿＿＿＿＿＿＿＿＿

3.　酸辣汤 / 碗 / 辣　　　　＿＿＿＿＿＿＿＿＿＿

4.　最近 / 天 / 做功课　　　＿＿＿＿＿＿＿＿＿＿

5.　这些菜 / 盘 / 好吃　　　＿＿＿＿＿＿＿＿＿＿

STRUCTURE NOTE 12.4

Use name/pronoun + 那儿 to talk about someone's location or home

Adding 那儿 *after someone's name or a pronoun can either refer to someone's home, as in "his place," or simply to their location. As is the case with the term "his place" in English, this expression has a colloquial feel in Chinese.*

> Noun / Pronoun + 那儿

From the Lesson Text:　我带你去他那儿看看好不好？
Wǒ dài nǐ qù tā nàr kànkan hǎo bu hǎo?
I'll take you to go see him, okay?

Other examples:　大东那儿有很多书。　　　你那儿有笔吗？
Dàdōng nàr yǒu hěn duō shū.　　Nǐ nàr yǒu bǐ ma?
There are a lot of books at Dadong's　Do you have a pen over there?
place.

Practice: Change the following sentences into Chinese, using the name/pronoun + 那儿 pattern.

Example:　Have you ever been to his place? → 你去过他那儿吗？

1.　Do they have a television at their place?

　　＿＿＿＿＿＿＿＿＿＿＿＿＿＿＿＿＿＿＿＿

2.　She has a cat at her place.

　　＿＿＿＿＿＿＿＿＿＿＿＿＿＿＿＿＿＿＿＿

3.　His place is huge; he has five bedrooms and three bathrooms!

　　＿＿＿＿＿＿＿＿＿＿＿＿＿＿＿＿＿＿＿＿

4.　Do you have a notebook over there?

　　＿＿＿＿＿＿＿＿＿＿＿＿＿＿＿＿＿＿＿＿

5.　My cellphone is over there with him.

　　＿＿＿＿＿＿＿＿＿＿＿＿＿＿＿＿＿＿＿＿

PRACTICE 12.1

Working with a partner, practice the following dialogue. You see that your friend isn't feeling well and you ask what's wrong with him/her. Your friend responds by describing his/her symptoms.

Example:

A: 你还好吗？你看起来不舒服，你生病了吗？

B: 我想是吧。我头很疼，身体觉得很累，每天都睡不着。

PRACTICE 12.2

Take a survey of the class to find out whether students would go to see a doctor of Traditional Chinese Medicine or a doctor of Western medicine if they were sick. Record the most popular answer choice below.

Kind of Doctor	Number of Students

PRACTICE 12.3

In the spaces provided, write down an appropriate description of how you think the person in the picture feels.

💬 PRACTICE 12.4

Look at the pictures below and suggest what each person should do using 最好.

Example:

A: 现在下雨了。

B: 你最好别出去。

现在下雨了。

我妹妹看起来生病了。

明天有考试。

今天天气冷得很。

我忘了带作业。

▦ PRACTICE 12.5

Type the following sentences on your computer.

1. 我跟男朋友分手了以后，天天睡不着。

2. 我肚子疼，头也很疼。

3. 你看起来很不舒服，眼睛和鼻子都红了。

4. 你最好去看中医。

5. 最近天气冷得很，你要多注意身体。

	Radical	Stroke Order
服	月 yuè moon	丿 刀 月 月 肝 肝 服 服
身	身 shēn body	丿 亻 勹 勹 自 身 身
体	亻(人) rén person	丿 亻 仁 什 什 休 体
头	大 dà big	丶 丷 三 头 头
疼	疒 nì sick	丶 亠 广 广 疒 疒 疒 疼 疼 疼
睡	目 mù eye	丨 冂 冂 月 目 目 肝 肝 肝 睡 睡 睡
舒	舌 shé tongue	丿 人 卢 卢 牟 舎 舎 舎 舒 舒 舒
病	疒 nì sick	丶 亠 广 广 疒 疒 疒 病 病 病
着	目 mù eye	丶 丷 丷 丷 兰 羊 羊 着 着 着 着
冷	冫(冰) bīng ice	丶 丷 冫 冸 冷 冷 冷
注	氵(水) shuǐ water	丶 丶 氵 氵 汁 汁 注 注
眼	目 mù eye	丨 冂 冂 月 目 肝 肝 肝 眼 眼 眼
睛	目 mù eye	丨 冂 冂 月 目 肝 肝 眭 睛 睛 睛 睛 睛
医	匸 xǐ box	一 厂 厂 互 圣 医 医
带	巾 jīn cloth	一 十 卄 卅 卅 卅 带 带 带

Make an audio recording and send it to your teacher. In the recording, describe what the weather in your hometown is like. Is it very hot in the summer? Does it snow in winter?

李中平：大东，要不要一起去健身房运动？
陈大东：对不起，我不太舒服。我现在要去看病。
李中平：你还好吧？身体哪儿不舒服？
陈大东：从昨天晚上开始我的肚子就很痛，可能昨天在派对吃太多东西了。
李中平：你下次还是少吃点东西吧。
陈大东：我知道了……
李中平：我开车送你去看医生吧。

Read the dialogue and answer the following questions.
1. Where is Chen Dadong going?
2. Why is he feeling sick?

安娜：

我今天有点不舒服，眼睛和鼻子都红红的，头也很疼。可能是最近天气冷了，昨晚又睡不着，所以生病了。大东昨天约了我今天下午五点半去看电影，可是我现在要去看医生。如果他来宿舍找我的话，你帮我跟他说我生病了不能跟他一起去看电影吧。还有，可不可以帮我买晚饭回来？谢谢。晚上见。

—— 小美

Read Wang Xiaomei's note and answer the following questions.
1. What symptoms does Wang Xiaomei describe in the note?
2. What does she ask Zhang Anna to tell Chen Dadong?

Sender   妈妈

Subject   注意身体

小美:

你们那儿天气怎么样? 你要多穿点儿衣服,别太晚睡觉。还有,要是身体不舒服,你要去看中医。你要注意身体啊!

Sender   小美

Subject   re: 注意身体

妈妈:

最近天气冷得很,昨晚还下雪了。你们那儿呢?妈妈,我不是小孩子了,生病的话我当然会去看医生啊!可是我们这儿找不到中医,只有西医。妈妈,你也要多注意身体啊!

Read the emails and answer the following questions.
1. What is Wang Xiaomei's mother's advice to her daughter?
2. What kind of doctor is Wang Xiaomei able to go see?

Massages

Chinese massages have a long history of providing health benefits. In the West, a massage would likely be had for recreation and relaxation. For the Chinese, however, massages not only relieve stress, they are also believed to affect organ, muscle, and mental performance. The traditional 按摩 (ànmó: "massage") employs a mixture of herbal remedies and massage to improve various facets of one's health. Compared to other methods, this type of massage is relatively pain-free and is popular for improving circulation and relieving muscle pain. Another common type of massage is 推拿 (tuīná: "press and rub"). This method stimulates the body's circulation of 气 (qì: "life force"), helping to boost energy flow and treat minor ailments such as insomnia, headaches, and hormonal imbalance.

For those brave enough to try a more intense treatment, the famous 足疗 (zúliáo: "foot massage") is performed by highly trained masseurs who, with great dexterity, apply heavy pressure to unique points in the foot which correspond to the sensory nerves of each of the body's internal organs. By manipulating these nerves, the procedure is thought to assist the function and operation of organs in a non-invasive manner.

Morning Exercises

Any visitor to China will likely notice the large numbers of people exercising in public squares, parks, and gardens in the early morning. Exercises like 太极拳 (tàijíquán: "Supreme Ultimate Fist"; known in the West as "Tai Chi") and 气功 (qìgōng: "qigong") are all popular methods of staying healthy and fit, particularly among older generations. Some of these habits also have more recent origins. During the Mao era, Chinese citizens regularly gathered for loudspeaker-regulated mass calisthenics. Perhaps one of the more curious exercises prescribed by the Chairman was eye rubbing, which he believed improved eyesight and averted the need for glasses.

Nowadays, China's public spaces play host to a broad range of different fitness activities. Many people are content to undertake exercises as simple as hand clapping or walking on cobbled roads, which is thought to stimulate acupuncture points in the palms and feet, and thus the organs they correspond to. Tai Chi is one of China's most popular forms of traditional exercise and its practitioners can be seen all over the country. It is based on the controlled movement of *qi*, which is achieved by orchestrated movements and careful concentration. Tai Chi is in fact so popular that one can even witness this early morning ritual in the populous cities of Europe and America.

黄祥安：	安娜，你还好吗？你看起来不舒服，你生病了吗？	Anna, are you OK? You don't look so well. Are you sick?
张安娜：	我想是吧。我跟男朋友分手了以后，天天睡不着。我肚子疼，头也很疼。	I think so. After I broke up with my boyfriend, I haven't been sleeping well. My stomach hurts and my head hurts too.
黄祥安：	最近天气冷得很，你要注意身体啊！你的眼睛和鼻子都红了，你最好去看病。	The weather has been very cold lately; you need to take care of yourself! Your eyes and nose are both red. You'd better go see a doctor.
张安娜：	可是现在下雨了，我不想出去……	But it's raining now, I don't feel like going outside...
黄祥安：	我可以送你去啊！你在这儿等我，我马上回来。	I can take you. Wait here, I'll be right back.
张安娜：	好吧，谢谢！	OK, thanks!

黄祥安：	我认识一个很好的中医。我带你去他那儿看看好不好？	I know of a really good Chinese doctor. I'll take you to see him, OK?
张安娜：	中医？为什么不去看西医？	A Chinese doctor? Why not a Western doctor?
黄祥安：	他真的很不错。	He's really good, honest.
张安娜：	好，试试吧。	OK, let's try it.

What Can You Do?

INTERPRETIVE
- I can understand terms for weather and the seasons.
- I can understand descriptions of illnesses.

INTERPERSONAL
- I can discuss someone's wellbeing with him or her.

PRESENTATIONAL
- I can describe the weather.
- I can talk about the state of someone's health and symptoms of illness.

看病
At the Doctor's

来，请坐。你哪儿不舒服？

tóu téng
我头疼，肚子也不舒服。

ér qiě
你的眼睛红红的，而且有
fā shāo   zhāng kāi zuǐ ba
点发烧了。请你张开嘴巴，让我看
shé tou
看你的舌头。

gǎn mào
你的感冒不
yán zhòng
是很严重。

dǎ zhēn
需要打针吗？

dǎ zhēn
中医不用打针。
kāi   zhōu   yào
我帮你开一周的药，
méi shì
吃完就没事了。

zhōng yào   kǔ
中药会很苦吗？

别担心。 等一会儿，护士会告诉你怎么吃。

记住，你要多喝水，好好儿地休息。

谢谢医生，我一定会记得。

医生说什么？

还好，他说我感冒了。

这是你的药，一天两次，吃七天。

大衣穿好，外面又下雨了。

你的男朋友对你真好。

他......只是好朋友！

LESSON TEXT 12.2

At the Doctor's 看病

At the doctor's office, Zhang Anna and the doctor discuss her symptoms and appropriate treatments while Huang Xiang'an waits outside.

医生：	来，请坐。你哪儿不舒服？	Lái, qǐng zuò. Nǐ nǎr bù shūfu?
张安娜：	我头疼，肚子也不舒服。	Wǒ tóuténg, dùzi yě bù shūfu.
医生：	你的眼睛红红的，而且有点发烧了。请你张开嘴巴，让我看看你的舌头。	Nǐ de yǎnjing hóng hóng de, érqiě yǒu diǎn fā shāo le. Qǐng nǐ zhāngkāi zuǐba, ràng wǒ kànkan nǐ de shétou.
医生：	你的感冒不是很严重。	Nǐ de gǎnmào bú shì hěn yánzhòng.
张安娜：	需要打针吗？	Xūyào dǎ zhēn ma?
医生：	中医不用打针。我帮你开一周的药，吃完就没事了。	Zhōngyī bú yòng dǎ zhēn. Wǒ bāng nǐ kāi yì zhōu de yào, chī wán jiù méi shì le.
张安娜：	中药会很苦吗？	Zhōngyào huì hěn kǔ ma?
医生：	别担心。等一会儿，护士会告诉你怎么吃。记住，你要多喝水，好好儿地休息。	Bié dānxīn. Děng yí huìr, hùshi huì gàosu nǐ zěnme chī. Jì zhù, nǐ yào duō hē shuǐ, hǎohāor de xiūxi.
张安娜：	谢谢医生，我一定会记得。	Xièxie yīshēng, wǒ yídìng huì jìde.

黄祥安：	医生说什么？	Yīshēng shuō shénme?
张安娜：	还好，他说我感冒了。	Hái hǎo, tā shuō wǒ gǎnmào le.
护士：	这是你的药，一天两次，吃七天。	Zhè shì nǐ de yào, yì tiān liǎng cì, chī qī tiān.
黄祥安：	大衣穿好，外面又下雨了。	Dàyī chuān hǎo, wàimian yòu xià yǔ le.

护士: 你的男朋友对你真好。

张安娜: 他……只是好朋友！

Nǐ de nánpéngyou duì nǐ zhēn hǎo.

Tā.... zhǐ shì hǎo péngyou!

LESSON VOCABULARY 12.2

	SIMPLIFIED	TRADITIONAL	PINYIN	WORD CATEGORY	DEFINITION
1.	头疼	頭疼	tóuténg	*adj, n*	to have a headache; headache
2.	而且		érqiě	*cj*	furthermore; and also
3.	发烧	發燒	fā shāo	*vo*	to have a fever
4.	张开	張開	zhāngkāi	*rv*	to open
5.	嘴巴		zuǐba	*n*	mouth
6.	舌头	舌頭	shétou	*n*	tongue
7.	感冒		gǎnmào	*v, n*	to catch/have a cold; a cold
8.	严重	嚴重	yánzhòng	*adj*	serious
9.	打针	打針	dǎ zhēn	*vo*	to give or have an injection
10.	开药	開藥	kāi yào	*vo*	to prescribe medicine
11.	周		zhōu	*n*	week
12.	没事	沒事	méi shì	*vo*	it doesn't matter; it's not a problem
13.	中药	中藥	zhōngyào	*n*	Chinese herbal medicine
14.	苦		kǔ	*adj*	bitter
15.	担心	擔心	dānxīn	*adj, vo*	anxious; to worry
16.	一会儿	一會兒	yí huìr	*adv*	in a while, in a moment
17.	护士	護士	hùshi	*n*	nurse
18.	水		shuǐ	*n*	water
19.	地		de	*p*	(used to express the manner in which an action is performed)
20.	休息		xiūxi	*v*	to rest
21.	医生	醫生	yīshēng	*n*	doctor
22.	一定		yídìng	*adj, adv*	certain(ly), definite(ly)
23.	记得	記得	jìde	*v*	to remember
24.	大衣		dàyī	*n*	overcoat

SIMPLIFIED	TRADITIONAL	PINYIN	WORD CATEGORY	DEFINITION
25. 外面		wàimian	*n*	outside
26. 又		yòu	*adv*	again; moreover

REQUIRED VOCABULARY 12.2

RELATED TO MEDICINE

SIMPLIFIED	TRADITIONAL	PINYIN	WORD CATEGORY	DEFINITION
27. 医院	醫院	yīyuàn	*n*	hospital
28. 吃药	吃藥	chī yào	*vo*	to take medicine

OPTIONAL VOCABULARY 12.2

RELATED TO MEDICINE

SIMPLIFIED	TRADITIONAL	PINYIN	WORD CATEGORY	DEFINITION
29. 开刀	開刀	kāi dāo	*vo*	to perform/have an operation
30. 血		xiě, xuè	*n*	blood

Body Parts

头
tóu
head

脖子
bózi
neck

手臂
shǒubì
arm

腿
tuǐ
leg

手
shǒu
hand

脚
jiǎo
foot

头发
tóufa
hair

耳朵
ěrduo
ear

眼睛
yǎnjing
eye

鼻子
bízi
nose

嘴巴
zuǐba
mouth

Online Resources
Visit *http://college.betterchinese.com* for a list of other body parts.

The Difference between 一会儿 and 一下

一会儿 means "a short while," and 一下 means "a moment." The two expressions differ very slightly in that 一下 emphasizes the action and 一会儿 stresses the duration. For example, 坐一下 means "have a seat" (emphasis on the action), while 坐一会儿 means "sit down for a while" (emphasis on the duration).

Different Ways to Talk about Weeks

There are several ways in Chinese to refer to weeks. The most common term is 星期，as in 星期一. The character 周 is sometimes used to refer to weeks, mainly in writing and formal speech. 周 can be used on its own to mean week, combined with other characters to create compound words (e.g., 周末, weekend), and also combined with numbers to create days of the week, as in 周一 (Monday).

STRUCTURE NOTE 12.5
Use 地 to express the manner in which an action is performed

In Structure Note 10.9, it was shown that the particle 得 is used to add modifying expressions after verbs. 地 (de, pronounced the same as 的) is also used to link modifying phrases to verbs, but in this case the modifier precedes the verb. In general, 得 tends to be used to describe how people perform actions on the whole (e.g., "he writes quickly"), while 地 is more often used for how an action is performed in a specific instance (e.g., "he quickly wrote something down").

The adjective in this pattern must be at least two characters long, one-character adjectives are therefore reduplicated. In many cases, the second character in these reduplicated adjectives switches to first tone. In northern China, it is also common to add 儿 after the second character, as in 好好儿. When disyllabic adjectives are reduplicated, they follow the AABB pattern covered in Structure Note 9.10.

Subject + Adjective + 地 + Verb

From the Lesson Text:
你要多喝水，好好儿地休息。
Nǐ yào duō hē shuǐ, hǎohāor de xiūxi.
You need to drink more water and rest well.

Other examples:
她认真地听。
Tā rènzhēn de tīng.
She listened attentively.

孩子们高高兴兴地出去玩儿。
Háizimen gāogāoxìngxìng de chūqu wánr.
The children happily went out to play.

Practice: Change the following adverbial sentences from 得 expressions to 地 expressions. Remember that the specificity of the statement may also need to be modified.

Example: 他看课文看得很快。→ 他很快地把课文看了一次。

1. 她们吃饭吃得很慢。

   _____

2. 弟弟做功课的时候做得很安静。

   _____

3. 她表演唱歌的时候唱得很紧张。

   _____

4. 他们打网球打得很开心。

   _____

5. 他开车开得小心。

   _____

STRUCTURE NOTE 12.6
Use 帮 to mean "for"

帮 (bāng) *has already been introduced as a verb meaning "to help." In some cases, however, a phrase which on the surface expresses "to help someone to do something" in fact means "to do something for someone." One can usually work this out from context.*

Subject + 帮 + Someone + Verb Phrase

From the Lesson Text:　我帮你开一周的药，吃完就没事了。
Wǒ bāng nǐ kāi yì zhōu de yào, chī wán jiù méi shì le.
I'll prescribe a week's worth of medicine for you; after you take it you'll be fine.

Other examples:

你可以帮我带那本书吗？
Nǐ kěyǐ bāng wǒ dài nà běn shū ma?
Could you bring that book for me?

我生病了，你可以帮我买药吗？
Wǒ shēng bìng le, nǐ kěyǐ bāng wǒ mǎi yào ma?
I'm sick; can you buy some medicine for me?

NOTE: *There are a few other verbs which can also act in the same way as* 帮 *to mean "for" or "on behalf of," one such example being* 给. *Once again, attention must be given to the context to distinguish this* 给 *from the preposition introduced in Structure Note 6.3, which means "to." Sometimes, however, the meaning may remain ambiguous.*

Practice: Respond to the following prompts using the verb provided and 帮 to mean "for."

Example:　我忘了带我的钱包，怎么办？（付钱）
→ 没问题，我帮你付钱。

1.　米饭做好了没有？（看看）

　　_____

2.　我借的书太多了。（还）

　　_____

3.　我吃饱了，这盘菜吃不完。（吃）

　　_____

4.　那个字我忘了怎么写。（写）

　　_____

5.　这里的菜都看起来好吃，不知道选哪一个好！（选）

　　_____

STRUCTURE NOTE 12.7
Use 好 as a resultative complement to describe a properly completed action
好 *can be used as a resultative complement with a very similar meaning to* 完, *"to finish." In some cases, the resultative complement* 好 *indicates that a certain action is being performed correctly or properly, for example* 坐好, *"to sit properly."*

Subject + Verb + 好

From the Lesson Text:

大衣穿好。
Dàyī chuān hǎo.
Make sure your coat is on properly. (Literally: Wear your coat properly)

Other examples:

同学们坐好!
Tóngxuémen zuò hǎo!
Students, sit properly!

书看好了没有?
Shū kàn hǎo le méiyǒu?
Did you finish reading the book?

Practice: Complete these fragments to create questions containing the resultative complement 好.

Example: 中文的语法... → 中文的语法你已经学好了吗?
1. 那本课本... _____
2. 下个星期的考试... _____
3. 今天的晚饭... _____
4. 明天的作业... _____
5. 那张画... _____

STRUCTURE NOTE 12.8
Use 又...了 to say "again"
In Structure Note 6.7, 再 *was introduced as a way to mark recurring actions.* 再 *is typically used to talk about future repetitions that have not yet occurred. To describe a recurring event that took place in the past, or an event that has just reoccurred in the present, the adverb* 又 *is used. The sentence-final particle* 了 *is often used with this pattern.*

Subject + 又 + Verb Phrase + 了

From the Lesson Text:

外面又下雨了。
Wàimian yòu xià yǔ le.
It has started raining again outside.

Other examples:

你又来了!
Nǐ yòu lái le!
You again!

她昨天又打网球了。
Tā zuótiān yòu dǎ wǎngqiú le.
She played tennis again yesterday.

Practice: Change the following sentences into Chinese using the 又…了 pattern.

Example: How did you forget your homework again!

→ 你的作业怎么又忘了！

1. Dad, are we lost again?

   _____

2. Yesterday he went to see that kung fu movie again.

   _____

3. My older brother borrowed my car again.

   _____

4. How come you're reading that book again?

   _____

5. I went to the bank again this morning.

   _____

练习 PRACTICE

💬 PRACTICE 12.11

Using the information given below, enact a roleplay with a partner in which one person plays the doctor and the other the patient.

    Example:

    A: 你哪儿不舒服？

    B: 我头疼，常常觉得很冷。

    A: 你感冒了，我开感冒药给你。

Name:	张安娜
Symptoms:	眼睛和鼻子红红的，常常觉得很冷
Diagnosis:	感冒
Presciption:	感冒药

Name:	李中平
Symptoms:	头疼，觉得很累
Diagnosis:	发烧
Presciption:	打针

Name:	陈大东
Symptoms:	肚子疼
Diagnosis:	东西吃太多
Presciption:	中药

Name:	王小美
Symptoms:	头疼，睡不着
Diagnosis:	感冒
Presciption:	头痛药

💬 PRACTICE 12.12

Working with a partner, take it in turns to give each other instructions about taking the medicine below.

    Example: 这是你的感冒药，一天两次，吃七天。

感冒药　每日：2 次　一共：7 天

感冒药　每日：3 次　一共：4 天

感冒药　每日：4 次　一共：5 天

感冒药　每日：1 次　一共：14 天

PRACTICE 12.13

Working with a partner, look at the information below and take it in turns to describe the problems (indicated by the text box), followed by an appropriate solution (indicated by the picture).

Example:
A: 我感冒了。
B: 我可以帮你买感冒药。

我感冒了。

我累了。

我很冷。

我饿了。

我发烧了。

PRACTICE 12.14

In the spaces provided, write the names for the body parts indicated.

	Radical	Stroke Order
拿	手 shǒu hand	ノ 人 亼 今 合 合 拿 拿 拿 拿
儿	儿 rén person	ノ 儿
周	口 kǒu mouth	ノ 刀 月 用 用 周 周 周
烧	火 huǒ fire	丶 丶 少 火 灯 灶 烁 烧 烧 烧
嘴	口 kǒu mouth	丨 口 口 口 叮 吵 吵 啮 啮 嘴 嘴 嘴 嘴 嘴 嘴 嘴
巴	己 jǐ oneself	フ 丆 尸 巴
冒	冂 jiōng down box	丨 冂 冃 曰 冐 冐 冒 冒 冒
严	一 yī one	一 丆 亚 严 严 亚 严
药	艹(草) cǎo grass	一 十 艹 艻 药 茐 苭 药 药
苦	艹(草) cǎo grass	一 十 艹 艹 芊 芐 苦 苦
担	扌(手) shǒu hand	一 十 扌 扣 扣 担 担
记	讠(言) yán speech	丶 讠 讠 记 记
休	亻(人) rén person	ノ 亻 仁 什 休 休
息	心 xīn heart	ノ 亻 白 白 自 自 息 息 息
外	夕 xī evening	ノ 夕 夕 列 外

PRACTICE 12.16

Type the following sentences on your computer and provide answers to the questions.

1. 请你张开嘴巴，让我看看你的舌头。
2. 我的病是不是很严重？
3. 我给你开一周的中药。
4. 感冒的时候要多喝水。
5. 你的眼睛红红的，而且还有点发烧。

PRACTICE 12.17

Make an audio recording and send it to your teacher. In the recording, describe a time that you went to see the doctor. Talk about how you were feeling and what the doctor recommended that you do.

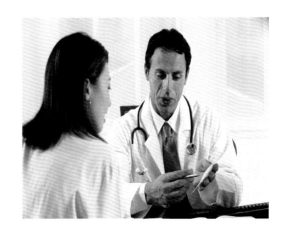

PRACTICE 12.18

护士： 张安娜，请跟我来。

张安娜：好的。

医生： 你哪儿不舒服？

张安娜：我常常头疼，晚上也睡不着。

医生： 让我先看看你的眼睛。

医生： 请你张开嘴巴，我看看你的舌头。

张安娜：我的病严重吗？

医生： 别担心，我给你开三天的药，好好儿地休息，吃完药就没事了。

张安娜：谢谢医生。

Read the dialogue and answer the following questions.

1. What symptoms does Zhang Anna describe to the doctor?
2. What does the doctor say that Zhang Anna should do?

安娜：

这是你的药。这是三天的感冒药，每六个小时吃一次，一天四次，最好饭后吃。护士说，如果三天以后你觉得还没好，你要再来看医生。还有，记得要多喝水，多休息。

——祥安

Read Huang Xiang'an's note and answer the following questions.
1. What are the instructions for taking the medicine?
2. What does the nurse remind Zhang Anna to do?

PRACTICE 12.20

我最近常常头疼，所以上个星期我去看西医了。医生说要给我打针，可是我不想打，医生只好开三天的药给我。我吃完以后还觉得不舒服，小美说我应该去试试看中医，但是我担心中药会很苦，所以我还是再去看西医了。

Read Zhang Anna's diary and answer the following questions.
1. Did Zhang Anna get an injection?
2. Why didn't Zhang Anna go to see a doctor of Chinese medicine?

Traditional Chinese Medicine

Contrary to the Western philosophy of treating illnesses on a case-by-case basis, Traditional Chinese Medicine (TCM) takes a holistic approach that aims to help the body heal itself. According to this system, the body may better equip itself to handle adverse symptoms by reconciling the opposing forces of 阴 (yīn) and 阳 (yáng). TCM makes use of a number of herbal concoctions and animal products that are largely alien to modern Western medicine. Many of these ingredients and combinations were developed by Daoists who, seeking to create elixirs of immortality, coincidentally discovered cures to various common ailments.

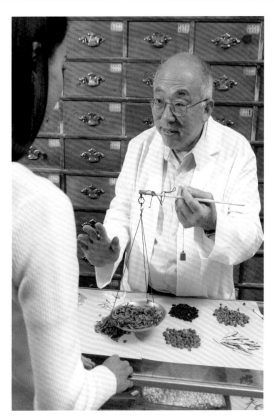

Processes such as acupuncture, moxibustion, and cupping are also common aspects of TCM. Acupuncture is a treatment method consisting of the insertion of stainless steel needles into the body at various *qi* points. The intention of the process is to reduce pain and alleviate various bodily afflictions. Moxibustion, a procedure which often accompanies acupuncture, involves burning certain herbs on or near the body. Cupping is a form of reverse-pressure massage. The practitioner will take a glass cup, light a match to heat the air inside, and then press the cup against the patient's back, creating a suction effect.

Hot and Cold Foods

食疗 (shíliáo: "food therapy") is a medical system which espouses the healing properties of certain foodstuffs. Medicine itself is in fact only one aspect of conventional Chinese beliefs regarding health and the body. In the Chinese medical tradition, all forms of consumption are believed to have different medicinal effects, both positive and negative. Medicine can be taken for ailments, but it does not necessarily take precedence over everyday food and drink. This close association of medicine and food is even reflected in the Chinese language itself. In English, one "takes" medicine. In Chinese, on the other hand, one "eats" it (吃药 chī yào).

Nutritional therapy relies on a systematic balancing of "hot" and "cold" foods, a dichotomy that also originates with the concept of 阴阳 (yīnyáng: "yin and yang"). Foodstuffs are not categorized by temperature, but rather by their associated benefits or the alterations to the body they may cause. *Yin* foods, such as carrots and crab, are considered "cold" foods that decrease the body's temperature, thus lowering metabolism. Conversely, *yang* foods, such as beef and mushrooms, are thought to be "hot" foods that increase the body's temperature and metabolism. The philosophy extends beyond substance to the method of preparation. For example, cooking by boiling, steaming, and poaching is associated with *yin*, while deep-frying, stir-frying, and roasting are all associated with *yang*.

医生:	来，请坐。你哪儿不舒服？	Here, please have a seat. What seems to be the problem?
张安娜:	我头疼，肚子也不舒服。	My head hurts and my stomach doesn't feel good either.
医生:	你的眼睛红红的，而且有点发烧了。请你张开嘴巴，让我看看你的舌头。	Your eyes are a little red and you have a bit of a fever. Please open your mouth and let me see your tongue.
医生:	你的感冒不是很严重。	Your cold is not that serious.
张安娜:	需要打针吗？	Do I need to get a shot?
医生:	中医不用打针。我给你开一周的药，吃完就没事了。	You don't need to get shots with Chinese medicine. Let me give you a week's worth of medicine. After you take it, you'll be fine.
张安娜:	中药会很苦吗？	Is Chinese medicine bitter?
医生:	别担心。等一会儿，护士会告诉你怎么吃。记住，你要多喝水，好好儿地休息。	Don't worry. The nurse will tell you how to take it in a moment. Remember, drink lots of water and rest well.
张安娜:	谢谢医生，我一定会记得。	Thanks, doctor. I will remember.

───────────

黄祥安:	医生说什么？	What did the doctor say?
张安娜:	还好，他说我感冒了。	It's fine, he said I have a cold.
护士:	这是你的药，一天两次，吃七天。	This is your medicine. Take it twice a day for seven days.
黄祥安:	大衣穿好，外面又下雨了。	Make sure your coat is on properly. It's started to rain again.
护士:	你的男朋友对你真好。	Your boyfriend is so good to you.
张安娜:	他……只是好朋友！	He's…just a good friend!

450 第十二单元 ▪ 第二课 ▪ 医

What Can You Do?

INTERPRETIVE

- I can understand the names of different ailments.
- I can understand the names for different parts of the body.
- I can understand doctors' advice and prescriptions.

INTERPERSONAL

- I can have a discussion with the doctor about how I am feeling.
- I can discuss treatments with the doctor or nurse.

PRESENTATIONAL

- I can give a presentation on some of the basic features of Chinese and Western medicine.
- I can give a presentation on a visit to a practitioner of Chinese medicine.

ACT IT OUT

Working in groups, compose an original three-minute skit that utilizes the vocabulary and structures introduced in Unit 12. Each of you should assume a role and have a roughly equal number of lines in the skit. Be prepared to perform your skit in class. You can either come up with your own story or choose from one of the following situations:

a) You're starting to feel sick so you discuss your symptoms with a friend.

b) You interview a doctor about what he does on the job.

c) It's starting to snow and your mother has some warnings and advice about the cold.

CHECK WHAT YOU CAN DO

RECOGNIZE

Adverbs
- □ 天天
- □ 最好
- □ 一会儿
- □ 一定
- □ 又

Adjectives
- □ 还好
- □ 舒服
- □ 疼
- □ 冷
- □ 痛
- □ 热
- □ 头疼
- □ 严重

- □ 苦
- □ 担心

Nouns
- □ 肚子
- □ 头
- □ 天气
- □ 身体
- □ 眼睛
- □ 鼻子
- □ 中医
- □ 西医
- □ 手
- □ 脚
- □ 春天
- □ 夏天

- □ 秋天
- □ 冬天
- □ 嘴巴
- □ 舌头
- □ 周
- □ 中药
- □ 医院
- □ 护士
- □ 水
- □ 医生
- □ 大衣
- □ 外面

Particles
- □ 地

Verbs
- □ 生病
- □ 睡不着
- □ 注意
- □ 看病
- □ 下雨
- □ 带
- □ 下雪
- □ 发烧
- □ 张开
- □ 感冒
- □ 打针
- □ 开药

- □ 没事
- □ 休息
- □ 记得
- □ 拿
- □ 吃药

Prepositions
- □ 从

WRITE
- □ 服
- □ 身体
- □ 头疼
- □ 睡
- □ 舒病
- □ 着
- □ 冷
- □ 注
- □ 眼睛
- □ 医
- □ 带

- □ 拿
- □ 儿
- □ 周
- □ 烧
- □ 嘴巴
- □ 冒
- □ 严
- □ 药
- □ 苦
- □ 担
- □ 记
- □ 休息
- □ 外

USE

- □ 最好 to make suggestions
- □ 带 to express bringing objects or people
- □ Noun or measure word reduplication to express "every"
- □ Name/pronoun + 那儿 to talk about someone's location or home

- □ 地 to express the manner in which an action is performed
- □ 帮 to mean "for"
- □ 好 as a resultative complement to describe a properly completed action
- □ 又 ... 了 to say "again"

Business

商

第十三单元
UNIT 13

Communication Goals

Lesson 1: 打工 **Part-Time Job**
- Talk about your full- or part-time job
- Offer words of encouragement
- Indicate that something is unexpected

Lesson 2: 去中国实习 **Internship in China**
- Discuss internships and working in China
- Talk about your employment experience and résumé
- Discuss your post-graduation plans
- Learn about the importance of guanxi, or "connections"

打工
Part-Time Job

小美！
méi xiǎng dào
没想到你
会来看我！

dǎ gōng
我想看看你打工的地方。

huán jìng
这里环境真不错，你每天
在这儿工作几小时？

我每天
晚上从八点
到十二点
shàng bān
上班。

xià bān   nán guài
你十二点才下班，难怪
hěn shǎo
晚上很少见到你。

LESSON TEXT 13.1

Part-Time Job 打工

Wang Xiaomei visits Chen Dadong at the coffee shop where he works and the two chat about his job.

陈大东：	小美！没想到你会来看我！	Xiǎoměi! Méi xiǎng dào nǐ huì lái kàn wǒ!
王小美：	我想看看你打工的地方。这里环境真不错，你每天在这儿工作几小时？	Wǒ xiǎng kànkan nǐ dǎ gōng de dìfang. Zhèli huánjìng zhēn bú cuò, nǐ měi tiān zài zhèr gōngzuò jǐ xiǎoshí?
陈大东：	我每天晚上从八点到十二点上班。	Wǒ měi tiān wǎnshang cóng bā diǎn dào shí èr diǎn shàng bān.
王小美：	你十二点才下班，难怪晚上很少见到你。	Nǐ shí èr diǎn cái xià bān, nánguài wǎnshang hěnshǎo jiàn dào nǐ.

王小美：	你在这儿都做些什么样的事？	Nǐ zài zhèr dōu zuò xiē shénme yàng de shì?
陈大东：	我要泡咖啡、做收银，还要打扫厨房。	Wǒ yào pào kāfēi, zuò shōu yín, hái yào dǎsǎo chúfáng.
王小美：	听起来很忙啊！	Tīngqilai hěn máng a!
陈大东：	我以前只管打扫。老板看我很努力，慢慢地就让我管更多的事了。	Wǒ yǐqián zhǐ guǎn dǎsǎo. Lǎobǎn kàn wǒ hěn nǔlì, mànman de jiù ràng wǒ guǎn gèng duō de shì le.
王小美：	你不但要上学，而且还要工作。这样一天到晚都很忙，不会太累吗？	Nǐ búdàn yào shàng xué, érqiě hái yào gōngzuò. Zhèyàng yì tiān dào wǎn dōu hěn máng, bú huì tài lèi ma?
陈大东：	虽然累一点，但是我想赚钱，这样的话，今年暑假可以出国旅行。	Suīrán lèi yì diǎn, dànshì wǒ xiǎng zhuàn qián, zhèyàng de huà, jīnnián shǔjià kěyǐ chū guó lǚxíng.
王小美：	大东，你一定做得到！加油！	Dàdōng, nǐ yídìng zuò de dào! Jiāyóu!

字 词 VOCABULARY

LESSON VOCABULARY 13.1

	SIMPLIFIED	TRADITIONAL	PINYIN	WORD CATEGORY	DEFINITION
1.	没想到	沒想到	méi xiǎng dào	ie	to not have expected or thought of
2.	打工		dǎ gōng	vo	to work part-time, to temp
3.	环境	環境	huánjìng	n	environment
4.	上班		shàng bān	vo	to go to work
5.	下班		xià bān	vo	to get off work
6.	难怪	難怪	nánguài	adv	no wonder
7.	很少		hěnshǎo	adv	very infrequently; rarely
8.	做事		zuò shì	vo	to work; to handle matters
9.	什么样	甚麼樣	shénme yàng	pr	what kind/sort
10.	泡		pào	v	to make (coffee or tea); to steep
11.	收银	收銀	shōu yín	vo	to collect money
12.	打扫	打掃	dǎsǎo	v	to clean up; to sweep
13.	厨房	廚房	chúfáng	n	kitchen
14.	以前		yǐqián	prep	before
15.	管		guǎn	v	to be in charge of
16.	老板		lǎobǎn	n	boss
17.	努力		nǔlì	adj, v	diligent; to work hard
18.	慢慢		mànmàn	adv	slowly; gradually
19.	不但		búdàn	cj	not only
20.	上学	上學	shàng xué	vo	to attend school
21.	一天到晚		yì tiān dào wǎn	adv	from morning until night; all day long
22.	虽然	雖然	suīrán	cj	even though
23.	赚钱	賺錢	zhuàn qián	vo	to earn money
24.	今年		jīnnián	n	this year
25.	暑假		shǔjià	n	summer vacation

LESSON VOCABULARY 13.1 (continued)

SIMPLIFIED	TRADITIONAL	PINYIN	WORD CATEGORY	DEFINITION
26. 出国	出國	chū guó	*vo*	to leave the country
27. 旅行		lǚxíng	*v, n*	to travel; travel
28. 加油		jiāyóu	*ie*	you can do it! (literally "add oil"; used when offering words of encouragement)

REQUIRED VOCABULARY 13.1

RELATED TO WORK

29. 整理		zhěnglǐ	*v*	to sort out; to put in order; to arrange
30. 干净	乾淨	gānjìng	*adj*	clean
31. 接待		jiēdài	*v*	to receive (guests)
32. 客人		kèrén	*n*	guests; customers

OPTIONAL VOCABULARY 13.1

OTHER PROFESSIONS

33. 家教		jiājiào	*n*	tutor
34. 助教		zhùjiào	*n*	teaching assistant
35. 厨师	廚師	chúshī	*n*	cook, chef

Work Titles

While in the past co-workers at a 单位 (dānwèi: "work unit") would most likely call each other 同志 (tóngzhì: "comrade"), these days people simply use the term 同事 (tóngshì: "colleague"). Other titles used in the workplace generally correspond to those used in English, but there are some notable exceptions. Below are some examples of common forms of address for professionals. Remember that as with other professional titles covered so far, a person's surname precedes the title.

Corporate titles

Title	Pinyin	Meaning
总经理	zǒngjīnglǐ	general manager
经理	jīnglǐ	manager
主席	zhǔxí	chairman
主任	zhǔrèn	director
董事长	dǒngshìzhǎng	president; chairman of the board

Other titles

Title	Pinyin	Use
师傅	shīfu	The term 师傅 literally means "master." While this term would indeed be employed for a master of a skill such as martial arts, it is also widely used to refer to any skilled worker. Taxi drivers, for example, are referred to as 师傅.
阿姨	āyí	阿姨 means "aunt." When used in a professional context, it is a generic form of address for females employed in such roles as maids, babysitters, or carers.
服务员	fúwùyuán	Literally "attendant" or "service person," this is the most common form of address for a male or female working in the service industry, from a humble tea house all the way to a high class restaurant.
老板	lǎobǎn	This term, akin to "boss" and mostly used in the same way, is also the common term for any shopkeeper or proprietor of a business. One may also hear 老板娘 (lǎobǎnniáng), the female equivalent, meaning "proprietress."
老(姓)	lǎo (xìng)	Calling someone old may seem a little offensive in the West, but in China, where Confucian principles have instilled veneration for older generations, addressing someone with the prefix 老 is both a marker of familiarity and respect.
小(姓)	xiǎo (xìng)	The opposite of 老, 小 is a prefix that would be given to a younger member of a working or social group.

STRUCTURE NOTE 13.1

Use 没想到 *to introduce an unexpected event*

The phrase 没想到 *(méi xiǎng dào) literally means "didn't think of." Its usage is similar to "didn't expect" or "who'd have thought" in English.*

(Subject +) 没想到 + Sentence

From the Lesson Text:

小美，没想到你会来看我！
Xiǎoměi, méi xiǎng dào nǐ huì lái kàn wǒ!
Xiaomei, I didn't expect that you'd come see me!

Other examples:

真的没想到我们学校会
有这么漂亮的学生。
Zhēnde méi xiǎng dào wǒmen xuéxiào
huì yǒu zhème piàoliang de xuésheng.
I really didn't think our school would
have students who were this pretty.

我没想到你们都会骗
我。
Wǒ méi xiǎng dào nǐmen dōu huì
piàn wǒ.
I didn't expect you all to cheat me.

Practice: Change the following statements into Chinese expressions containing the 没想到 pattern.

Example: I didn't think he'd go to bed that late.
→ 没想到他那么晚才去睡觉。

1.   I didn't expect that she would break up with her boyfriend.

   _____

2.   I didn't think the test would be that easy.

   _____

3.   Who'd have thought that he plays the guitar so well.

   _____

4.   We didn't expect that leaving the country to go travelling would be so expensive.

   _____

5.   I didn't expect that she planned to go to Russia to find a job.

   _____

STRUCTURE NOTE 13.2

Use 难怪 *to express "no wonder"*

难怪 *(nánguài) expresses the equivalent of "no wonder."* 难怪 *is placed before the subject at the beginning of the phrase.*

难怪 + Subject + Verb Phrase

From the Lesson Text:

难怪晚上很少见到你。
Nánguài wǎnshang hěnshǎo jiàn dào nǐ.
No wonder I rarely see you in the evenings.

Other examples:

难怪你找不到女朋友，
你一直都在工作啊！
Nánguài nǐ zhǎo bu dào nǚpéngyou,
nǐ yìzhí dōu zài gōngzuò a!
No wonder you can't find a girlfriend,
you're always working!

他从来没打扫过房
间，难怪他不喜欢在
那儿住。
Tā cónglái méi dǎsǎo guo fángjiān,
nánguài tā bù xǐhuan zài nàr zhù.
He's never cleaned his room, no
wonder he doesn't like to live there.

Practice: Match the following sentences on this basis of the information given.

这家饭馆的饺子真好吃，	难怪外面没有人。
她一天到晚都上班，	难怪客人这么多。
天气冷得很，	难怪肚子饿。
他感冒了，	难怪鼻子那么红。
你今天没吃早饭，	难怪那么累。

STRUCTURE NOTE 13.3
Use 什么样的 *to ask "what kind?"*

什么样的 (shénme yàng de) *can be added to nouns in order to elicit a more specific response. It is equivalent to "what kind of?" or "what sort of?" in English.*

> Subject + Verb + 什么样 + 的 + Noun Phrase

From the Lesson Text:

你在这儿都做些什么样的事？
Nǐ zài zhèr dōu zuò xiē shénme yàng de shì?
What kind of work do you do here?

Other examples:

你喜欢什么样的菜？
Nǐ xǐhuan shénme yàng de cài?
What kind of food do you like?

那是什么样的手机？
Nà shì shénme yàng de shǒujī?
What kind of cellphone is that?

NOTE: *In the example from the Lesson Text,* 都 *is added to the question to imply that a response containing more than one thing is expected (i.e., Xiaomei anticipates that Dadong does more than one thing at the coffee shop).* 什么样的 *pairs quite naturally with this use of* 都 *as it is a question that usually anticipates a multiple response.*

Practice: For each of the following statements, provide a question containing 什么样的 that could elicit such a response, following the example shown below.

Example: 我喜欢中国菜。→ 你喜欢什么样的菜？

1. 我的老板是个很认真的人。

    _____

2. 我觉得她应该看中医。

    _____

3. 我想找个很聪明的女朋友。

    _____

4. 我们今年都选了语言课。

    _____

5. 那里天气冷，你应该带一件毛衣。

    _____

STRUCTURE NOTE 13.4
Use 不但…而且… to express "not only…but also..."

There are a number of two-part sentence patterns in Chinese. In this particular pattern, the initial part, 不但 (búdàn), means "not only." It pairs with 而且 (érqiě), meaning "moreover." As in other structures of this type, if the subject of the two clauses remains the same, the subject can precede 不但.

> Subject + 不但 + Verb Phrase A + , + 而且 + Verb Phrase B

> 不但 + Clause A + , + 而且 + Clause B

From the Lesson Text: 你不但要上学，而且还要工作。
Nǐ búdàn yào shàng xué, érqiě hái yào gōngzuò.
Not only do you have to study, you also have to work.

Other examples:

不但中平知道了，
而且别的同学也知道
了！
Búdàn Zhōngpíng zhīdào le, érqiě bié de tóngxué yě zhīdào le!
Not only Zhongping knew it, the other classmates also knew it!

他不但会接待客人，
而且会泡咖啡。
Tā búdàn huì jiēdài kèrén, érqiě huì pào kāfēi.
Not only does he know how to serve customers, he also knows how to brew coffee.

Practice: *Create complete sentences using* 不但...而且... *and the word pairs provided below.*

Example:　这个孩子 / 打扫客厅 / 泡茶
→ 这个孩子不但帮妈妈打扫客厅，而且给她泡茶。

1. 安娜 / 唱歌 / 拉小提琴

   _____

2. 饺子 / 好吃 / 便宜

   _____

3. 大东 / 准备考试 / 上班

   _____

4. 小美 / 聪明 / 漂亮

   _____

5. 她 / 没结婚 / 分手了

   _____

STRUCTURE NOTE 13.5

Use 虽然...但是... to express "although...however..."

In English, it would sound strange to say both "although" and "however" in the same sentence – usually we pick one or the other. In Chinese, however, these sayings appear together as a set pattern. The second clause is generally introduced by 但是 *or* 可是. *As in Structure Note 13.4, if the subject remains the same for both clauses, it can precede* 虽然 (suīrán).

Subject + 虽然 + Verb Phrase A + , + 但是 / 可是 + Verb Phrase B

虽然 + Subject + Verb Phrase A + , + 但是 / 可是 + Verb Phrase B

From the Lesson Text:　虽然累一点，但是我想赚钱。
Suīrán lèi yì diǎn, dànshì wǒ xiǎng zhuàn qián.
Although it's a bit tiring, I want to make money.

Other examples:

她虽然没有钱，可是对朋友很好。
Tā suīrán méiyǒu qián, kěshì duì péngyou hěn hǎo.
Although she doesn't have money, she treats her friends very well.

虽然我很忙，但是我很高兴。
Suīrán wǒ hěn máng, dànshì wǒ hěn gāoxìng.
Although I'm busy, I'm very happy.

Practice: Create complete sentences using the following word pairs with the 虽然...但是... construction.

Example:　这家饭馆 / 青菜 / 有点咸 / 味道还不错
→ 这家饭馆的青菜虽然有点咸，但是味道还不错。

1.　这家饭馆 / 不便宜 / 客人还很多

　　_____

2.　教室 / 打扫过 / 看起来不干净

　　_____

3.　课文 / 有点难 / 很有意思

　　_____

4.　我 / 生病了 / 不想看病

　　_____

5.　我和她 / 分手了 / 还是好朋友

　　_____

STRUCTURE NOTE 13.6
Use 从...到... to express length of time

In Structure Note 7.7, 从 *A* 到 *B* was used to express "from location A to location B." As well as distance in space, this pattern can also be used to express distance between two points in time. As with the pattern introduced previous, the main verb of the sentence follows the 从...到... construction.

> Subject + 从 + Time A + 到 + Time B + Verb Phrase

From the Lesson Text:　我每天晚上从八点到十二点上班。
Wǒ měi tiān wǎnshang cóng bā diǎn dào shí èr diǎn shàng bān.
I work every day from 8pm to 12am.

Other examples:

她从晚上十一点到早上七点半睡觉。
Tā cóng wǎnshang shí yī diǎn dào zǎoshang qī diǎn bàn shuì jiào.
She sleeps from 11pm to 7:30am.

他从下午到晚上都要学习。
Tā cóng xiàwǔ dào wǎnshang dōu yào xuéxí.
He has to study from the afternoon through to the evening.

Practice: Use 从…到… to create sentences with the times given below and the activity in parentheses.

Example: 从7:30pm ／ 到 9:00pm
→ 我昨天晚上从七点半到九点看电视。

1. 从 9:00am ／ 到 1:00pm（上课）

_____

2. 从 2:30pm ／ 到 3:30pm（打球）

_____

3. 从 4:00pm ／ 到 6:00pm（看电影）

_____

4. 从 6:10pm ／ 到 7:20pm（跟朋友吃饭）

_____

5. 从 8:00pm ／ 到 9:30pm（做作业）

_____

练习 PRACTICE

PRACTICE 13.1

Working with a partner, write profiles for the pictured characters using the words provided, then ask and answer questions about their work schedules and duties.

Work place: 咖啡店
Work time:
每天晚上从八点
到十二点
Duties:
泡咖啡，做收银

Example:

A: 你每天在这儿工作几个小时？
B: 我每天晚上从八点到十二点上班。
A: 你在这儿都做些什么样的事？
B: 我泡咖啡、做收银。

Work places: 餐厅 医院 饭馆 商店
Duties: 打扫厨房 卖衣服 表演 开药 接待客人 开刀 做收银

Work place:

Work time:

Duties:

Work place:

Work time:

Duties:

Work place:

Work time:

Duties:

Work place:

Work time:

Duties:

PRACTICE 13.2

Working with a partner, first change the responses of the characters on the right into 虽然…但是 sentences, then practice the dialogues using the new sentences that you have made.

你早上没吃东西，不会饿吗？

中午我会跟小美吃饭。

Example:
虽然有点饿，但是中午我会跟小美吃饭。

你第一次表演，不会紧张吗？

我会好好地表演。

你跟男朋友分手了，不会难过吗？

我会找到一个更好的男朋友。

这条项链卖一百块，不会太贵吗？

我要把它送给玛丽。

	Radical	Stroke Order
工	工 gōng work	一 丁 工
房	户 hù door	丶 ⼀ ⼆ 户 户 户 房 房
银	钅(金) jīn gold	丿 𠂉 𠂉 𠂉 钅 钅 钅 钅 钔 银 银
假	亻(人) rén person	丿 亻 亻 𠂆 𠂊 作 作 假 假 假
班	玉 yù jade	一 二 干 王 玎 玎 玵 班 班
板	木 mù wood	一 十 才 木 朾 朾 板 板
环	玉 yù jade	一 二 干 王 环 环 环 环
境	土 tǔ earth	一 十 土 圵 圹 圹 圹 垆 垆 培 培 培 境 境
怪	忄(心) xīn heart	丶 ⼀ 忄 忉 忆 怪 怪
前	刂(刀) dāo knife	丶 丷 丷 丷 前 前 前 前 前
管	竹(竹) zhú bamboo	丿 𠂉 𠂉 𠂉 竺 竺 竺 筲 筲 管 管 管 管
但	亻(人) rén person	丿 亻 亻 但 但 但
而	而 ér and	一 丆 丆 丙 而 而
且	一 yī one	丨 𠀀 日 月 且
虽	虫 chóng insect	丨 口 口 吊 吊 吊 虽 虽

🎤 Make an audio recording and send it to your teacher. In the recording, describe a part time job that you have had. What were the hours like? What kind of responsibilities did you have?

PRACTICE 13.5

Type the following sentences on your computer.

1. 这里环境真不错，我也想在这儿打工。
2. 没想到你每天晚上十二点才下班！
3. 你这么努力工作，难怪老板让你管更多的事。
4. 他不但要泡咖啡、做收银，还要打扫厨房。
5. 虽然工作累一点，但是赚了钱就可以出国旅行了。

PRACTICE 13.6

Sender	祥安
Subject	音乐会

大东：
最近晚上很少见到你，你在忙什么？
安娜说上个星期在医院里看到你了，
你怎么了？下个周末你有空吗？我们
一起去听小美的音乐会吧！

Sender	大东
Subject	re: 音乐会

祥安：
我上个星期身体不舒服，所以去看医生了。医
生说可能是我工作太累了。最近不但要上学，
而且还要工作，真是太忙了！我也想去听小美
的音乐会，可是我得问问我的老板，看看可不
可以早一点下班。

Read the emails and answer the following questions.
1. What does the doctor suggest is the reason for Chen Dadong not feeling well?
2. Will Chen Dadong go to Wang Xiaomei's concert?

陈大东：你每天打几个小时的工？
孙玛丽：差不多三个小时，从下午三点到六点。
陈大东：你都做些什么？
孙玛丽：卖衣服、做收银，还要打扫。
陈大东：你喜欢你的工作吗？
孙玛丽：这里环境不错，可是我有点忙。
陈大东：你不但要上学，而且还要打工，会不会太累？
孙玛丽：还好，我会找时间做作业和准备考试。
陈大东：那你要注意身体！

Read the dialogue and answer the following questions.
1. How many hours does Sun Mali work each day?
2. What are her duties at work?

中平：
我找到了一份新的工作，我在学校餐厅后面的咖啡店打工。星期一到星期五从晚上八点到十点，每天工作两个小时。周末的工作时间比较长，从下午五点到晚上十点，所以以后晚上不能跟你们去看足球了。

Read Huang Xiang'an's note and answer the following questions.
1. Where does Huang Xiang'an work?
2. What are his working hours?

Guanxi

关系 (guānxi) is a powerful force in Chinese business culture. The closest English rendering of the term would be "connections" or "networking," but its actual usage refers to a complex cultural system of personal relationships and moral obligations.

Implications of the Term

Although *guanxi* is considered a vital aspect of conducting business in China, it has also acquired a slightly unethical reputation over the years. In terms of its implications, the concept of guanxi is to some extent comparable to the English saying "if you scratch my back, I'll scratch yours," so it is perhaps unsurprising that, for some people, there is a fine line between *guanxi* and corruption. While this negative view may be accurate in some instances, *guanxi* has also been used to gain valid favors, such as helping one's company win a contract, negotiate better rates, or secure better quality products.

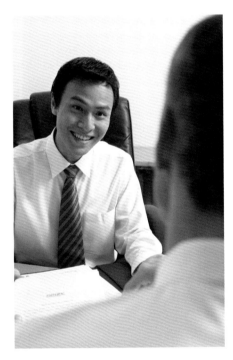

Chinese and Western Business Culture

There are a number of ways in which the system of *guanxi* has made Chinese business culture different from Western business culture. *Guanxi* does not always signify a straightforward exchange between companies. Instead, it tends to involve a further connection between representatives from the organizations at a personal level. For instance, it is common for individuals to visit the residences of their business acquaintances bearing gifts such as alcohol, cigarettes, and sports accessories. Furthermore, it is perfectly appropriate to inquire about a client's family and other matters that may seem overly personal to a Western businessperson.

Though *guanxi* is in some ways a trait unique to Chinese business culture, in other ways it is not so different to how trade is conducted in the West. As the saying goes, "it's not about what you know, it's about who you know." Networking and connections are just as essential in the Western business environment as they are in China, and while gift-giving may not be so common in the West, wining and dining is an integral part of wooing potential clients in any business culture.

Above all, when conducting business in China, one must bear in mind the phrase 入境随俗 (rùjìngsuísú): "When you enter a place, follow its customs," equivalent to the English "When in Rome, do as the Romans do." Undoubtedly the most effective way to avert undesired strife is to gain a thorough understanding of modern business practices in China, and to adapt oneself to them accordingly.

陈大东： 小美！没想到你会来看我！

Xiaomei! I didn't expect that you'd come to see me!

王小美： 我想看看你打工的地方。这里环境真不错，你每天在这儿工作几小时？

I wanted to see your workplace. This place isn't bad at all. How many hours do you work a day here?

陈大东： 我每天晚上从八点到十二点上班。

I work every evening from 8pm to 12am.

王小美： 你十二点才下班，难怪晚上很少见到你。

You don't get off work until 12am; no wonder I rarely see you at night.

———————

王小美： 你在这儿都做些什么样的事？

What kind of work do you do here?

陈大东： 我要泡咖啡、做收银，还要打扫厨房。

I make coffee, man the register, and also clean the kitchen.

王小美： 听起来很忙啊！

Sounds like you're really busy!

陈大东： 我以前只管打扫。老板看我很努力，慢慢地就让我管更多的事了。

I used to only be responsible for cleaning. After seeing how hard I work, the boss gradually started giving me more to do.

王小美： 你不但要上学，而且还要工作。这样一天到晚都很忙，不会太累吗？

Not only do you have to go to school, you also have to work. You're so busy all day long; isn't it tiring?

陈大东： 虽然累一点，但是我想赚钱，这样的话，今年暑假可以出国旅行。

Although it is a little tiring, I want to earn some money. That way I can travel abroad during summer vacation.

王小美： 大东，你一定做得到！加油！

Dadong, you can do it! Go for it!

What Can You Do?

INTERPRETIVE

- I can understand instructions regarding the tasks involved in doing a job.
- I can distinguish different professional titles and use them in the correct context.

INTERPERSONAL

- I can have a discussion about employment with someone.
- I can ask and answer questions about lengths of time.

PRESENTATIONAL

- I can present information about a job and what it entails.
- I can give a more formal presentation by using structures like "not only... but also..." and "although... however..."

去中国实习
Internship in China

刘老师，我打算今年夏天去中国，在中国公司里实习。您有什么建议吗？

liú
xià tiān
gōng sī　shí xí

我已经准备了一份简历，介绍我的背景和工作经验。

jiǎn lì
bèi jǐng
jīng yàn

好极了！你想找什么样的工作？在中国有很多机会。

jí le
jī huì

我毕业后想要做跟商务有关的事。

bì yè
xiǎng yào
shāng wù yǒu guān

LESSON TEXT 13.2

Internship in China 去中国实习

Sun Mali wants to find a summer internship in China and asks Teacher Liu for advice. Teacher Liu gives her some tips.

孙玛丽：　刘老师，我打算今年夏天去中国，在中国公司里实习。您有什么建议吗？

Liú lǎoshī, wǒ dǎsuan jīnnián xiàtiān qù Zhōngguó, zài Zhōngguó gōngsī li shíxí. Nín yǒu shénme jiànyì ma?

　　　　　我已经准备了一份简历，介绍我的背景和工作经验。

Wǒ yǐjīng zhǔnbèi le yí fèn jiǎnlì, jièshào wǒ de bèijǐng hé gōngzuò jīngyàn.

刘老师：　好极了！你想找什么样的工作？在中国有很多机会。

Hǎo jíle! Nǐ xiǎng zhǎo shénme yàng de gōngzuò? Zài Zhōngguó yǒu hěn duō jīhuì.

孙玛丽：　我毕业后想要做跟商务有关的事。

Wǒ bì yè hòu xiǎngyào zuò gēn shāngwù yǒu guān de shì.

―――――――――――――――

刘老师：　首先，在中国关系很重要。你可以先问问你的中国朋友。他们可以帮你跟他们认识的公司联络。

Shǒuxiān, zài Zhōngguó guānxi hěn zhòngyào. Nǐ kěyǐ xiān wènwen nǐ de Zhōngguó péngyou. Tāmen kěyǐ bāng nǐ gēn tāmen rènshi de gōngsī liánluò.

　　　　　我也可以帮你问一下我的朋友。在那里有很多外国公司和中国公司都需要你这样的人才。

Wǒ yě kěyǐ bāng nǐ wèn yí xià wǒ de péngyou. Zài nàli yǒu hěn duō wàiguó gōngsī hé Zhōngguó gōngsī dōu xūyào nǐ zhèyàng de réncái.

孙玛丽：　谢谢老师！

Xièxie lǎoshī!

刘老师：　祝你今年夏天实习成功！

Zhù nǐ jīnnián xiàtiān shíxí chénggōng!

字 词 VOCABULARY

LESSON VOCABULARY 13.2

	SIMPLIFIED	TRADITIONAL	PINYIN	WORD CATEGORY	DEFINITION
1.	刘	劉	liú	*surname*	Liu
2.	夏天		xiàtiān	*n*	summer
3.	公司		gōngsī	*n*	company
4.	实习	實習	shíxí	*v*	to intern; to have an internship
5.	简历	簡歷	jiǎnlì	*n*	résumé; curriculum vitae
6.	背景		bèijǐng	*n*	background
7.	经验	經驗	jīngyàn	*n*	experience
8.	极了	極了	jíle	*adv*	extremely
9.	机会	機會	jīhuì	*n*	opportunity
10.	毕业	畢業	bì yè	*vo*	to graduate
11.	想要		xiǎngyào	*av*	want; wish; would like
12.	商务	商務	shāngwù	*n*	business
13.	有关	有關	yǒu guān	*vo*	to be relevant; to be about; to do with
14.	首先		shǒuxiān	*prep*	first
15.	关系	關係	guānxi	*n*	relation; relationship; connections
16.	外国	外國	wàiguó	*adj, n*	foreign; foreign country
17.	人才		réncái	*n*	a person of ability/talent
18.	成功		chénggōng	*v, n*	to succeed; success

REQUIRED VOCABULARY 13.2

SIMPLIFIED	TRADITIONAL	PINYIN	WORD CATEGORY	DEFINITION
RELATED TO PROFESSIONS				
19. 当	當	dāng	v	to serve as, to be (a profession)

OPTIONAL VOCABULARY 13.2

SIMPLIFIED	TRADITIONAL	PINYIN	WORD CATEGORY	DEFINITION
BUSINESS				
20. 做生意		zuò shēngyì	vo	to do business
21. 官员	官員	guānyuán	n	official
22. 翻译	翻譯	fānyì	v, n	to translate; translation; translator
OTHER PROFESSIONS				
23. 家庭主妇	家庭主婦	jiātíng zhǔfù	n	homemaker
24. 工程师	工程師	gōngchéngshī	n	engineer
25. 作家		zuòjiā	n	writer, author
26. 画家	畫家	huàjiā	n	artist

Review of Professions

Profession	Pinyin	Meaning
老师	lǎoshī	teacher
医生	yīshēng	doctor
护士	hùshi	nurse
服务员	fúwùyuán	waiter, waitress
教授	jiàoshòu	professor
律师	lùshī	lawyer

Profession	Pinyin	Meaning
商人	shāngrén	businessman
家教	jiājiào	tutor
助教	zhùjiào	teaching assistant
厨师	chúshī	chef
家庭主妇	jiātíngzhǔfù	homemaker
工程师	gōngchéngshī	engineer

Online Resources

Visit *http://college.betterchinese.com* for a list of other professions.

Chinese Resumes

Resumes in Mainland China and Taiwan look similar to English resumes, but there are a few different conventions. In Mainland China, for example, it is common to include one's birthdate, ethnicity, and health status on a resume. Here are some common terms used in Chinese resumes:

Term	Pinyin	Meaning
个人简历	gèrén jiǎnlì	résumé, c.v.
性别	xìngbié	gender
年龄	niánlíng	age
教育	jiàoyù	education
工作经历	gōngzuò jīnglì	work experience
推荐	tuījiàn	recommendation / reference

Use 想要 *to express a desire*

Individually, 想 *and* 要 *can both be used to express "to want to do something." Together, they form a two-character word that is a more polite, formal way of expressing the same meaning.*

> Subject + 想要 + Verb Phrase

From the Lesson Text:
我毕业后想要做跟商务有关的事。
Wǒ bì yè hòu xiǎngyào zuò gēn shāngwù yǒu guān de shì.
After I graduate, I would like to do work related to business.

Other examples:
您想要吃什么样的菜？
Nín xiǎngyào chī shénme yàng de cài?
What type of food would you like to eat?

我不想要在这儿工作了。
Wǒ bù xiǎngyào zài zhèr gōngzuò le.
I don't want to work here anymore.

Practice: Change the following sentences into English sentences containing the verb 想要.

Example: I would like to go to a restaurant tonight.
→ 今天晚上我想要去饭馆吃饭。

1. If you wish to go to China to attend university, you must study diligently.

_____

2. This summer, he wants to do an internship at a company in California.

_____

3. She has always wanted to go traveling abroad.

_____

4. If you want to find a job, you should prepare a résumé first.

_____

5. She doesn't want to go to piano lessons anymore.

_____

STRUCTURE NOTE 13.8

Use 极了 *as an intensifier*

Structure Note 11.1 discussed complements of degree that may follow an adjective when used with the particle 得. 极了 *(jíle), meaning "to a great extent" or "extremely," is another such intensifier that is placed after an adjective. Its meaning is similar to* 得很 *or* 得不得了*, but, unlike these complements,* 极了 *follows on directly from an adjective, without the connecting* 得.

> Subject + Adjective + 极了

| From the Lesson Text: | 好极了！
Hǎo jíle!
Great! |

| Other examples: | 我最近忙极了。
Wǒ zuìjìn máng jíle.
Recently I've been extremely busy. | 今天冷极了。
Jīntiān lěng jíle.
It's extremely cold today. |

Practice: Modify the following sentences so that they express the same meaning but with the intensifier 极了 instead of the existing intensifiers.

Example: 昨天天气非常冷。→ 昨天天气冷极了。

1. 你拉小提琴拉得很好。

_____

2. 他的卧室干净得很。

_____

3. 夏天出国旅行非常贵。

_____

4. 你的中文太好了。

_____

5. 她画的画儿漂亮得不得了。

_____

STRUCTURE NOTE 13.9

Use 跟...有关 *to express relevance to a subject*

跟...有关 (gēn... yǒu guān) *indicates that a noun is related to a particular topic, as in "books about China."* 有关 *is a contraction of* 有关系, *which can also be used in the same structure.*

> 跟 + Topic + 有关 (+ 的 + Noun)

| From the Lesson Text: | 我毕业后想要做跟商务有关的事。
Wǒ bì yè hòu xiǎngyào zuò gēn shāngwù yǒu guān de shì.
After I graduate, I would like to do work related to business. |

| Other examples: | 我想找几本跟中国有关的书。
Wǒ xiǎng zhǎo jǐ běn gēn Zhōngguó yǒu guān de shū.
I want to find a few books about China. | 你有没有什么跟买手机有关的建议？
Nǐ yǒu méiyǒu shénme gēn mǎi shǒujī yǒu guān de jiànyì?
Do you have any advice about buying a cellphone? |

Practice: Complete the following sentences using 跟...有关.

Example:　　　这本书...(历史) → 这本书跟历史有关。
1.　　这部电影...(功夫)　　　_____
2.　　第十三单元...(工作)　　_____
3.　　她唱的歌...(感情)　　　_____
4.　　老师的话...(考试)　　　_____
5.　　他写的信...(商务)　　　_____

STRUCTURE NOTE 13.10
Use Noun + 这样/那样 *to say "this/that type of..."*

Adding 这样 *or* 那样 *after a noun conveys the meaning "things like this" or "things like that." A greater degree of specificity is introduced to the structure by adding* 的 *and a noun after the expression, which indicates the type of "thing" one is referring to, for example "this type of book" or "that type of teacher."*

> Noun + 这样 / 那样 + 的 + Noun

From the Lesson Text:　在那里有很多外国公司和中国公司都需要你这样的人才。
Zài nàli yǒu hěn duō wàiguó gōngsī hé Zhōngguó gōngsī dōu xūyào nǐ zhèyàng de réncái.
There are many foreign and Chinese companies there that need talents like yours.

Other examples:

我很喜欢吃饺子那样的东西。
Wǒ hěn xǐhuan chī jiǎozi nàyàng de dōngxi.
I really like to eat things like dumplings.

你应该找他那样的老师。
Nǐ yīnggāi zhǎo tā nàyàng de lǎoshī.
You should look for teachers like him.

Practice: Insert 这样/那样 and a 'type' category of noun to the sentences below, following the pattern in the example given.

Example: 吃素的人当然不吃醉鸡。（菜）
→ 吃素的人当然不吃醉鸡那样的菜。

1. 她对数学没有兴趣。（课）

   _____

2. 去上课不应该忘记带笔。（文具）

   _____

3. 他喜欢跳舞、唱歌。（活动）

   _____

4. 故宫、长城我都去过。（地方）

   _____

5. 这家商店卖小提琴。（乐器）

   _____

PRACTICE 13.9

Interview 5 of your classmates about what they are planning to do during the summer vacation, the winter vacation, and after graduation.

Example:

A: 你暑假／寒假打算做什么？
   你毕业后打算做什么工作？
B: 我暑假打算出国旅行。
   我毕业后打算当老师。

名字	暑假／寒假	毕业后

PRACTICE 13.10

Have a discussion with a partner in which you cover the following:
1. Where do you want to go for an internship and why?
2. What kind of internship do you want to do?
3. Tell your partner what to prepare and what is important.

PRACTICE 13.11

Take a survey of the class to find out which of the following factors people think is most important in finding a job: 工作经验 (gōngzuò jīngyàn: "work experience"), 关系 (guānxi: "connections"), 教育 (jiàoyù: "education"). Record the most popular answer choice below.

Most Important Factor	Number of Students

PRACTICE 13.12

Make an audio recording and send it to your teacher. In the recording, talk about some of your plans for after graduation.

PRACTICE 13.13

Working with a partner, practice asking each other the questions shown and respond on the basis of the information in the pictures.

Example:

A: 你想做什么样的实习？

B: 我想做跟商务有关的实习。

你想做什么样的实习？

你想做什么样的工作？

你想选什么样的课？

你想找什么样的书？

你想做什么样的活动？

PRACTICE 13.14

Read the passage and help Sun Mali to write her résumé in Chinese. Refer to the Language Notes for vocabulary relating to résumés.

我是孙玛丽，今年十九岁。我是成功大学的一年级学生。我当过售货员，也当过服务员。毕业后我想做跟商务有关的工作。我认识这家公司的老板陈先生。

简历

姓名：

年龄：

性别：

教育：

工作经验：

推荐人：

	Radical	Stroke Order
务	力 lì power	ノ ク 夂 冬 务
关	八 bā eight	丶 丷 ㅛ 关 关
系	纟(糸) sī silk	一 乙 幺 玄 系 系 系
简	竹(竹)zhú bamboo	ノ ト 彳 个 竹 竹 竹 竿 竿 简 简 简 简
商	口 kǒu mouth	丶 亠 六 亣 产 产 产 商 商 商
先	儿 rén person	ノ ㇒ 牛 生 先 先
实	宀 mián roof	丶 ㇒ 宀 宀 空 实 实
习	乙 yǐ second heav- enly stem	丁 刁 习
司	口 kǒu mouth	丁 刁 司 司 司
背	肉 ròu meat	丨 ㇇ ㇈ 北 北 北 背 背 背
景	日 rì sun	丶 ㇆ 日 旦 旦 旱 昊 昌 景 景 景
验	马 mǎ horse	丁 马 马 马 驴 验 验 验 验 验
极	木 mù wood	一 十 才 木 朽 极 极
首	首 shǒu head	丶 丷 丷 ㅛ 产 首 首 首
成	戈 gē spear	一 厂 厅 成 成 成

Type the following sentences on your computer and provide answers to the questions.
1. 我打算今年夏天去中国实习。
2. 你大学毕业以后想做什么样的工作?
3. 我想做跟商务有关的工作。

4. 很多外国公司都需要这样的人才。

5. 你可以帮我跟你认识的公司联络一下吗?

PRACTICE 13.17

因为我毕业以后想要做跟商务有关的工作,所以今年暑假我想找一个实习的机会。朋友都说现在中国有很多工作机会,可是我不知道怎样去找。老师建议我先准备一份简历,她可以帮我问一下她的朋友。

Read Sun Mali's diary and answer the following questions.
1. What does Sun Mali want to do this summer?
2. What does the teacher suggest?

PRACTICE 13.18

Sender　玛丽

Subject　工作

爸爸:
听说现在中国有很多工作机会,所以我打算毕业后去中国工作。可是,老师说在中国关系很重要。爸爸你在中国有没有朋友?可以帮我问一下吗?
谢谢!

Sender　爸爸

Subject　re: 工作

玛丽:
我有个老同学是中国公司的老板,我可以跟他联络一下。我想他的公司很需要你这样的人才。

Read the emails and answer the following questions.
1. What does the teacher say is important for finding a job in China?
2. How does Sun Mali's dad offer to help her?

PRACTICE 13.19

孙玛丽:您好,这是我的简历。

陈先生:你有跟商务有关的工作经验吗?

孙玛丽:有,去年夏天我在中国实习了两个月。

陈先生:你的中文读写怎么样?

孙玛丽:我在大学学了一点中文。

陈先生:你还会说哪些语言?

孙玛丽:我会说英语,也会说一点法语和西班牙语。

陈先生:好极了!我们很需要这样的人才。

Read the dialogue and answer the following questions.
1. Does Sun Mali have any experience in business?
2. What skill does Mr. Chen emphasize the most?

China's Special Economic Zones

Since their inception in the late 1970s, Special Economic Zones (SEZs) have been a cornerstone of China's economic reforms. Initially, five coastal locations were classified as SEZs: Shenzhen, Zhuhai, Shantou, Xiamen, and Hainan. These regions enjoyed preferential economic policies and relaxed governmental regulations exclusively designed to bring about greater international exchange. The intention of the plan was to create powerful models of economic progress that could eventually be emulated by other cities and districts across the country. The project was indeed a great success; since the 1980s numerous other regions have been granted SEZ status.

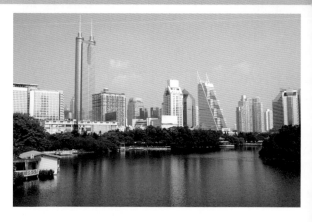

The favorable policies offered to these zones included assistance in establishing new infrastructure, upgrading of industries, and cultivating science and technology. The policies were largely based around five points:

1. Special tax incentives for foreign investment in the SEZ
2. Greater independence for international trade activities
3. Export-oriented production of goods
4. Market driven economic activity
5. Attraction and utilization of foreign capital for local development

These policies have not only brought colossal amounts of money into the Chinese market, they have also increased China's exposure to foreign expertise, which in turn has helped China build towards establishing its own companies and presence on the global market.

Breaking the Iron Rice Bowl

Before the economic reforms towards a market economy that began in 1979, work in China was state-run and collectivized. Many people worked for large factories that also provided social benefits, including education, pensions, housing, and healthcare. With many thousands of people working and living in a factory complex and organized by work unit (单位 dānwèi), they resembled small villages: there were schools, clinics, and even theatres.

People working in the factories also enjoyed what was called the 'iron rice bowl' (铁饭碗 tiěfànwǎn)—their jobs were secure from cradle to grave.

With reforms, the nature of work in China changed significantly. Instead of being tied to the factory town and to one area, workers were able to choose between jobs in both the public and private sectors all across China. However, their jobs are no longer guaranteed for life, and companies no longer provide social benefits. Some parts of the system do remain, depending on the company—some may offer housing, and others may offer a company lunch.

While the iron rice bowl may be no more, new and varied opportunities have arisen in its place, and further changes no doubt lie in wait as the country continues its rapid development.

孙玛丽：	刘老师，我打算今年夏天去中国，在中国公司实习。您有什么建议吗？	Teacher Liu, I plan to go to China this summer and do an internship at a Chinese Company. Do you have any advice?
	我已经准备了一份简历，介绍我的背景和工作经验。	I already prepared a resume detailing my background and work experience.
刘老师：	好极了！你想找什么样的工作？在中国有很多机会。	That's great! What kind of job are you looking for? There are many opportunities in China.
孙玛丽：	我毕业后想要做跟商务有关的事。	After I graduate, I want to do something related to business.

刘老师：	首先，在中国关系很重要。你可以先问问你的中国朋友。他们可以帮你跟他们认识的公司联络。	Firstly, networking is very important in China. You can start by asking your Chinese friends; they can help you get in touch with Chinese companies that they are familiar with.
	我也可以帮你问一下我的朋友。在那里有很多外国公司和中国公司都需要你这样的人才。	I can also ask my friends. There are many foreign and Chinese companies there that need talents like yours.
孙玛丽：	谢谢老师！	Thank you, Teacher Liu!
刘老师：	祝你今年夏天实习成功！	Hope you have a successful internship this summer!

What Can You Do?

INTERPRETIVE
- I can understand terms related to employment experiences.
- I can understand advice about employment.

INTERPERSONAL
- I can discuss plans for after graduation with others.
- I can attend a job interview in China.

PRESENTATIONAL
- I can give a presentation about my future plans and the kind of employment I am seeking.
- I can describe my employment history.

ACT IT OUT

Working in groups, compose an original three-minute skit that utilizes the vocabulary and structures introduced in Unit 13. Each of you should assume a role and have a roughly equal number of lines in the skit. Be prepared to perform your skit in class. You can either come up with your own story or choose from one of the following situations:

A) You are at a job interview and discuss the details of the job with the interviewer, such as hours, location, your job interests, previous experience, etc.

B) You and a friend are discussing what types of professions you are considering after graduation and share your interests.

C) Your friend has a new job and you ask him/her for details about it.

CHECK WHAT YOU CAN DO

RECOGNIZE

Adjectives
- □ 努力
- □ 干净
- □ 外国

Adverbs
- □ 难怪
- □ 很少
- □ 慢慢
- □ 一天到晚
- □ 极了

Auxiliary Verbs
- □ 想要

Conjunctions
- □ 不但
- □ 虽然

Idiomatic Expressions
- □ 没想到
- □ 加油

Names
- □ 刘

Nouns
- □ 环境
- □ 厨房
- □ 老板
- □ 今年
- □ 暑假
- □ 客人
- □ 夏天
- □ 公司
- □ 简历
- □ 背景
- □ 经验
- □ 机会
- □ 商务
- □ 关系
- □ 人才

Prepositions
- □ 以前
- □ 首先

Pronouns
- □ 什么样
- □ 这样

Verbs
- □ 打工
- □ 上班
- □ 下班
- □ 泡
- □ 收银
- □ 打扫
- □ 管
- □ 上学

- □ 赚钱
- □ 出国
- □ 旅行
- □ 整理
- □ 接待
- □ 实习
- □ 毕业
- □ 有关
- □ 成功
- □ 努力
- □ 做事
- □ 当

WRITE
- □ 工
- □ 房
- □ 银
- □ 假
- □ 班
- □ 板
- □ 环
- □ 境
- □ 怪
- □ 前
- □ 管
- □ 但
- □ 而
- □ 且
- □ 虽

- □ 务
- □ 关
- □ 系
- □ 简
- □ 商
- □ 先
- □ 实
- □ 习
- □ 司
- □ 背
- □ 景
- □ 验
- □ 极
- □ 首
- □ 成

USE
- □ 没想到 to introduce an unexpected event
- □ 难怪 to express "no wonder"
- □ 什么样的 to ask "what kind?"
- □ 不但…而且… to express "not only…but also…"
- □ 虽然…但是… to express "although…however…"
- □ 从…到… to express length of time

- □ 想要 to express a desire
- □ 极了 as an intensifier
- □ 跟…有关 to express relevance to a subject
- □ Noun + 这样/那样 to say "this/that type of…"

节

Festivals

第十四单元
UNIT 14

Communication Goals

Lesson 1: 新年快乐! **Happy Chinese New Year!**
- Talk about the customs and traditions of Chinese New Year
- Use the appropriate expressions to convey New Year's greetings and wishes
- Indicate that something is an ongoing action

Lesson 2: 中国和西方节日 **Chinese and Western Holidays**
- Compare and contrast various Chinese and Western holidays
- Discuss the different foods that are eaten during Chinese holidays
- Expand on a topic by providing examples

新年快乐!
Happy Chinese New Year!

小美，你家真漂亮，有这么多红色的装饰。
zhuāng shì

中国人过春节喜欢用红色来装饰，这是传统习惯。
guò chūn jié
zhuāng shì   chuán tǒng xí guàn

难怪你要我们今天穿红色的衣服。你看，我戴了红帽子。
dài
mào zi

那，祥安，你呢?

我穿着红袜子!
zhe   wà zi

你们见到我的爸妈的时候，要说"恭喜发财"!
gōng xǐ fā cái

LESSON TEXT 14.1

Happy Chinese New Year! 新年快乐！

Sun Mali, Chen Dadong, Li Zhongping, Zhang Anna, and Huang Xiang'an visit Wang Xiaomei's house to celebrate Chinese New Year with her and her parents.

孙玛丽：	小美，你家真漂亮，有这么多红色的装饰。	Xiǎoměi, nǐ jiā zhēn piàoliang, yǒu zhème duō hóngsè de zhuāngshì.
王小美：	中国人过春节喜欢用红色来装饰，这是传统习惯。	Zhōngguó rén guò Chūnjié xǐhuan yòng hóngsè lái zhuāngshì, zhè shì chuántǒng xíguàn.
张安娜：	难怪你要我们今天穿红色的衣服。你看，我戴了红帽子。那，祥安，你呢？	Nánguài nǐ yào wǒmen jīntiān chuān hóngsè de yīfu. Nǐ kàn, wǒ dài le hóng màozi. Nà, Xiáng'ān, nǐ ne?
黄祥安：	我穿着红袜子！	Wǒ chuān zhe hóng wàzi!
王小美：	你们见到我的爸妈的时候，要说"恭喜发财"！	Nǐmen jiàn dào wǒ de bàmā de shíhou, yào shuō "gōngxǐfācái"!

大家：	伯父伯母，恭喜发财！	Bófù bómǔ, gōngxǐfācái!
小美妈：	新年快乐！	Xīnnián kuàilè!
小美爸：	来来来，每个人都有一个红包，祝你们学业进步，万事如意。	Lái lái lái, měi ge rén dōu yǒu yí ge hóngbāo, zhù nǐmen xuéyè jìn bù, wànshì rúyì.
孙玛丽：	谢谢！祝伯父伯母身体健康。	Xièxie! Zhù bófù bómǔ shēntǐ jiànkāng.
小美妈：	请坐，先吃些糖果，我去拿年糕和瓜子。	Qǐng zuò, xiān chī xiē tángguǒ, wǒ qù ná niángāo hé guāzǐ.
李中平：	伯父，您这儿有那么多的花灯啊！	Bófù, nín zhèr yǒu nàme duō de huādēng a!

字 词 VOCABULARY

小美爸： 是啊，元宵节快要到了，我们会挂花灯，放烟火，会非常热闹。到时候欢迎你们再来玩儿！

Shì a, Yuánxiāojié kuài yào dào le, wǒmen huì guà huādēng, fàng yānhuǒ, huì fēicháng rènao. Dào shíhou huānyíng nǐmen zài lái wánr!

LESSON VOCABULARY 14.1

	SIMPLIFIED	TRADITIONAL	PINYIN	WORD CATEGORY	DEFINITION
1.	装饰	裝飾	zhuāngshì	v, n	to decorate; decoration
2.	过	過	guò	v	to spend (the holiday, an occasion)
3.	春节	春節	Chūnjié	n	Spring Festival
4.	传统	傳統	chuántǒng	adj, n	traditional; tradition
5.	习惯	習慣	xíguàn	n, v	habit; to be used to
6.	戴		dài	v	to wear (for glasses and hats)
7.	帽子		màozi	n	hat
8.	着		zhe	p	(added to verb or adjective to indicate a continued action or state)
9.	袜子	襪子	wàzi	n	socks
10.	恭喜发财	恭喜發財	gōngxǐfācái	ie	wishing you happiness and property (greeting used during the New Year)
	恭喜		gōngxǐ	v	to congratulate
11.	伯父		bófù	n	uncle (polite term of address for a man of one's parents' generation)
12.	伯母		bómǔ	n	aunt (polite term of address for a woman of one's parents' generation)
13.	新年		xīnnián	n	new year
14.	红包	紅包	hóngbāo	n	red envelope
15.	学业	學業	xuéyè	n	studies; academics
16.	万事如意	萬事如意	wànshìrúyì	ie	(wishing you) all the best (greeting used during the New Year)
17.	健康		jiànkāng	adj, n	healthy; health
18.	糖果		tángguǒ	n	candy

LESSON VOCABULARY 14.1 (continued)

SIMPLIFIED	TRADITIONAL	PINYIN	WORD CATEGORY	DEFINITION
19. 拿		ná	v	to hold; to get; to take
20. 年糕		niángāo	n	New Year's rice cake
21. 瓜子		guāzǐ	n	melon seeds
22. 花灯	花燈	huādēng	n	festive/decorative lantern
23. 元宵节	元宵節	Yuánxiāojié	n	Lantern Festival
24. 挂	掛	guà	v	to hang
25. 放		fàng	v	to put; to set off
26. 烟火	煙火	yānhuǒ	n	fireworks
27. 热闹	熱鬧	rènao	adj	lively

OPTIONAL VOCABULARY 14.1

RELATED TO FESTIVALS

SIMPLIFIED	TRADITIONAL	PINYIN	WORD CATEGORY	DEFINITION
28. 猜谜	猜謎	cāi mí	vo	to guess a riddle
29. 除夕		Chúxī	n	(Chinese) New Year's Eve
30. 正月		zhēngyuè	n	first month of the lunar year
31. 锣鼓	鑼鼓	luó gǔ	n	gong and drum
32. 舞龙舞狮	舞龍舞獅	wǔlóngwǔshī	n	dragon and lion dance

Spring Festival Greetings

An important part of celebrating the Spring Festival is visiting family and friends. People often greet each other with traditional phrases, generally containing good wishes for the new year. Children often request 红包 from adults with the joking phrase, 恭喜发财，红包拿来! (gōngxǐ fācái, hóngbāo nálái!: "Happy New Year, bring out my red envelope!"). Below are a few common greetings used at the Spring Festival.

Phrase	Pinyin	Meaning	Usage
恭喜发财	gōngxǐfācái	congratulations and be prosperous	equivalent to "Happy New Year!"
万事如意	wànshìrúyì	all things as you wish	general greeting
心想事成	xīnxiǎngshìchéng	your wishes come true	general greeting
学业进步	xuéyèjìnbù	progress in your studies	for students
身体健康	shēntǐjiànkāng	healthy body	for the elderly
生意兴隆	shēngyìxīnglóng	prosperous business	for businesspeople

Idioms

Idioms are a challenging and fascinating feature of any language, and Chinese is no exception. In Chinese, the majority of idioms come in the form of phrases that consist of four characters, known as 成语 (chéngyǔ).

成语 are not to be confused with what this book terms "idiomatic expressions," which covers phrases like 你好，对不起, and 欢迎光临. Although it can sometimes be hard to differentiate, a 成语 is also distinct from a 四个字的结构 (sì ge zì de jiégòu: "four-character expression"). The New Year's greetings listed above, for example, do not fall under the category of 成语 because the characters directly express the meaning of the phrase. 成语, on the other hand, are idiomatic – that is, their intended meaning is other than their literal meaning.

As a general rule, a four-character expression is only a 成语 if it has a story attached to it. Most of these stories derive from historical and literary sources; novels like *Romance of the Three Kingdoms* and *Dream of the Red Chamber* alone contain scores of idioms.

There are countless 成语 in Chinese; even a highly literate person may find the need to consult a dictionary when faced with a more obscure one. Nevertheless, they are a significant feature of the written language, and often come in handy in everyday speech. Some examples of 成语 are provided below.

Idiom	Pinyin	Meaning
对牛弹琴	duìniútánqín	Literally "playing the zither to an ox," this is equivalent to the English idiom "casting pearls before swine" and means to give something valuable to someone who can't appreciate it.
井底之蛙	jǐngdǐzhīwā	Literally "a frog at the bottom of a well," this idiom describes a person with limited outlook and experience.
一箭双雕	yíjiànshuāngdiāo	Literally "one arrow, two vultures," this idiom is the same as the English "to kill two birds with one stone."
如鱼得水	rúyúdéshuǐ	Literally "like a fish that gets water," this describes someone who is very happy or in their element, like the English idiom "like a duck to water."

STRUCTURE NOTE 14.1

Use 用...来...*to describe the means of doing something*

The 用...来... *(yòng... lái...) pattern is used with a noun phrase and a verb phrase to express "use A to do B." The noun phrase follows* 用, *and the verb phrase is placed after* 来.

> Subject + 用 + Noun Phrase + 来 + Verb Phrase

From the Lesson Text:

中国人过春节喜欢用红色来装饰。
Zhōngguó rén guò Chūnjié xǐhuan yòng hóngsè lái zhuāngshì.
During Spring Festival, Chinese people like to use the color red to decorate.

Other examples:

请你用笔来写作业。
Qǐng nǐ yòng bǐ lái xiě zuòyè.
Please use a pen to write your homework.

他们要用爸爸妈妈的钱来买车。
Tāmen yào yòng bàba māma de qián lái mǎi chē.
They are going to use their parents' money to buy a car.

Practice: Use the following noun/verb pairs to form complete sentences.

Example: 笔 / 写作业 → 我今天想用笔来写作业。

1. 筷子 / 吃米饭 _____

2. 手机 / 玩游戏 _____

3. 关系 / 找工作 _____

4. 录音 / 练习听力 _____

5. 信用卡 / 付钱 _____

STRUCTURE NOTE 14.2
Use 着 to indicate an ongoing action

Structure Note 8.14 introduced 在 *as a way of describing ongoing action, as in* 我们在说中文, *"we are speaking Chinese." A similar effect is created by adding the particle* 着 *(zhe) after a verb. Rather than describing an ongoing action, however,* 着 *tends to indicate an ongoing or settled state. As a result, activities that involve a significant duration of time, such as "waiting" and "sitting," are often paired with* 着*. Like* 在, 着 *is negated by* 没*.*

Subject + Verb + 着 (+ Object)

From the Lesson Text:

我穿着红袜子。
Wǒ chuān zhe hóng wàzi.
I'm wearing red socks.

Other examples:

他带着本子。
Tā dài zhe běnzi.
He's carrying a notebook.

我们在餐厅里坐着。
Wǒmen zài cāntīng li zuò zhe.
We're sitting in the cafeteria.

NOTE: (正)在…(呢) *and* 着 *are not mutually exclusive. They can both be used in the same sentence to emphasize an ongoing action.*

Practice: Change the following sentences into Chinese using the ongoing state particle 着.

Example: They are sitting on the sofa. → 他们在沙发上坐着。

1. He's waiting outside.

   _____

2. The children are carrying red envelopes.

   _____

3. She's sitting in the kitchen.

   _____

4. That musician is wearing black clothes.

   _____

5. Xiaomei is wearing yellow socks.

   _____

STRUCTURE NOTE 14.3

Use 快要...了 *to say "be about to"*

快要...了 (kuài yào...le) *expresses that an event is about to take place. The* 了 *in this pattern denotes imminent action. It can be seen as an extension of the change of state* 了 *discussed in Structure Note 3.10, as it implies that the situation will soon be changing.*

Subject + 快要 + Verb Phrase + 了

From the Lesson Text:　元宵节快要到了。
Yuánxiāojié kuài yào dào le.
The lantern festival is fast approaching.

Other examples:

我们快要走了。
Wǒmen kuài yào zǒu le.
We are about to leave.

他们快要放烟火了。
Tāmen kuài yào fàng yānhuǒ le.
They are about to set off fireworks.

Practice: Complete the sentences below using the 快要...了 pattern and the verb in parentheses.

Example:　你不用泡茶，我...（走）
→ 你不用泡茶，我快要走了。

1.　请大家安静点，表演...（开始）

　　_____

2.　你们别吃糖果，我们...（吃饭）

　　_____

3.　四点十七分的火车...（到）

　　_____

4.　他刚给我打电话，说...（来）

　　_____

5.　鼻子都红了，我好像...（感冒）

　　_____

STRUCTURE NOTE 14.4

Use 到时候 *to express "when the time comes"*

到时候 (dào shíhou) *is a phrase equivalent to the English "when the time comes," "at that time," or simply "then." Unlike* 的时候 *sentences,* 到时候 *precedes the verb phrase.*

到时候 + Verb Phrase

From the Lesson Text:

到时候欢迎你们再来玩儿!
Dào shíhou huānyíng nǐmen zài lái wánr!
You're all welcome to come back and visit then!

Other examples:

到时候再说吧。
Dào shíhou zài shuō ba.
We'll talk about it when the time comes.

到时候你就知道了。
Dào shíhou nǐ jiù zhīdào le.
You'll know when the time comes.

Practice: Add 到时候 to the expressions below to form complete sentences, following the example given.

Example: 考试要好好儿地准备
→ 到时候考试要好好儿地准备。

1. 上课要带课本。 _____
2. 用手机再联系吧。 _____
3. 付钱要刷卡。 _____
4. 表演不要紧张。 _____
5. 回老家要坐飞机。 _____

PRACTICE 14.1

Working with a partner, ask whether each of the pictures shown below is a Chinese New Year custom, then describe the custom.

Example:
A: 这是过春节的传统习惯吗？
B: 是，中国人过春节喜欢用红色来装饰。

PRACTICE 14.2

Go on the internet or ask your teacher to try to find out more about traditional foods of the Spring Festival. Ask your classmates which Spring Festival food they like the most. What does it taste like?

Name	Favorite Food	Taste

💬 PRACTICE 14.3

Working in a group, act out a dialogue that might occur on a visit to a Chinese friend's house during Chinese New Year. In your dialogue, cover the following points:

1. Spring Festival greetings
2. Traditional decorations
3. Traditional foods

💬 PRACTICE 14.4

Working with a partner, ask and describe the means of doing something.

Example:

A: 他用什么来接待客人？
B: 他用咖啡来接待客人。

接待客人

付钱

写信

吃饺子

打电话

💬 PRACTICE 14.5

Make an audio recording and send it to your teacher. In the recording, describe what you have learned about the traditions of Chinese New Year.

PRACTICE 14.6

	Radical	Stroke Order
闹	门 mén door	丶 丬 门 闩 闩 闩 闱 闹
装	衣 yī clothing	丶 丬 丬 壮 壮 壮 苿 娄 装 装 装
春	日 rì sun	一 二 三 声 夫 表 春 春 春
节	艹(草) cǎo grass	一 十 艹 节 节
传	亻(人) rén person	丿 亻 亻 仁 传 传
统	纟(糸) sī silk	乙 纟 纟 纟 纟 纺 统 统 统
恭	心 xīn heart	一 十 廾 世 共 共 恭 恭 恭
财	贝 bèi shell	丨 冂 冂 贝 贝 财 财
包	勹 bāo wrap	丿 勹 勺 匀 包
万	一 yī one	一 丁 万
如	女 nǚ female	乚 女 女 如 如 如
果	木 mù wood	丨 冂 冂 日 旦 甲 甲 果
元	儿 rén person	一 二 テ 元
火	火 huǒ fire	丶 丷 少 火
热	灬(火) huǒ fire	一 十 扌 扌 执 执 热 热 热

PRACTICE 14.7

Type the following sentences on your computer and provide answers to the questions.

1. 为什么你家有这么多红色的装饰?
2. 这是中国人的传统习惯。
3. 春节时，记得要对人说"恭喜发财"！
4. 祝你身体健康、万事如意。
5. 元宵节时我们会挂花灯、放烟火。

PRACTICE 14.8

Write three more Spring Festival greetings on the red banners below. Refer to the Language Notes for more on phrases related to the Spring Festival.

Example:

PRACTICE 14.9

Sender   王小美

Subject   春节

明天是中国的春节，你来我家玩吧！中国人过年都会穿红色的衣服，你要记得穿我上个月买给你的中国传统衣服喔！春节前我们会先把家里打扫干净，再准备过年的晚饭。我们会准备饺子和年糕，可是你也要带点儿小礼物来。还有，你看到我爸妈的时候，记得要说"恭喜发财"！

Read Wang Xiaomei's email and answer the following questions.
1. What will Wang Xiaomei's family do to prepare for the Spring Festival?
2. What does Wang Xiaomei ask Chen Dadong to remember?

张安娜：小美，我来了！
王小美：你真的穿了红色的衣服呀！
张安娜：我还穿了红色的袜子，戴了红色的手套。
王小美：来，我给你介绍 — 这是我爸爸和妈妈。
张安娜：伯父伯母，恭喜发财！
王爸爸：来来来，这个红包给你。
张安娜：谢谢伯父！
王妈妈：这是中国人的传统习惯，祝你学业进步。

Read the dialogue and answer the following questions.
1. What does Zhang Anna wear to the Chinese New Year celebration?
2. What do Wang Xiaomei's parents give to Zhang Anna?

PRACTICE 14.11

今天，我的中国朋友请我去她家过春节。我学了一些中国人的传统习惯。过年时去中国人的家，要注意很多事。第一，要说些新年应该说的话，像"恭喜发财"、"新年快乐"、"万事如意"。第二，要带点儿小礼物去，像糖果或者蛋糕都可以。

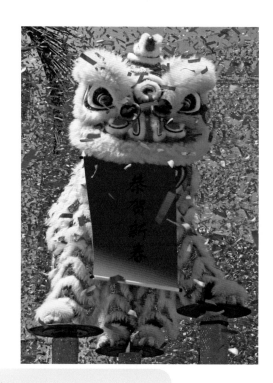

Read Chen Dadong's diary and answer the following questions.
1. What Spring Festival greetings did Chen Dadong learn?
2. What kinds of gifts does Chen Dadong suggest are appropriate to give the hosts?

Tomb Sweeping Festival

清明节 (Qīngmíngjié: "Qingming Festival," also known as "Ancestors Day," and "Tomb Sweeping Day") is a traditional Chinese festival that is celebrated in early April. Qingming is a time to honor one's ancestors, so it is common for people to spend the day sweeping away the dust and dirt from their family tombs, hence the English translation of "Tomb Sweeping Day." During this festival, prayers are given and symbolic offerings are made in order to pay respect to one's departed ancestors. The most common offerings are paper effigies of luxury items that are set alight and thereby symbolically passed to the deceased for use in the afterlife. These paper replicas can be anything from money and gold to houses and cars. Although it is a traditional festival, Qingming has certainly kept up with the times: in 2011, the most in-demand offering was an iPad2 replica boasting a capacity of 888 gigabytes!

The Dragon Boat Festival

端午节 (Duānwǔjié: "the Dragon Boat Festival") is held on the fifth day of the fifth month of the Chinese calendar. In addition to the consumption of 粽子 (zòngzi: "rice dumplings"), this midsummer celebration involves a lively boat race, from which it derives its name. These races feature long, slender vessels called 龙舟 (lóngzhōu: "dragon boats") and can have as many as eighty rowers in participation.

The Dragon Boat Festival has a long history. Among the various explanations of its origins, one ranks as the most popular. In 278 BCE the famous poet 屈原 (Qū Yuán) drowned himself in the Miluo River when the kingdom to which he belonged was conquered by the state of Qin. The locals took boats out onto the river to search for the poet, which is said to be the origin of the dragon boat race. In addition, in an attempt to keep fish from eating his body, they threw rice dumplings into the river, which is why this food is eaten during the Dragon Boat Festival today.

The Mid-Autumn Festival

中秋节 (Zhōngqiūjié: the Mid-Autumn Festival) is another festival with a long and rich history. It is celebrated on the 15th day of the eighth month of the Chinese lunar calendar, which falls in September or October. The Mid-Autumn Festival celebrates the successful completion of the harvest cycle, and represents a time of rest after hard work and strain.

The traditional delicacy of the festival is the moon cake, which is usually placed in a gift box and exchanged between friends. In cities and some larger towns, performances and street fairs are held to celebrate the festival, which include popular customs such as burning incense and hanging lanterns.

孙玛丽：	小美，你家真漂亮，有这么多红色的装饰。
王小美：	中国人过春节喜欢用红色来装饰，这是传统习惯。
张安娜：	难怪你要我们今天穿红色的衣服。你看，我戴了红帽子。那，祥安，你呢？
黄祥安：	我穿着红袜子！
王小美：	你们见到我的爸妈的时候，要说"恭喜发财"！
大家：	伯父伯母，恭喜发财！

Xiaomei, your house is so pretty. There are so many red decorations.

During Spring Festival, Chinese people like to use the color red to decorate — it's tradition.

No wonder you had us wear red clothing today. Look, I'm wearing a red hat. What about you, Xiang'an?

I'm wearing red socks!

When you see my parents, you must say "may you be happy and prosperous!"

Mr. and Mrs. Wang, may you be happy and prosperous!

小美妈：	新年快乐！
小美爸：	来来来，每个人都有一个红包，祝你们学业进步，万事如意。
孙玛丽：	谢谢！祝伯父伯母身体健康。
小美妈：	请坐，先吃些糖果，我去拿年糕和瓜子。
李中平：	伯父，您这儿有那么多的花灯啊！
小美爸：	是啊，元宵节快要到了，我们会挂花灯，放烟火，会非常热闹。到时候欢迎你们再来玩儿！

Happy New Year!

Here you go, everyone gets a red envelope. I wish you progress in your studies and success in all things.

Thank you! May you both enjoy the best of health.

Please have a seat. First have some candies and I'll go get the New Year's rice cake and the melon seeds.

Mr. Wang, you have a lot of lanterns here!

Indeed, the Lantern Festival is fast approaching. We will hang lanterns and set off firecrackers; it will be very festive. You're all welcome to come back and visit then!

What Can You Do?

INTERPRETIVE
- I can understand the traditional greetings given at Chinese New Year.
- I can understand the meanings of some Chinese idioms.

INTERPERSONAL
- I can offer and receive Chinese New Year's greetings using culturally appropriate expressions.
- I can discuss some of the features of Chinese New Year and the Lantern Festival with someone.

PRESENTATIONAL
- I can give a presentation about Chinese New Year and its customs.

中国和西方节日
Chinese and Western Holidays

今天我们吃年夜饭。
nián yè fàn
过年，我们习惯吃鱼。因
yú
为"鱼"听起来像"多余"
duō yú
的"余，"所以吃鱼就是
yú   yú
希望"年年有余。"
nián nián yǒu yú

吃年夜饭，最重要的是全家人
nián yè fàn   quán
在一起，跟圣诞节一样耶。
shèng dàn jié   ye

我们过节都
guò jié
有传统的食物。
shí wù
中秋节要吃月饼，
zhōng qiū jié   yuè bǐng
春节吃鱼、吃年糕。
yú
你们呢？

我们家感恩节一定会吃火鸡。
gǎn ēn jié   huǒ jī

我们家
好像每天都
hǎo xiàng
在过节，每天
guò jié
都吃大餐！
dà cān

我记得有一个中国节日是吃
zòng zi
粽子的……

duān wǔ jié　　duān wǔ jié
那是端午节。端午节的时候
huá lóng zhōu
还会有划龙舟比赛。

哇，中国的节日那么多，
xī fāng
中国人还过西方节日吗？

现在有一些
xī fāng
西方节日在
yuè lái yuè
中国越来越
liú xíng
流行。

bǐ fāng shuō　　　　　　nián qīng
比方说，在中国有的年轻人
cān jiā wàn shèng jié
会参加万圣节派对。

没想到中国人
lián wàn shèng jié
连万圣节都会
过啊！

LESSON TEXT 14.2

Chinese and Western Holidays 中国和西方节日

The group sits down for a reunion dinner on Chinese New Year with Wang Xiaomei's family and discusses various Chinese festivals.

王小美：	今天我们吃年夜饭。过年，我们习惯吃鱼。因为"鱼"听起来像"多余"的"余，"所以吃鱼就是希望"年年有余。"	Jīntiān wǒmen chī niányèfàn. Guò nián, wǒmen xíguàn chī yú. Yīnwèi "yú" tīngqilai xiàng "duōyú" de "yú," suǒyǐ chī yú jiùshì xīwàng "niánnián yǒu yú."
李中平：	吃年夜饭，最重要的是全家人在一起，跟圣诞节一样耶。	Chī niányèfàn, zuì zhòngyào de shì quán jiā rén zài yìqǐ, gēn Shèngdànjié yíyàng ye.
小美爸：	我们过节都有传统的食物。中秋节要吃月饼，春节吃鱼、吃年糕 。你们呢？	Wǒmen guò jié dōu yǒu chuántǒng de shíwù. Zhōngqiūjié yào chī yuèbǐng, Chūnjié chī yú, chī niángāo. Nǐmen ne?
孙玛丽：	我们家感恩节一定会吃火鸡。	Wǒmen jiā Gǎn'ēnjié yídìng huì chī huǒjī.

黄祥安：	我们家好像每天都在过节，每天都吃大餐！	Wǒmen jiā hǎoxiàng měi tiān dōu zài guò jié, měi tiān dōu chī dàcān!
孙玛丽：	我记得有一个中国节日是吃粽子的……	Wǒ jìde yǒu yí ge Zhōngguó jiérì shì chī zòngzi de...
王小美：	那是端午节。端午节的时候还会有划龙舟比赛。	Nà shì Duānwǔjié. Duānwǔjié de shíhou hái huì yǒu huá lóngzhōu bǐsài.
张安娜：	哇，中国的节日那么多，中国人还过西方节日吗？	Wā, Zhōngguó de jiérì nàme duō, Zhōngguó rén hái guò Xīfāng jiérì ma?
王小美：	现在有一些西方节日在中国越来越流行。	Xiànzài yǒu yì xiē Xīfāng jiérì zài Zhōngguó yuèláiyuè liúxíng.

字词 VOCABULARY

小美爸： 比方说，在中国有的年轻人会参加万圣节派对。

陈大东： 没想到中国人连万圣节都会过啊！

Bǐfāngshuō, zài Zhōngguó yǒude niánqīng rén huì cānjiā Wànshèngjié pàiduì.

Méi xiǎng dào Zhōngguó rén lián Wàn-shèng-jié dōu huì guò a!

LESSON VOCABULARY 14.2

	SIMPLIFIED	TRADITIONAL	PINYIN	WORD CATEGORY	DEFINITION
1.	年夜饭	年夜飯	niányèfàn	n	a reunion dinner for the whole family on Chinese New Year's Eve
2.	过年	過年	guò nián	vo	to celebrate the New Year
3.	鱼	魚	yú	n	fish
4.	像		xiàng	v, adj	to resemble; like; similar
5.	多余	多餘	duōyú	n, adj	surplus; superfluous
6.	年年有余	年年有餘	niánnián yǒu yú	ie	may you have abundance every year (greeting used at New Year)
7.	全		quán	adj, adv	complete, whole; completely
8.	圣诞节	聖誕節	Shèngdànjié	n	Christmas
9.	耶		ye	p	(particle used at end of a sentence)
10.	过节	過節	guò jié	vo	to celebrate a festival
11.	食物		shíwù	n	food
12.	中秋节	中秋節	Zhōngqiūjié	n	Mid-Autumn Festival
13.	月饼	月餅	yuèbǐng	n	mooncake
14.	感恩节	感恩節	Gǎn'ēnjié	n	Thanksgiving
15.	火鸡	火鷄	huǒjī	n	turkey
16.	好像		hǎoxiàng	adv	apparently; it appears; it seems like
17.	大餐		dàcān	n	a large feast
18.	节日	節日	jiérì	n	holiday; festival
19.	粽子		zòngzi	n	pyramid-shaped dumpling made of glutinous rice wrapped in bamboo leaves

LESSON VOCABULARY 14.2 (continued)

	SIMPLIFIED	TRADITIONAL	PINYIN	WORD CATEGORY	DEFINITION
20.	端午节	端午節	Duānwǔjié	n	Dragon-Boat Festival
21.	划		huá	v	to row
22.	龙舟	龍舟	lóngzhōu	n	dragon boat
23.	西方		Xīfāng	n	the West
24.	越来越	越來越	yuèláiyuè	adv	more and more
25.	流行		liúxíng	adj	popular
26.	比方说	比方說	bǐfāngshuō	ie	for example
27.	年轻人	年輕人	niánqīng rén	n	young people
	年轻	年輕	niánqīng	adj	young
28.	参加	參加	cānjiā	v	to take part in, to participate in
29.	万圣节	萬聖節	Wànshèngjié	n	Halloween
30.	连	連	lián	prep	even

REQUIRED VOCABULARY 14.2

HOLIDAYS

31.	母亲节	母親節	Mǔqīnjié	n	Mother's Day
32.	父亲节	父親節	Fùqīnjié	n	Father's Day
33.	情人节	情人節	Qíngrénjié	n	Valentine's Day

OPTIONAL VOCABULARY 14.2

HOLIDAYS

34.	光明节	光明節	Guāngmíngjié	n	Hanukkah
35.	复活节	復活節	Fùhuójié	n	Easter
36.	元旦		Yuándàn	n	New Year's Day
37.	清明节	清明節	Qīngmíngjié	n	Tomb Sweeping Festival

语言注释 LANGUAGE NOTES 语言注释

Holiday Foods

Spring Festival Foods

Foods	Pinyin	Meaning	Symbolism/Significance
年糕	niángāo	New Year's rice cake	年年高升 (niánnián gāoshēng): "advance every year"
饺子	jiǎozi	dumplings	symbolize wealth as they resemble old Chinese currency
汤圆	tāngyuán	rice dumplings	团圆 (tuányuán): family reunion and togetherness
鱼	yú	fish	年年有余 (niánnián yǒu yú): "abundance every year"
瓜子	guāzǐ	melon seeds	a wish for offspring (子: "son")

Other Holiday Foods

月饼	yuèbǐng	moon cakes	eaten at Mid-Autumn Festival, they represent the moon
粽子	zòngzi	leaf-wrapped dumplings	a commemoration of the poet Qu Yuan (see Cultural Spotlight 14.1)

Online Resources

Visit *http://college.betterchinese.com* for a list of other words related to Chinese festivals.

Horizontal and Vertical Text

Historically, Chinese script was written and read from top to bottom, right to left. Formal inscriptions in temples and palaces could be written horizontally, but were still read from the right. In the early 20th Century, reformers began to print magazines in horizontal script, citing the fact that this format was better suited to incorporating Western words and scientific formulae into the text. In territories that use traditional characters, such as Taiwan and Hong Kong, many newspapers and books continue to use vertical text, whereas publications in Mainland China are by and large printed in the Western style. Nevertheless, it is not unusual to see vertical or right to left text on a restaurant or shop in any Chinese community, a touch that gives the establishment a more traditional feel.

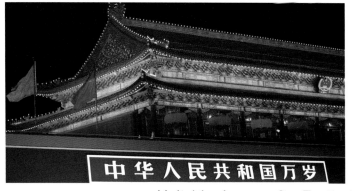

Unit 14 ▪ Lesson 2 ▪ Festivals **515**

STRUCTURE NOTE 14.5
Use 像 to express "resemble" or "is like"

像 (xiàng) *can act as a verb meaning "to resemble" or as an adjective meaning "similar." When* 像 *is used as a verb, it is simply placed between the two noun phrases, as in the pattern A* 是 *B. When used as an adjective, it comes after the noun phrases, which are joined by a conjunction.*

> Noun Phrase A (+ 不) + 像 + Noun Phrase B

> Noun Phrase A + 跟 + Noun Phrase B (+ 很 / 不) + 像

From the Lesson Text:

因为 "鱼" 听起来像 "多余" 的 "余。"
Yīnwèi "yú" tīngqilai xiàng "duōyú" de "yú".
Because the word "yu" (fish) sounds like the "yu" in "duoyu" (surplus).

Other examples:

你跟你妈妈很像。
Nǐ gēn nǐ māma hěn xiàng.
You look a lot like your mom.

他有点像我们的老师。
Tā yǒu diǎn xiàng wǒmen de lǎoshī.
He looks a bit like our teacher.

Practice: Use one of the 像 patterns shown above in conjunction with the information below to create complete sentences. Remember that you may negate either of the patterns.

Example: 这里的天气 / 北京的天气
→ 这里的天气跟北京的天气很像。

1. 母亲节 / 父亲节 _____
2. 黄祥安 / 李中平 _____
3. 中医 / 西医 _____
4. 拉小提琴 / 拉大提琴 _____
5. 英语 / 法语 _____

STRUCTURE NOTE 14.6
Use 越来越 to mean "increasingly"

To express that something is "becoming more and more (adjective)," Chinese uses the phrase 越来越 (yuèláiyuè) *followed by the relevant adjective.*

> Subject + 越来越 + Adjective

From the Lesson Text:

现在有一些西方节日在中国越来越流行。
Xiànzài yǒu yì xiē Xīfāng jiérì zài Zhōngguó yuèláiyuè liúxíng.
There are several Western holidays that are becoming more and more popular in China now.

Other examples:	会说中文的人越来越多。	我们的公司越来越大。
	Huì shuō Zhōngwén de rén yuèláiyuè duō.	Wǒmen de gōngsī yuèláiyuè dà.
	More and more people can speak Chinese.	Our company is getting bigger and bigger.

Practice: Complete the following sentences using 越来越 and an adjective of your choice.

Example:　最近天气… → 最近天气越来越冷。

1. 爸爸最近看起来…

   _____

2. 中文的语法好像…

   _____

3. 快要考试的时候…

   _____

4. 这家商店的东西…

   _____

5. 你的儿子看起来每天…

   _____

STRUCTURE NOTE 14.7
Use 比方说 to say "for example"

The phrase 比方说 (bǐfāngshuō) can be used to introduce an example. It is equivalent to the English "for example" or "to give an example."

> 比方说 + Example Sentence

From the Lesson Text:　比方说，在中国有的年轻人会参加万圣节派对。
Bǐfāngshuō, zài Zhōngguó yǒude niánqīng rén huì cānjiā Wànshèngjié pàiduì.
For example, in China some young people go to Halloween parties.

Other examples:	中国人有很多春节传统。比方说，吃饺子的传统。	有的人不喜欢过节日。比方说，我妹妹不太喜欢。
	Zhōngguó rén yǒu hěn duō Chūnjié chuántǒng. Bǐfāngshuō, chī jiǎozi de chuántǒng.	Yǒude rén bù xǐhuan guò jiérì. Bǐfāngshuō, wǒ mèimei bú tài xǐhuan.
	Chinese people have many Spring Festival traditions. For example, the tradition of eating dumplings.	Some people don't like to celebrate holidays. For example, my younger sister doesn't like to that much.

Practice: Provide examples to support the following statements, using 比方说.

Example: 周末有很多活动做。 → 比方说，去看电影。

1. 手机现在可以用来做很多事，

    _____

2. 出国旅行有很多国家可以去，

    _____

3. 北京好玩的地方很多，

    _____

4. 我的同学会玩很多乐器，

    _____

5. 大东有很多打工的经验，

    _____

STRUCTURE NOTE 14.8

Use 连...都 to say "even..."

连...都 (lián...dōu) *is a pattern used to express "even," as in "even he came to my party." Remember to pay attention to the position of the subject and object in relation to* 连. *For example,* 连他们都不会写那个字 *means "even they can't write that character," but* 他们连那个字都不会写 *means "they can't even write that character." Note that the* 都 *in this pattern can also be replaced with* 也.

> 连 + Subject + 都/也 + Verb Phrase

> Subject + 连 + Object / Time Phrase + 都/也 + Verb Phrase

From the Lesson Text:　没想到中国人连万圣节都会过啊！
Méi xiǎng dào Zhōngguó rén lián Wànshèngjié dōu huì guò a!
I never expected that Chinese people would even celebrate Halloween!

Other examples:　连我妈妈都会用手机。　　她连星期天也练习中文。
Lián wǒ māma dōu huì yòng shǒujī.　Tā lián Xīngqī tiān yě liànxí Zhōngwén.
Even my mother knows how to use a　She even practices Chinese on Sundays.
cellphone.

Practice: Change the following sentences into Chinese using the 连...都 pattern.

Example: She doesn't even drink coffee. →她连咖啡都不喝。

1. Even Chinese people forget how to write that character.

   _____

2. My roommate has never even cleaned the kitchen.

   _____

3. He doesn't even know where Spain is.

   _____

4. My classmate can even speak Russian.

   _____

5. She can't even find a job now.

   _____

练习 PRACTICE

PRACTICE 14.12

In the space provided below, record the details of a Western or Chinese festival that you like. Share the details of the festival with your classmates.

Festival: _____   Date: _____

Country of Origin: _____   Customs: _____

PRACTICE 14.13

Working with a partner, identify the foods below and the festivals that they are related to, then practice the dialogue shown. Refer to Cultural Spotlight 14.1 if you need help.

Example:

A: 过年的时候你们习惯吃什么?

B: 过年的时候我们习惯吃糖果。

糖果

鱼　年糕　月饼　粽子

520 第十四单元 ▪ 第二课 ▪ 节

PRACTICE 14.14

Take a survey of the class to find out which Chinese festival they like the most. Record your findings below.

Festival	Number of Students

PRACTICE 14.15

Working with a partner, use the Cultural Spotlights in Unit 14 to identify the holidays associated with the pictures and the traditions that they depict. Record the traditions in the spaces provided.

Example:

A: 春节的时候会有很多传统活动。

B: 比方说，春节的时候会有舞龙舞狮。

舞龙舞狮

Unit 14 ▪ Lesson 2 ▪ Festivals **521**

	Radical	Stroke Order
午	十 shí ten	ノ ㇒ 乍 午
餐	食 shí food	⺋ ⺊ ⺅ 歺 歺 歺 夗 多 癶 癶 夗 夗 夗 餐 餐 餐
划	刂(刀) dāo knife	一 ㇆ 戈 戈 戈 划
夜	夕 xī evening	丶 亠 广 亠 疒 疒 疒 夜
像	亻(人) rén person	ノ 亻 亻 伫 伫 侉 侉 侉 傄 傄 像 像
余	人 rén person	ノ 人 人 今 今 余 余
秋	禾 hé grain	ノ 二 千 千 禾 禾 秋 秋
食	食 shí food	ノ 人 人 今 今 今 食 食 食
端	立 lì stand	丶 亠 亠 立 立 立 䇦 䇦 䇦 䇦 䇦 端 端 端
龙	龙 lóng dragon	一 ナ 尢 龙 龙
越	走 zǒu walk	一 十 土 キ キ 走 走 走 赺 越 越 越
流	氵(水) shuǐ water	丶 氵 氵 氵 汸 泸 浐 浐 浐 流
轻	车 chē cart	一 七 车 车 轵 轵 轵 轻 轻
参	厶 sī private	厶 厶 厸 叅 叅 叅 参 参
连	辶 chuò walk	一 七 七 车 连 连 连

PRACTICE 14.16

Make an audio recording and send it to your teacher. In the recording, use what you have learned to compare and contrast a Western holiday and a Chinese holiday of your choosing.

PRACTICE 14.17

Typing the following sentences on your computer.

1. 过春节的时候，中国人一定要回家吃年夜饭。
2. 每个节日都有传统的食物。
3. 现在有一些西方节日在中国越来越流行。
4. 你会参加学校的万圣节派对吗？
5. 没想到中国的年轻人也会过圣诞节！

PRACTICE 14.19

陈大东：昨天我跟小美的家人一起吃年夜饭了。
李中平：你吃些什么了？
陈大东：小美的妈妈做了很多中国菜，每个菜都是有意思的。
李中平：你说说看！
陈大东：比方说，吃鱼就是希望"年年有余。"
李中平：你有没有吃过年糕？
陈大东：当然吃过，好吃极了！
李中平：中国人吃年糕有什么特别的意思？
陈大东：哎呀！我吃完就忘了。

Read the dialogue and answer the following questions.
1. What did Chen Dadong eat with Xiaomei's family?
2. What symbolic value did the food have?

中国的春节跟西方的圣诞节一样，都是一年中最重要的节日，也是全家人一起过的节日。圣诞节的时候很多西方人吃火鸡，春节的时候中国人吃年夜饭。现在有一些西方节日，像圣诞节、万圣节，在中国越来越流行。中国的传统节日，像元宵节、端午节、中秋节，以后可能也会在西方越来越流行。

Read the passage and answer the following questions.
1. What are the similarities and differences between Chinese New Year and Christmas?
2. What Western festivals are becoming popular in China?

Chinese New Year

春节 (Chūnjié: "the Spring Festival," also referred to as "Chinese New Year") is celebrated by millions every year and is undoubtedly the most important annual celebration for the Chinese. The Spring Festival is a time to be with one's family and enjoy foods such as 饺子 (jiǎozi: "dumplings") and to celebrate by setting off firecrackers and fireworks.

The Spring Festival is typically a weeklong festival in Mainland China. It is China's busiest travel season; only those prepared enough (and indeed lucky enough) to get tickets well in advance are able to go traveling. During this time, migrant workers around the country also make the trip to their ancestral homes to reunite with their families and celebrate the New Year.

The New Year period typically involves some vigorous spring cleaning, which, aside from its practical benefits, is believed to rid the house of negative energy from the previous year and to make room for good luck to move in. Children are given 红包 (hóngbāo: "red envelopes") containing money from their parents or older relatives, and new clothes and haircuts are frequently in order for a fresh start to the New Year.

Spring Festival is so important in Chinese culture that even other countries with large Chinese populations such as Indonesia and Malaysia have adopted it as a national holiday. In addition, major cities in the West also recognize the significance of the holiday by holding parades and celebrations for Chinese New Year.

Lantern Festival

元宵节 (Yuánxiāojié: "the Lantern Festival") marks the end of the Chinese New Year celebrations. It takes place on the fifteenth day of the New Year, the first full moon of the year and an auspicious night to celebrate. Traditional activities associated with the Lantern Festival include solving puzzles and riddles, eating 汤圆 (tāngyuán: "glutinous rice balls"), and making colorful paper lanterns for children to carry around. Like most of the oldest Chinese festivals, the exact origin of the holiday is unclear. One legend states that the festival derives its name from 元宵 (Yuán Xiāo), a lonely palace maid who concocted a complex plan to reunite with her family. Whatever its origins, the Chinese people have been celebrating the Lantern Festival in one form or another for centuries.

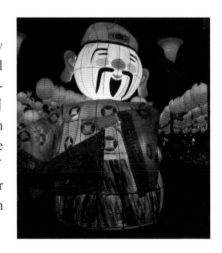

Originally, the lanterns used at the festival were made of simple, unadorned paper. These days, they come in all shapes and sizes and are decorated with a variety of elaborate and eye-catching designs. In major cities like Shanghai and Hangzhou, competitions are held to find the most attractive lantern, an event that draws visitors from far and wide.

王小美： 今天我们吃年夜饭。过年，我们习惯吃鱼。因为"鱼"听起来像"多余"的"余，"所以吃鱼就是希望"年年有余。"

Today we are having a New Year's Eve dinner. At New Year it is a custom to have fish. Because the Chinese word for "fish" sounds like the word for "plentiful," eating fish represents a wish to "enjoy abundance year after year."

李中平： 吃年夜饭，最重要的是全家人在一起，跟圣诞节一样耶。

The most important thing about the New Year's Eve dinner is to have the whole family together, just like Christmas.

小美爸： 我们过节都有传统的食物。中秋节要吃月饼，春节吃鱼，吃年糕 。你们呢？

When we celebrate Chinese holidays, there are always traditional foods. For the Mid-Autumn Festival, we have moon cakes; for Chinese New Year, we have fish and New Year's rice cake. How about you?

孙玛丽： 我们家感恩节一定会吃火鸡。

At Thanksgiving, my family has turkey.

黄祥安： 我们家好像每天都在过节，每天都吃大餐！

My family seems like it's celebrating a holiday every day. Every day we have a feast!

孙玛丽： 我记得有一个中国节日是吃粽子的……

I remember there is a Chinese festival where people eat leaf-wrapped dumplings…

王小美： 那是端午节。端午节的时候还会有划龙舟比赛。

That is the Dragon Boat Festival. During that festival, there are also dragon boat races.

张安娜： 哇，中国的节日那么多，中国人还过西方节日吗？

Wow, there are so many Chinese holidays. Do Chinese people also celebrate Western holidays?

王小美： 现在有一些西方节日在中国越来越流行。

There are several Western holidays that are becoming more and more popular in China now.

小美爸： 比方说，在中国有的年轻人会参加万圣节派对。

For example, some young people in China go to Halloween parties.

陈大东： 没想到中国人连万圣节都会过啊！

Who'd have thought that Chinese people even celebrate Halloween!

What Can You Do?

INTERPRETIVE

- I can understand why certain foods are eaten at certain festivals.
- I can interpret the significance of customs and activities associated with Chinese festivals.

INTERPERSONAL

- I can discuss holidays and festivals with others.
- I can inquire as to what kinds of food or activities are traditionally associated with a festival.

PRESENTATIONAL

- I can present information about a variety of Chinese holidays.
- I can compare and contrast Western festivals with Chinese festivals.

单元复习 UNIT REVIEW

ACT IT OUT

Working in groups, compose an original three-minute skit that utilizes the vocabulary and structures introduced in Unit 14. Each of you should assume a role and have a roughly equal number of lines in the skit. Be prepared to perform your skit in class. You can either come up with your own story or choose from one of the following situations:

A) You visit your Chinese friend for Chinese New Year and he/she explains the customs of Chinese New Year to you.

B) You work in a store that sells party supplies and some customers want to buy supplies for a Chinese festival.

C) You and your spouse decide whose family to visit for the different holidays of the year.

CHECK WHAT YOU CAN DO

Recognize

Adjectives
- □ 传统
- □ 健康
- □ 热闹
- □ 多余
- □ 流行

Adverbs
- □ 好像
- □ 越来越

Idiomatic Expressions
- □ 恭喜发财
- □ 万事如意
- □ 年年有余
- □ 比方说

Nouns
- □ 春节
- □ 习惯
- □ 帽子
- □ 袜子
- □ 伯父
- □ 伯母
- □ 新年
- □ 红包

- □ 学业
- □ 糖果
- □ 年糕
- □ 瓜子
- □ 花灯
- □ 元宵节
- □ 烟火
- □ 年夜饭
- □ 圣诞节
- □ 中秋节
- □ 食物
- □ 月饼
- □ 感恩节
- □ 火鸡
- □ 大餐

- □ 节日
- □ 粽子
- □ 端午节
- □ 龙舟
- □ 西方
- □ 年轻人
- □ 万圣节
- □ 母亲节
- □ 父亲节
- □ 情人节

Prepositions
- □ 连

Verbs
- □ 装饰
- □ 戴
- □ 挂
- □ 放
- □ 过年
- □ 像
- □ 过节
- □ 划
- □ 参加

Particles
- □ 着
- □ 耶

Write

- □ 闹
- □ 装
- □ 春
- □ 节
- □ 传
- □ 统
- □ 恭
- □ 财
- □ 包
- □ 万
- □ 如
- □ 果
- □ 元
- □ 火
- □ 热

- □ 午
- □ 餐
- □ 划
- □ 夜
- □ 像
- □ 余
- □ 秋
- □ 食
- □ 端
- □ 龙
- □ 越
- □ 流
- □ 轻
- □ 参
- □ 连

Use

- □ 用...来... to describe the means of doing something
- □ 着 to indicate an ongoing action
- □ 快要...了 to say "be about to"
- □ 到时候 to express "when the time comes"
- □ 像 to express "resemble" or "is like"
- □ 越来越 to mean "increasingly"
- □ 比方说 to say "for example"
- □ 连...都 to say "even..."

礼

Chinese Ways

第十五单元
UNIT 15

Lesson 1: 有礼貌 **Being Respectful**
- Politely ask someone to do something
- Understand and follow Chinese social conventions
- Use the correct etiquette towards one's elders

Lesson 2: 了解中国文化 **Understanding Chinese Culture**
- Name some features of traditional Chinese culture
- Express that one has "just" done something
- Make basic comparisons between ancient and modern Chinese culture

有礼貌
Being Respectful

服务员，麻烦您，买单。

小美，今天晚上应该是我请客，让我来买单吧。

今天晚饭是我父母请你。

为什么？

因为中国传统是长辈要照顾晚辈，所以你让他们请客是尊敬他们。

可是我真的很想请他们。

下次吧。今天，你应该给他们一点儿面子，要不然他们会不高兴。

LESSON TEXT 15.1

Being Respectful 有礼貌

At a dinner with Wang Xiaomei and her parents, Chen Dadong wants to pay for the check, but Wang Xiaomei tells him to let her parents pay. Following social etiquette, Chen Dadong gives a gift instead.

小美爸：	服务员，麻烦您，买单。	Fúwùyuán, máfan nín, mǎi dān.
陈大东：	小美，今天晚上应该是我请客，让我来买单吧。	Xiǎoměi, jīntiān wǎnshang yīnggāi shì wǒ qǐng kè, ràng wǒ lái mǎi dān ba.
王小美：	今天晚饭是我父母请你。	Jīntiān wǎnfàn shì wǒ fùmǔ qǐng nǐ.
陈大东：	为什么？	Wèishénme?
王小美：	因为中国传统是长辈要照顾晚辈，所以你让他们请客是尊敬他们。	Yīnwèi Zhōngguó chuántǒng shì zhǎngbèi yào zhàogù wǎnbèi, suǒyǐ nǐ ràng tāmen qǐng kè shì zūnjìng tāmen.

———————

陈大东：	可是我真的很想请他们。	Kěshì wǒ zhēnde hěn xiǎng qǐng tāmen.
王小美：	下次吧。今天，你应该给他们一点儿面子，要不然他们会不高兴。	Xiàcì ba. Jīntiān, nǐ yīnggāi gěi tāmen yì diǎnr miànzi, yàoburán tāmen huì bù gāoxìng.
陈大东：	给他们面子是什么意思？	Gěi tāmen miànzi shì shénme yìsi?
王小美：	就是说，今天让他们请你吃饭。	Jiùshì shuō, jīntiān ràng tāmen qǐng nǐ chī fàn.
陈大东：	好吧，我应该对你的父母表示尊敬。	Hǎo ba, wǒ yīnggāi duì nǐ de fùmǔ biǎoshì zūnjìng.
王小美：	第一次见面，你可以送他们一份礼物。我正好买了一盒茶叶，给你送他们吧。	Dì yī cì jiàn miàn, nǐ kěyǐ sòng tāmen yí fèn lǐwù. Wǒ zhènghǎo mǎi le yì hé cháyè, gěi nǐ sòng tāmen ba.
陈大东：	小美，你太好了！	Xiǎoměi, nǐ tài hǎo le!

字 词 VOCABULARY

陈大东：	谢谢伯父伯母。	Xièxie bófù bómǔ.
小美爸：	哪里哪里。	Nǎlǐ nǎlǐ.
陈大东：	这是我送你们的小礼物，很希望下次可以请你们吃饭。	Zhè shì wǒ sòng nǐmen de xiǎo lǐwù, hěn xīwàng xiàcì kěyǐ qǐng nǐmen chī fàn.
小美妈：	别客气！你们还是学生，我们是长辈，应该照顾你们。	Bié kèqi! Nǐmen hái shì xuésheng, wǒmen shì zhǎngbèi, yīnggāi zhàogù nǐmen.

LESSON VOCABULARY 15.1

	SIMPLIFIED	TRADITIONAL	PINYIN	WORD CATEGORY	DEFINITION
1.	麻烦	麻煩	máfan	v, n, adj	to trouble someone to do something; trouble; troublesome
2.	买单	買單	mǎi dān	vo, n	to pay the bill; bill
3.	父母		fùmǔ	n	parents (formal)
4.	长辈	長輩	zhǎngbèi	n	elder generation
5.	照顾	照顧	zhàogù	v	to take care of
6.	晚辈	晚輩	wǎnbèi	n	younger generation
7.	尊敬		zūnjìng	v	to pay respect to (used for people)
8.	面子		miànzi	n	reputation; face; feelings
9.	要不然		yàoburán	cj	otherwise
10.	就是说	就是說	jiùshìshuō	ie	that is to say; in other words
11.	表示		biǎoshì	v	to express
12.	正好		zhènghǎo	adv	happen to, as it happens
13.	盒		hé	n, mw	box; a box of
14.	茶叶	茶葉	cháyè	n	tea leaves
15.	客气	客氣	kèqi	adj, v	polite; to be polite

REQUIRED VOCABULARY 15.1

SIMPLIFIED	TRADITIONAL	PINYIN	WORD CATEGORY	DEFINITION
PEOPLE				
16. 大人		dàrén	*n*	adults
17. 老人		lǎorén	*n*	elders
ETIQUETTE				
18. 礼貌	禮貌	lǐmào	*n*	manners; politeness

OPTIONAL VOCABULARY 15.1

SIMPLIFIED	TRADITIONAL	PINYIN	WORD CATEGORY	DEFINITION
ETIQUETTE				
19. 孝顺	孝順	xiàoshùn	*v, adj*	to show filial obedience; filial
孝		xiào	*n, v*	filial piety; to be filial
20. 侮辱		wǔrǔ	*n, v*	insult; to insult; to humiliate
21. 得罪		dézuì	*v*	to offend; to displease
22. 谦虚	謙虚	qiānxū	*adj*	modest
23. 高傲		gāo'ào	*adj*	arrogant

Face

One of the most important features of Chinese etiquette is "face." Face refers to a person's public image. When someone is embarrassed or weakened in public, they "lose face" (丢脸 diū liǎn). When one allows someone to display or maintain their social status, one "gives them face" (给他面子 gěi tā miànzi). Chinese has a few different terms that refer to face. Here are some common expressions.

Phrase	Pinyin	Meaning	Use
请给我点儿面子	qǐng gěi wǒ diǎnr miànzi	Please give me some face	Request for someone not to embarrass the speaker
很丢脸啊！	hěn diū liǎn a!	It's disgraceful!	Something is embarrassing
你让我没面子！	nǐ ràng wǒ méi miànzi!	You made me lose face!	The addressee has embarrassed the speaker

Terms for Politeness

The term 客气 is primarily used as an adjective meaning "polite," and 礼貌 is primarily used as a noun meaning "politeness" or "manners." They can express the same meaning, but as they are different parts of speech, they are generally used in different ways.

Phrase	Pinyin	Meaning
他很客气	tā hěn kèqi	he is very polite
他很有礼貌	tā hěn yǒu lǐmào	
客气的话	kèqi de huà	polite words
有礼貌的话	yǒu lǐmào de huà	

Certain expressions can only use one term or the other:

Phrase	Pinyin	Meaning
不客气	bú kèqi	You're welcome (lit: don't be polite)
不懂礼貌	bùdǒng lǐmào	doesn't have manners (lit: doesn't understand manners)
没礼貌	méi lǐmào	doesn't have manners

STRUCTURE NOTE 15.1
Use 麻烦 *to make requests*

As a noun, 麻烦 *(máfan) means "trouble," and as an adjective it is "troublesome" or "inconvenient." It can also be used as a verb when one wishes to make a request, in which case it is the same as the English "could I trouble you to…" As this is a polite form of request,* 麻烦 *is often used with the polite second person pronoun* 您.

麻烦 + 你/您 + Verb Phrase

From the Lesson Text:

服务员，麻烦您买单。
Fúwùyuán, máfan nín mǎi dān.
Waiter, please could you bring the bill.

Other examples:

麻烦你把纸给我。
Máfan nǐ bǎ zhǐ gěi wǒ.
Please could you give the paper to me.

对不起，麻烦你了。
Duìbuqǐ, máfan nǐ le.
Sorry to have troubled you.

Practice: Change the sentences below into Chinese using the expression 麻烦.

Example: Could you please help me for a moment? → 麻烦你帮我一下。

1.   Please could you read my résumé for me.

    _____

2.   Could you please help me to hang this lantern?

    _____

3.   Could I trouble you to call him again?

    _____

4.   Please help me to clean up the living room.

    _____

5.   Could you please carry those textbooks for me.

    _____

STRUCTURE NOTE 15.2

Use 来 before verbs to express commencing an activity

When it is placed before a verb phrase, 来 serves the purpose of emphasizing that someone will commence or engage in an activity presently.

> Subject + 来 + Verb Phrase

From the Lesson Text:

让我来买单吧。
Ràng wǒ lái mǎi dān ba.
How about you let me go ahead and pay the bill.

Other examples:

请你来说一说你的建议。
Qǐng nǐ lái shuō yi shuō nǐ de jiànyì.
Please go ahead and share some of your thoughts on this.

现在我们来看一下这个问题。
Xiànzài wǒmen lái kàn yí xià zhèi gè wèntí.
Now we're going to take a look at this question.

Practice: Change the following into English.

Example: 让我来看一下。 → Let me take a look.

1. 你不喜欢饺子吗？ 那我来吃。

   _____

2. 让我们来看第十五课的练习。

   _____

3. 你去休息吧，厨房我来打扫。

   _____

4. 明天我来放烟火吧。

   _____

5. 我们今天晚上去什么地方你来选吧。

   _____

STRUCTURE NOTE 15.3
Use 要不然 *to say "or else" or "otherwise"*

In Chinese, there are no special verb forms used to express counterfactual or hypothetical situations. Instead, context and certain key words indicate when a situation has not actually taken place. The conjunction 要不然 (yàoburán) expresses the meaning "otherwise, ..." It is preceded by a condition, and followed by what would result if this condition were not met.

Condition + 要不然 + Sentence

From the Lesson Text:

你应该给他们一点儿面子，要不然他们会不高兴。
Nǐ yīnggāi gěi tāmen yì diǎnr miànzi, yàoburán tāmen huì bù gāoxìng.
You should give them some face, otherwise they'll be unhappy.

Other examples:

你先把作业做好，要不然不可以去跳舞。
Nǐ xiān bǎ zuòyè zuò hǎo, yàoburán bù kěyǐ qù tiào wǔ.
Finish your homework first, otherwise you may not go dancing.

我应该学点中文，要不然去中国的时候会有很多问题。
Wǒ yīnggāi xué diǎn Zhōngwén, yàoburán qù Zhōngguó de shíhou huì yǒu hěn duō wèntí.
I should study some Chinese, otherwise I'll have lots of problems when I go to China.

Practice: Complete the follow sentences using 要不然.

Example:　　我周末得复习，...
→ 我周末得复习，要不然考试一定考不好。

1.　　明天是母亲节，你要给妈妈买花，...

　　_____

2.　　春节快要到了，我们快去买票，...

　　_____

3.　　你应该准备一份简历，...

　　_____

4.　　你要对女朋友好，...

　　_____

5.　　你要注意身体，...

　　_____

STRUCTURE NOTE 15.4
Use 正好 *to express "as it happens"; "happen to…"*
The adverb 正好 (zhènghǎo) expresses that the following event is a coincidence, similar to "as it happens." As in English, this pattern is generally used to describe a positive event.

> Subject + 正好 + Verb Phrase

From the Lesson Text:

我正好买了一盒茶叶。
Wǒ zhènghǎo mǎi le yì hé cháyè.
Luckily I happen to have bought a box of tea leaves.

Other examples:

我想找玛丽借书，正好在街上看到她。
Wǒ xiǎng zhǎo Mǎlì jiè shū, zhènghǎo zài jiē shang kàn dào tā.
I wanted to go and find Mali to borrow a book, and I just happened to spot her on the street.

我今天没带我的本子，他正好带了很多纸。
Wǒ jīntiān méi dài wǒ de běnzi, tā zhènghǎo dài le hěn duō zhǐ.
Today I didn't bring my notebook, but as it happens, he brought a lot of paper.

Practice: Match the sentence beginnings below with the appropriate 正好 phrase to form complete expressions.

Example: 你说你想学西班牙语，我正好认识一位西班牙语老师。

你说你想学西班牙语，	那边正好有个公园。
没想到今天有客人来，	我今天正好打扫客厅了。
她想去散散步，	我正好在那边实习。
我的手机没电了，	我正好带了一点糖果。
他去北京旅游的时候，	他正好带了他的。
她的孩子开始哭了，	我正好认识一位西班牙语老师。

🗨 **PRACTICE 15.1**
Working with a partner, use the word box and the pictures below to enact dialogues containing the appropriate respectful language.

Example:
A: 让我请你吃饭吧。
B: 谢谢伯父。
A: 哪里哪里。我是长辈，应该照顾你。

伯父请她吃饭

谢谢　别客气　哪里哪里　长辈　晚辈　照顾　尊敬　礼貌

爷爷送他们去机场

孙小姐带他去看医生

学生帮她拿东西

奶奶帮她们做饭

PRACTICE 15.2

Use the following pattern to politely request something from your classmates. Record the requests you have made in the table below. Remember to respond politely by using the phrases you have learned.

Example:

A: 玛丽, 麻烦你借一张纸给我。

B: 没问题。

A: 谢谢。

B: 不客气。

Name	Request
Example: 玛丽	麻烦你借一张纸给我

PRACTICE 15.3

Find two partners to script a roleplay based on the following scenario. You are invited by a Chinese friend to have dinner with his/her father. At the dinner, discuss the idea of 'face,' showing respect to older generations, and who will pay the bill.

PRACTICE 15.4

Make an audio recording and send it to your teacher. In the recording, discuss what you have learned about being respectful to one's elders in Chinese culture.

PRACTICE 15.5

Type the following sentences on your computer.

1. 今天晚饭让我来买单吧！

2. 中国的传统习惯是长辈照顾晚辈。

3. 请你给我父母一点儿面子。

4. 服务员！麻烦您，我要买单。

5. 你让长辈请客就是尊敬他们。

	Radical	Stroke Order
单	十 shí ten	丶 丷 丷 ⺌ ⺌ 甲 旦 单
客	宀 mián roof	丶 丶 宀 宀 冬 安 安 客 客
次	欠 qiàn owe	丶 冫 冫 沙 汐 次
气	气 qì air	丿 仁 仁 气
父	父 fù father	丿 八 分 父
母	毋 wú not	乚 囗 毋 母 母
麻	麻 má hemp	丶 一 广 广 庁 庁 床 庄 庥 麻 麻
烦	火 huǒ fire	丶 丶 火 火 灯 灯 灯 炳 烦 烦
辈	车 chē cart	丿 丨 ヨ ヨ 非 非 非 非 辈 辈 辈 辈
尊	寸 cùn inch	丶 丷 酋 酋 酋 酋 酋 酋 酋 尊 尊
敬	攵(攴) pū knock	一 十 艹 艹 芀 芀 苟 苟 苟 苟 敬 敬
照	灬(火) huǒ fire	丨 冂 日 日 昭 昭 昭 昭 昭 照 照 照 照
顾	页 yè page	一 厂 厂 厄 厄 厄 厄 顾 顾 顾
茶	艹(草) cǎo grass	一 十 艹 艾 艾 苳 茶 茶 茶
叶	口 kǒu mouth	丿 丨 口 口 叶 叶

王小美：大东，你记得下个周末要来我家过节吗？
陈大东：当然！
王小美：第一次来我家，要对我父母表示尊敬，
　　　　最好带一份礼物。
陈大东：我打算买一盒月饼送给你父母。
王小美：不要闹了，现在是春节，不是中秋节！
陈大东：我只是骗骗你！我昨天已经买了一盒茶叶。
王小美：我爸爸最喜欢喝茶！他一定会喜欢你的礼物。
陈大东：太好了！我昨天还在担心你父母会不喜欢。

Read the dialogue and answer the following questions.
1. What does Wang Xiaomei advise Chen Dadong to do when he comes to her home?
2. What did Chen Dadong buy?

陈大东：伯父伯母，你们好！这是送你们的小礼物。
王妈妈：你太客气了！你还是学生，不要花钱给我
　　　　们买东西。
陈大东：第一次见面，我要有礼貌。
王爸爸：大东，虽然你不是中国人，可是很懂中国的传
　　　　统。
陈大东：哪里哪里，都是小美教我的。
王妈妈：欢迎你以后常常来我们家玩。
陈大东：我有空会常常来看伯父伯母。

Read the dialogue and answer the following questions.
1. How do Wang Xiaomei's parents respond when Chen Dadong gives them a present?
2. How do Wang Xiaomei's parents praise Chen Dadong?

中国人喜欢请客吃饭。长辈常常请晚辈吃饭是因为他们觉得应该照顾晚辈，晚辈也想请客是因为他们觉得要尊敬长辈，所以在饭馆会常常看到中国人吵着谁应该请客。中国人觉得面子是很重要的，可是我想西方没有这样的请客习惯是比较简单的。

Read Huang Xiang'an's diary and answer the following questions.
1. What does Huang Xiang'an say that you might see Chinese people doing in a restaurant?
2. What does Huang Xiang'an think about the idea of 'face'?

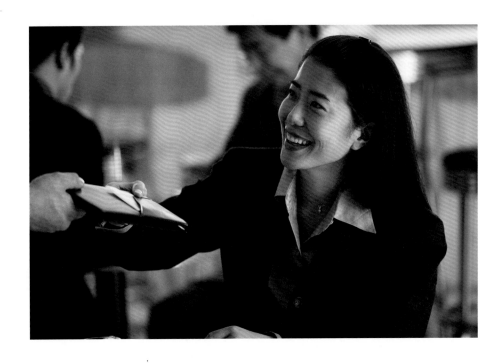

Confucius and Confucianism

孔子 (Kǒngzǐ: "Confucius") is the most influential philosopher and teacher in the history of China. His ideas are based on ethical, respectful relationships between individuals, and emphasize the importance of moral righteousness when interacting with family members and the outside community.

Confucius lived during the Spring and Autumn period (770 — 476 BC). During this time of instability, Confucianism arose as a philosophy which addressed issues of governance and correct social behavior. Confucius saw filial relationships within the family as a model for relationships between a ruler and his subjects, and preached that rulers who wished to unify the scattered Chinese states could only do so by practicing benevolence towards their people.

Confucian Ideals

Confucian ideals are a series of abstract ideas and noble characteristics that, according to Confucius, all people must work tirelessly to attain. One who exemplifies these traits is considered to be a 君子 (jūnzi: "ideal gentleman"). The ideal gentleman is said to follow the 道 (Dào: "the Way"), the ideal path of moral existence for man.

孝 (xiào: "filial piety") is one of the key concepts of Confucian philosophy. Confucius saw filial piety as the cornerstone of society. He expected people to treat their elders with respect, to care for them in their old age, and to acknowledge their teachings. This respect also extended to one's ancestors, who were still considered honored parts of the Chinese family even though they had passed on.

Even today, the Confucian emphasis on filial piety is extremely prevalent in Chinese culture. Grandparents and other elders are considered the most respected members of the family, and their children and grandchildren are expected to tend to their needs before their own.

Shaping Chinese Culture

Confucian philosophy has played a huge part in defining Chinese civilization, as well as the cultures of other East Asian nations. During the Han Dynasty (202 BCE – 220 BCE), Confucianism was adopted as the official national ideology. The Civil Service Examination, designed to appoint government officials based on merit, assessed proficiency in Confucian concepts from his writings and sayings. Testing candidates on these ideas did not necessarily evaluate their ability to contribute to governmental affairs; instead, the exam determined their moral character. Beyond the Civil Service Examination, Confucianism became the foundation of education and schooling in China, and the philosophy continues to exert a strong influence on Chinese culture today.

小美爸：	服务员，麻烦您，买单。	Excuse me waiter, check please.
陈大东：	小美，今天晚上应该是我请客，让我来买单吧。	Xiaomei, I should be paying for tonight's dinner, let me pay the bill.
王小美：	今天晚饭是我父母请你。	Tonight my parents are treating you to dinner.
陈大东：	为什么？	Why?
王小美：	因为中国传统是长辈要照顾晚辈，所以你让他们请客是尊敬他们。	Because in Chinese tradition the older generation takes care of the younger, so letting them pay for dinner is a sign of respect.
陈大东：	可是我真的很想请他们。	But I really would like to treat them.

———————

王小美：	下次吧。今天，你应该给他们一点儿面子，要不然他们会不高兴。	You can do it next time. Today, you should give them face, or else they won't be happy.
陈大东：	给他们面子是什么意思？	What do you mean by "give them face"?
王小美：	就是说，今天让他们请你吃饭。	It means you should let them treat you.
陈大东：	好吧，我应该对你的父母表示尊敬。	OK, I should show your parents the proper respect.
王小美：	第一次见面，你可以送他们一份礼物。我正好买了一盒茶叶，给你送他们吧。	When you meet them for the first time, you can offer them a present. I just bought a box of tea, why don't you give them that?
陈大东：	小美，你太好了！	Xiaomei, you're the best!
陈大东：	谢谢伯父伯母。	Thank you Mr. and Mrs. Wang.
小美爸：	哪里哪里。	Don't mention it.

陈大东： 这是我送你们的小礼物，很希望下次可以请你们吃饭。

小美妈： 别客气！你们还是学生，我们是长辈，应该照顾你们。

This is a little present I got for you. I hope next time I can treat you both to dinner.

You're welcome! You are still students, and we are your elders. We should take care of you.

What Can You Do?

INTERPRETIVE
- I can respond using the proper social etiquette in various social situations.
- I can respond to a situation to allow someone to save face.

INTERPERSONAL
- I can interact with elders whilst showing them the proper respect.
- I can have a discussion to decide who will pay the bill at a restaurant.

PRESENTATIONAL
- I can give a presentation on aspects of manners and etiquette in Chinese culture.
- I can give a presentation on the meaning and significance of "face" in Chinese culture.

了解中国文化
Understanding Chinese Culture

中平，快来看看这些书，我刚刚在中文书店买的。
(kuài / gāng gāng)

武术、京剧、书法……怎么都是中国传统文化的东西？
(wǔ shù / jīng jù / shū fǎ / wén huà)

我暑假要去中国实习，所以想先了解一下中国的文化。
(liǎo jiě / wén huà)

什么？那些都太古老了，现代的中国很不一样吧。
(gǔ lǎo / xiàn dài)

LESSON TEXT 15.2

Understanding Chinese Culture 了解中国文化

Sun Mali has bought some books on Chinese culture and asks Li Zhongping to take a look with her. They discuss the influence of traditional culture on modern China and Sun Mali gives Li Zhongping some pointers.

孙玛丽： 中平，快来看看这些书，我刚刚在中文书店买的。

Zhōngpíng, kuài lái kànkan zhè xiē shū, wǒ gānggāng zài Zhōngwén shūdiàn mǎi de.

李中平： 武术、京剧、书法……怎么都是中国传统文化的东西？

Wǔshù, Jīngjù, shūfǎ—zěnme dōu shì Zhōngguó chuántǒng wénhuà de dōngxi?

孙玛丽： 我暑假要去中国实习，所以想先了解一下中国的文化。

Wǒ shǔjià yào qù Zhōngguó shíxí, suǒyǐ xiǎng xiān liǎojiě yí xià Zhōngguó de wénhuà.

李中平： 什么？那些都太古老了，现代的中国很不一样吧。

Shénme? Nà xiē dōu tài gǔlǎo le, xiàndài de Zhōngguó hěn bù yíyàng ba.

孙玛丽： 虽然中国已经现代化了，可是传统文化还很重要。比方说，孔子的想法还是很被重视的。

Suīrán Zhōngguó yǐjīng xiàndài huà le, kěshì chuántǒng wénhuà hái hěn zhòngyào. Bǐfāngshuō, Kǒngzǐ de xiǎngfǎ hái shì hěn bèi zhòngshì de.

孙玛丽： 中国人的礼节很复杂，如果你做得不对，很容易发生误会。

Zhōngguó rén de lǐjié hěn fùzá, rúguǒ nǐ zuò de bú duì, hěn róngyì fāshēng wùhuì.

黄祥安： 没错，比如，一个人把东西交给你，你该怎么样？

Méi cuò, bǐrú, yí ge rén bǎ dōngxi jiāogěi nǐ nǐ gāi zěnmeyàng?

孙玛丽： 我要用双手接受。用一只手接是不礼貌的。

Wǒ yào yòng shuāngshǒu jiēshòu. Yòng yì zhī shǒu jiē shì bù lǐmào de.

黄祥安： 这样我就放心了，你已经学了很多了。你可以去中国交很多新朋友！

Zhèyàng wǒ jiù fàngxīn le, nǐ yǐjīng xué le hěn duō le. Nǐ kěyǐ qù Zhōngguó jiāo hěn duō xīn péngyou!

李中平： 有了新朋友，不要忘记老朋友喔！

Yǒu le xīn péngyou, bú yào wàngjì lǎo péngyou o!

字 词 VOCABULARY

LESSON VOCABULARY 15.2

	SIMPLIFIED	TRADITIONAL	PINYIN	WORD CATEGORY	DEFINITION
1.	快		kuài	adj	fast; quick
2.	刚刚	剛剛	gānggāng	adv	just
3.	武术	武術	wǔshù	n	martial arts
4.	京剧	京劇	Jīngjù	n	Peking opera
5.	书法	書法	shūfǎ	n	calligraphy
6.	文化		wénhuà	n	culture
7.	了解		liǎojiě	v	to understand
8.	古老		gǔlǎo	adj	ancient; old-fashioned
9.	现代	現代	xiàndài	adj, n	modern; modern times
10.	现代化	現代化	xiàndài huà	adj, v, n	modernized; modernize; modernization
11.	孔子		Kǒngzǐ	name	Confucius
12.	想法		xiǎngfǎ	n	idea; opinion; way of thinking
13.	重视	重視	zhòngshì	v	think highly of; attach importance to
14.	礼节	禮節	lǐjié	n	etiquette; courtesy
15.	复杂	複雜	fùzá	adj	complex, complicated
16.	误会	誤會	wùhuì	v	to misunderstand
17.	没错	沒錯	méi cuò	adj	not wrong; (that's) right
18.	比如		bǐrú	cj	for instance
19.	交给	交給	jiāogěi	v	to hand/give to
20.	双手	雙手	shuāngshǒu	n	both hands
21.	接受		jiēshòu	v	to accept
22.	礼貌	禮貌	lǐmào	n	manners
23.	放心		fàngxīn	v	to put one's mind at ease
24.	交朋友		jiāo péngyou	vo	to make friends

REQUIRED VOCABULARY 15.2

SIMPLIFIED	TRADITIONAL	PINYIN	WORD CATEGORY	DEFINITION
NOUNS				
25. 思想		sīxiǎng	*n*	thought, idea
26. 太极拳	太極拳	tàijíquán	*n*	Taichi

OPTIONAL VOCABULARY 15.2

RELATED TO CLASSICAL CULTURE

SIMPLIFIED	TRADITIONAL	PINYIN	WORD CATEGORY	DEFINITION
27. 哲学家	哲學家	zhéxuéjiā	*n*	philosopher
28. 孟子		Mèngzǐ	*name*	Mencius
29. 庄子	莊子	Zhuāngzǐ	*name*	Zhuangzi
OTHER				
30. 办法	辦法	bànfǎ	*n*	way; means
31. 看法		kànfǎ	*n*	opinion; perspective
32. 古代		gǔdài	*adj, n*	ancient; ancient times

Classical and Modern Chinese

Until the early twentieth century, the majority of written Chinese was composed in 文言文 (wényánwén: "Classical Chinese"). In one form or another, 文言文 had existed since as early as the Spring and Autumn Period (771 – 403 BC). 文言文 was notably different from the spoken vernacular, but the latter was not considered appropriate for refined writing and so it remained largely a means of verbal communication. During the 1920s momentous changes in China swept away the ancient language and replaced it with 白话 (báihuà: literally, "plain speech"), so that written Chinese resembled the everyday spoken variety, unifying the language into the form we know today.

Although the structures and vocabulary of 文言文 are by and large completely different from present day Mandarin, the historical continuity of Chinese characters still allows the student of the modern language to understand some classical texts. Here, for example, is the poem 静夜思 (Jìng Yè Sī: "Thoughts On a Quiet Night") by the famous Tang Dynasty (618 – 907) poet 李白 (Lǐ Bái):

Poem	Pinyin	Meaning
床前明月光，	Chuáng qián míng yuè guāng	The moon shines bright before my bed,
疑是地上霜。	Yí shì dì shàng shuāng	I wonder if it is frost on the ground.
举头望明月，	Jǔ tóu wàng míng yuè	Lifting my head I look at the bright moon,
低头思故乡。	Dī tóu sī gù xiāng	Lowering it, I think of my home.

It is important to note that Classical Chinese still exerts a significant influence on the modern language, particularly in formal written Chinese. There is a predilection for 'balanced' sentences or phrases consisting of four characters, as was often the classical style, as well as the many 成语 (chéngyǔ: "idioms") derived from classical stories. In addition, certain particles of Classical Chinese grammar still find their way into modern written Chinese. When writing formally, one may replace 的 with 之 (zhī), its classical equivalent. Similarly, formal notices may substitute 的人 with 者 (zhě), for example 年长者 (年长的人: "elderly people").

STRUCTURE NOTE 15.5

Use 刚 or 刚刚 to express "just now"

刚 (gāng) and 刚刚 (gānggāng) can both express the meaning "just now" or "only just." The single-character version 刚 is slightly more formal than 刚刚.

> Subject + 刚(刚) + Verb Phrase

From the Lesson Text:

我刚刚在中文书店买的。
Wǒ gānggāng zài Zhōngwén shūdiàn mǎi de.
I just bought them at a Chinese bookstore.

Other examples:

你是刚来的吗？
Nǐ shì gāng lái de ma?
Did you just get here?

我刚看到你的女儿。
Wǒ gāng kàn dào nǐ de nǚ'ér.
I just saw your daughter.

Practice: Change the following sentences into Chinese using 刚 or 刚刚.

Example:　　I just finished my homework. → 我刚把作业做完了。

1.　　I'm sorry, the manager just left.

　　_____

2.　　He only just broke up with his girlfriend, no wonder he's so sad.

　　_____

3.　　Dad just finished putting up the lanterns.

　　_____

4.　　They've just returned from China.

　　_____

5.　　It's no problem; the match only just started.

　　_____

STRUCTURE NOTE 15.6

Use nouns with 化 to form "-ize" verbs or "-ized" adjectives

化 (huà), when added onto certain adjectives and nouns, is equivalent to the English suffixes "-ize" and "-ized," as in "modernize." Depending on the context, a noun or an adjective with the 化 suffix in Chinese will become a verb or an adjective when translated into English.

Adjective/Noun + 化

From the Lesson Text:

虽然中国已经现代化了，可是传统文化还很重要。
Suīrán Zhōngguó yǐjīng xiàndài huà le, kěshì chuántǒng wénhuà hái hěn zhòngyào.
Even though China has already modernized, traditional culture is still very important.

Other examples:

北京人说话常常带儿化音。
Běijīng rén shuō huà chángcháng dài ér huà yīn.
People from Beijing often rhotacize their words.
("rhotacize": to add an "-r" sound to the end of a word)

住在西方这么多年了，他们当然西化了。
Zhù zài Xīfāng zhème duō nián le, tāmen dāngrán Xī huà le.
They've lived in the West all these years; of course they've become Westernized.

Practice: Put the words from the word bank into the correct places below.

儿化音，中国化，现代化，加州化，西化，美国化

Example: 这本书跟中国现代化的问题有关。

1. 每天打太极拳、用筷子吃饭，看起来你已经 _____ 了！

2. 他说的这个 _____ 是什么意思呢？

3. 长辈重视传统文化，可是被 _____ 的晚辈没有这个想法。

4. 北京人说话带 _____ 我有的时候听不懂。

5. 他看了那么多美国电影以后，朋友都说他 _____ 了。

6. 这本书跟中国 _____ 的问题有关。

STRUCTURE NOTE 15.7

Use 比如(说) to say "for instance" and give examples

In Structure Note 14.7, the phrase 比方说 *was introduced as a way to present examples.* 比如(说) *(bǐrú [shuō]) is a another way to do this, but it carries a slightly more formal tone.*

比如(说), + Example Sentence

From the Lesson Text:

比如，一个人把东西交给你，你该怎么样？
Bǐrú, yí ge rén bǎ dōngxi jiāogěi nǐ, nǐ gāi zěnmeyàng?
For example, when someone gives you something, what should you do?

Other examples:

我很喜欢中国电影，比如说，《一个都不能少》。
Wǒ hěn xǐhuan Zhōngguó diànyǐng, bǐrúshuō, "Yí Ge Dōu Bù Néng Shǎo."
I really like Chinese movies, for example, "Not One Less."

他交了很多朋友。比如，小美。
Tā jiāo le hěn duō péngyou. Bǐrú, Xiǎoměi.
He made a lot of friends. For example, Xiaomei.

Practice: Complete the following statements using 比如(说) and one or more examples.

Example: 她会说很多语言，...
→ 她会说很多语言，比如说英语、法语，跟中文。

1. 中国有很多节日，...

_____

2. 他在家里常常帮妈妈的忙，...

_____

3. 我爸爸对中国传统文化有兴趣，...

_____

4. 中国的春节跟西方的新年不太一样，...

_____

5. 我妈妈做过很多工作，...

_____

STRUCTURE NOTE 15.8

Use double-了 to describe an action continuing up to the present

It has been shown that the particle 了 is sometimes placed after the verb and sometimes at the end of a sentence. When the verb-suffix 了 and the sentence-final 了 are both used in the same sentence, it indicates that an action is continuing up to the present. For example, 我学了三年的中文 *means that the speaker studied Chinese for three years at some point in the past, but is not studying it anymore. However,* 我学了三年的中文了 *means the speaker has studied for three years now and is still studying. The first* 了 *in this pattern is followed by a quantity (see Structure Note 6.11) or a duration (see Structure Note 10.11).*

> Subject + Verb + 了 + Quantity (+ Object) + 了

> Subject + Verb + Object + Verb + 了 + Duration + 了

> Subject + Verb + 了 + Duration + 的 + Object + 了

From the Lesson Text:

你已经学了很多了。
Nǐ yǐjīng xué le hěn duō le.
You've already learned a lot.

Other examples:

我们学中文学了一年半了。
Wǒmen xué Zhōngwén xué le yī nián bàn le.
We have been studying Chinese for a year and a half.

这里下了三天的雨了。
Zhèli xià le sān tiān de yǔ le.
It has been raining for three days here.

Practice: Use double-了 to change the meaning of these sentences so that they indicate an action continuing up to the present.

Example: 我学了六个月的西班牙语。
→ 我学了六个月的西班牙语了。

1. 弟弟吃了十五个饺子！他真能吃。
_____

2. 元宵节的花灯你已经挂了很多，休息一下吧！
_____

3. 她学了四年的钢琴，现在弹得很不错。
_____

4. 今天下了一个早上的雪，你快来看！
_____

5. 老板讲了两个小时，大家好像快要睡觉了。
_____

练习 PRACTICE

PRACTICE 15.10

Working with a partner, enact a dialogue based on the information below. Following the structure in the example, person A should list a number of items associated with the picture and form a question about them, and person B should offer a corresponding explanation.

Example:

A: 武术、京剧、书法……怎么都是中国传统文化的书？

B: 因为我想了解中国传统文化。书店里卖关于中国传统文化的书还有很多，比如说太极拳、中国舞，跟孔子思想。

我在图书馆借了很多出国旅游的书。

我在饭馆点了很多中国菜。

我在商店买了很多红色的东西。

我在中国参加了很多过节的传统活动。

PRACTICE 15.11

Take a survey of the class to find out which aspect of traditional Chinese culture your classmates would most like to learn. Write the most popular response below.

Aspect of Traditional Culture	Number of Students

PRACTICE 15.12

Make an audio recording and send it to your teacher. In the recording, talk about some of the ways in which the influence of traditional Chinese culture can still be seen in China today.

PRACTICE 15.13

Type the following sentences on your computer.

1. 我在图书馆借了一本介绍中国京剧的书。
2. 虽然中国已经现代化了，可是传统文化还很重要。
3. 中国人很重视孔子的想法。
4. 中国人的礼节很复杂，你要多学习！
5. 如果做得不对，很容易发生误会。

PRACTICE 15.14

Help Chen Dadong to reply to his dad's postcard from Beijing. Respond to his dad's inquiry about Chinese customs.

大东：

我到北京了，这里天气很热。我打算工作完以后，去长城看看才回去加拿大。

我很喜欢这里，人们都对我很好，可是我不太了解这里的文化。昨天我到一位中国朋友的家去，他送了我一份礼物。我很高兴，想马上看看里面是什么，可是他叫我回家才看。我不明白，为什么我不可以马上看看他送我什么礼物呢？

爸爸

	Radical	Stroke Order
放	攵(攴) pū knock	丶 一 亠 方 方 放 放 放
刚	刂(刀) dāo knife	丨 冂 刀 冈 刚 刚
武	止 zhǐ stop	一 二 干 于 武 正 武 武
术	木 mù wood	一 十 才 木 术
剧	刂(刀) dāo knife	乛 冂 尸 尸 尸 居 居 剧 剧
化	匕 bǐ ladle	丿 亻 仁 化
解	角 jiǎo horn	丿 ⺈ 广 勹 角 角 角 觖 觖 解 觧 觧 解
古	口 kǒu mouth	一 十 古 古 古
代	亻(人) rén person	丿 亻 仁 代 代
复	夂 suī go slowly	丿 ⺈ 仁 仁 白 白 勹 复 复
杂	木 mù wood	丿 九 九 杂 杂 杂
误	讠(言) yán speech	丶 讠 讠 讠 误 误 误 误
双	又 yòu again	乛 又 双 双
接	扌(手) shǒu hand	一 十 扌 扩 扩 扩 护 拉 接 接 接
受	又 yòu again	一 ⺈ 爫 爫 爫 严 受 受

王小美：玛丽，这是我送你的生日礼物。

孙玛丽：哦！是跟中国书法有关的书，谢谢你！

王小美：我刚刚在中文书店买的，希望你喜欢。

孙玛丽：我非常喜欢，最近我就想开始学习写书法。

王小美：真的吗？我也对书法很有兴趣。

孙玛丽：你可以教我吗？

王小美：那我先带你去书店买写书法的文具。

孙玛丽：怎么才能把书法学好呢？

王小美：你得多多练习，每天练习一个小时，你很
快就会进步。

孙玛丽：那我明天就开始练习！

Read the dialogue and answer the following questions.
1. What did Wang Xiaomei buy for Sun Mali at the bookshop?
2. What else do they plan to buy?

Sender 玛丽
Subject 中国文化

爸爸：
我暑假要去中国实习，想先了解
一下中国的文化。我特别喜欢中
国的传统文化，可是不知道应该
从哪里开始学习。还有，我朋友
说中国的礼节很复杂，如果做得
不对，很容易发生误会。所以请
你教教我，应该特别注意中国人
的哪些礼节。

Sender 爸爸
Subject re:中国文化

玛丽：
你可以到图书馆去借一些中国文
化的书来看。你也可以在中文书
店买一些跟中国传统文化有关的
书，比如说京剧、武术、中国
画、还有中国菜，这些都不错。
还有，中国的礼节需要注意的地
方很多，比方说，别人送礼物给
你，你不能用一只手接受，要用
双手接受才有礼貌。

Read the emails and answer the following questions.
1. Why does Sun Mali want to know about traditional Chinese culture?
2. What kind of books does her dad suggest that she should buy?

PRACTICE 15.18

孔子是中国历史上最重要的老师。有些地方在孔子的生日那天会有尊敬老师的节日活动。有些学校也会有很多文化活动让学生学习孔子思想。虽然中国已经现代化了，孔子的想法还是很被重视的。

Read the passage and answer the following questions.
1. What do some places do to mark Confucius' birthday?
2. What do some schools do to mark the occasion?

Daoism

道教 (Dàojiào: "Daoism") is a philosophy with ancient origins that is commonly associated with the philosopher 老子 (Lǎozǐ) and his text 道德经 (Dàodéjīng: "The Daodejing"). As Daoism became more popular over time, more organized rituals and practices emerged, and the philosophy eventually evolved into a religious faith.

Daoism espouses belief in the 道 (Dào: "the Way"), which represents the basis of all living things and dictates the flow of the universe. Daoist ideas encourage one to embrace the simplicity of life and acknowledge the nature of reality.

Among the central themes associated with Daoism are balance and interdependence. This idea is represented by the well-known Daoist symbol, the 阴阳 (yīnyáng: "yin and yang"). Yin, the black portion of the symbol, represents passivity, softness and femininity, while yang, the white portion of the symbol, represents solidity, aggression, and masculinity. However, each side still contains a portion of the other, representing the interaction of opposites and the balance of complementary forces that brings order to nature.

One of Laozi's most famous disciples, 庄子 (Zhuāngzǐ), is also credited with developing many Daoist ideas. Zhuangzi emphasized the importance of recognizing relativity in all situations. Famously, he once dreamt that he was a carefree butterfly, roaming the skies. Once he awoke, he proclaimed, "I do not know whether I was then a man dreaming I was a butterfly, or whether I am now a butterfly dreaming I am a man."

Enduring Influence

Despite the great prominence of Confucian philosophy and Daoist beliefs in Chinese culture, the schools of thought have undergone a number of challenges throughout Chinese history. During the Qin dynasty (221 – 207 BC), the emperor 秦始皇 (Qín Shǐhuáng) governed by one philosophy, Legalism, and sought to eliminate all other schools of thought. He ordered that all non-Legalist texts be burned, and is rumored to have ordered hundreds of Confucian scholars to be buried alive.

In more recent years, too, traditional philosophies have had to endure tough times. During the Cultural Revolution (1966 – 1976), mass movements were undertaken to rid China of old influences, with Confucianism and Daosim being identified as targets for criticism. Despite these setbacks, however, Confucian and Daoist influences are still found in Chinese society, a fact that stands as a testament to how deeply ingrained they are in the fabric of Chinese civilization.

孙玛丽： 中平，快来看看这些书，我刚刚在中文书店买的。

Zhongping, come take a look at these books. I just bought them at the Chinese bookstore.

李中平： 武术、京剧、书法……怎么都是中国传统文化的东西？

Martial arts, Peking opera, calligraphy… how come they're all about traditional Chinese culture?

孙玛丽： 我暑假要去中国实习，所以想先了解一下中国的文化。

I am going to China for a summer internship, so I thought I should first learn more about Chinese culture.

李中平： 什么？那些都太古老了，现代的中国很不一样吧。

What? Those things are all so old-fashioned, China nowadays is probably very different.

孙玛丽： 虽然中国已经现代化了，可是传统文化还很重要。比方说，孔子的想法还是很被重视的。

Even though China has become modernized, old traditions and customs are still important. For example, Confucius' thinking is still very much respected.

孙玛丽： 中国人的礼节很复杂，如果你做得不对，很容易发生误会。

Chinese customs are very complicated. If you commit a cultural faux pas, it's very easy for misunderstandings to occur.

黄祥安： 没错，比如，一个人把东西交给你，你该怎么样？

That's right. For example, if someone hands you something, what should you do?

孙玛丽： 我要用双手接受。用一只手接是不礼貌的。

I should receive it with both hands. If you use only one hand, it is impolite.

黄祥安： 这样我就放心了，你已经学了很多了。你可以去中国交很多新朋友！

You have set my mind at ease; you've already learned a lot. You can go to China and make lots of new friends!

李中平： 有了新朋友，不要忘记老朋友喔！

Once you've made new friends, don't forget about your old ones!

What Can You Do?

INTERPRETIVE
- I can understand some of the significant features of traditional Chinese culture.

INTERPERSONAL
- I can hold a discussion with someone on aspects of traditional and modern Chinese culture, and support my statements by giving examples.

PRESENTATIONAL
- I can give a presentation about the main aspects of traditional Chinese culture.
- I can compare some features of traditional and modern culture in China.

ACT IT OUT

Working in groups, compose an original three-minute skit that utilizes the vocabulary and structures introduced in Unit 15. Each of you should assume a role and have a roughly equal number of lines in the skit. Be prepared to perform your skit in class. You can either come up with your own story or choose from one of the following situations:

A) You and a group of friends discuss where you were all born and your family histories.

B) Your friend will be studying abroad next semester. You discuss how your local customs differ from those of his/her destination.

C) You will be staying with a host family in Beijing for a week. You ask your friend from China for tips regarding Chinese etiquette.

CHECK WHAT YOU CAN DO

RECOGNIZE				WRITE	
Adjectives □ 客气 □ 快 □ 古老 □ 现代 □ 现代化 □ 复杂 □ 没错 *Adverbs* □ 正好 □ 刚刚 *Conjunctions* □ 要不然 □ 比如	*Idiomatic Expressions* □ 就是说 *Measure Words* □ 盒 □ 双 *Names* □ 孔子 *Nouns* □ 父母 □ 长辈 □ 晚辈 □ 面子 □ 礼貌	□ 茶叶 □ 大人 □ 老人 □ 武术 □ 京剧 □ 书法 □ 文化 □ 想法 □ 礼节 □ 双手 □ 思想 □ 太极拳	*Verbs* □ 麻烦 □ 买单 □ 尊敬 □ 照顾 □ 了解 □ 重视 □ 误会 □ 交给 □ 接受 □ 放心 □ 交朋友	□ 单 □ 客 □ 次 □ 气 □ 父 □ 母 □ 麻 □ 烦 □ 辈 □ 尊 □ 敬 □ 照 □ 顾 □ 茶 □ 叶	□ 放 □ 刚 □ 武 □ 术 □ 剧 □ 化 □ 解 □ 古 □ 代 □ 复 □ 杂 □ 误 □ 双 □ 接 □ 受

USE	
□ 麻烦 to make requests □ 来 before verbs to express commencing an activity □ 要不然 to say "or else" or "otherwise" □ 正好 to express "as it happens"; "happen to…"	□ 刚 or 刚刚 to express "just now" □ Nouns with 化 to form "-ize" verbs or "-ized" adjectives □ 比如(说) to say "for instance" and give examples □ Double-了 to describe an action continuing up to the present

Technology & Modern China

第十六单元
UNIT 16

Communication Goals

Lesson 1: 线上聊天 **Chatting Online**
- Use expressions related to computers and the internet
- Discuss city lifestyles
- Understand and use the "besides" construction

Lesson 2: 一路顺风！ **Have a Safe Trip!**
- Express that you will miss someone
- Use terms for posting letters and packages as well as sending emails
- Wish someone a safe trip

线上聊天
Chatting Online

小美，我在北京找到了一份暑假实习的工作！

恭喜你！
chú le
除了了解中国的
qíng kuàng yǐ wài
工作情况以外，你
cān guān
还可以参观北京
yǒu míng jǐng diǎn
有名的景点。

北京那么大，
rén kǒu
人口那么多，我
pà
怕我会不习惯
shēng huó
那儿的生活。

biǎo gē
别担心，我的表哥
住在北京。

来，我们看看他
zài xiàn
在不在线上。

嗨，
biǎo gē
表哥，这是
我的好朋友
孙玛丽，

她今年暑假要去北京，你一定要照顾她喔！

没问题！

rén kǒu
北京虽然人口多，
shēng huó fāng biàn
但是生活很方便。可以
说是一个最现代化
chéng shì
的大城市。

有什么好玩儿的活动？

guàng hú tong
什么都有！可以逛胡同、
bù tóng   bó wù guǎn
吃很多不同的食物、去博物馆。
guàng jiē
你当然也可以去逛街、看电影。

听起来真不错。在北京
shàng wǎng
怎么能上网呢？

zì jǐ
你可以带自己的
bǐ jì běn diàn nǎo
笔记本电脑来，买
wú xiàn shàng wǎng kǎ
无线上网卡，或者
wǎng bā
去网吧。

děng
好，等我到了北京以后，
再麻烦你了！

LESSON TEXT 16.1

Chatting Online 线上聊天

Sun Mali tells Wang Xiaomei that she will be going to Beijing for an internship but that she is worried about her inability to adjust to life in a new place. Wang Xiaomei suggests they talk to her cousin, who lives there.

孙玛丽：	小美，我在北京找到了一份暑假实习的工作！	Xiǎoměi, wǒ zài Běijīng zhǎo dào le yí fèn shǔjià shíxí de gōngzuò!
王小美：	恭喜你！除了了解中国的工作情况以外，你还可以参观北京有名的景点。	Gōngxǐ nǐ! Chúle liǎojiě Zhōngguó de gōngzuò qíngkuàng yǐwài, nǐ hái kěyǐ cānguān Běijīng yǒumíng de jǐngdiǎn.
孙玛丽：	北京那么大，人口那么多，我怕我会不习惯那儿的生活。	Běijīng nàme dà, rénkǒu nàme duō, wǒ pà wǒ huì bù xíguàn nàr de shēnghuó.
王小美：	别担心，我的表哥住在北京。来，我们看看他在不在线上。	Bié dānxīn, wǒ de biǎogē zhù zài Běijīng. Lái, wǒmen kànkan tā zài bu zài xiàn shàng.

———————————

王小美：	嗨，表哥，这是我的好朋友孙玛丽，她今年暑假要去北京，你一定要照顾她喔！	Hāi, biǎogē, zhè shì wǒ de hǎo péngyou Sūn Mǎlì, tā jīnnián shǔjià yào qù Běijīng, nǐ yídìng yào zhàogù tā o!
小美的表哥：	没问题！北京虽然人口多，但是生活很方便。可以说是一个最现代化的大城市。	Méi wèntí! Běijīng suīrán rénkǒu duō, dànshì shēnghuó hěn fāngbiàn. Kěyǐ shuō shì yí ge zuì xiàndài huà de dà chéngshì.
孙玛丽：	有什么好玩儿的活动？	Yǒu shénme hǎo wánr de huódòng?
小美的表哥：	什么都有！可以逛胡同、吃很多不同的食物、去博物馆。你当然也可以去逛街、看电影。	Shénme dōu yǒu! Kěyǐ guàng hútong, chī hěn duō bù tóng de shíwù, qù bówùguǎn. Nǐ dāngrán yě kěyǐ qù guàng jiē, kàn diànyǐng.

孙玛丽：	听起来真不错。在北京怎么能上网呢？	Tīngqilai zhēn bú cuò. Zài Běijīng zěnme néng shàng wǎng ne?
小美的表哥：	你可以带自己的笔记本电脑来，买无线上网卡，或者去网吧。	Nǐ kěyǐ dài zìjǐ de bǐjìběn diànnǎo lái, mǎi wúxiàn shàng wǎng kǎ, huòzhě qù wǎngbā.
孙玛丽：	好，等我到了北京以后，再麻烦你了！	Hǎo, děng wǒ dào le Běijīng yǐhòu, zài máfan nǐ le!

LESSON VOCABULARY 16.1

	SIMPLIFIED	TRADITIONAL	PINYIN	WORD CATEGORY	DEFINITION
1.	除了		chúle	cj	in addition to; apart from; besides
2.	情况	情況	qíngkuàng	n	situation
3.	以外		yǐwài	cj	other than; except
4.	参观	參觀	cānguān	v	to tour; to visit
5.	有名		yǒumíng	adj	famous
6.	景点	景點	jǐngdiǎn	n	scenic spot
7.	人口		rénkǒu	n	population
8.	怕		pà	v	to fear, to be afraid of
9.	生活		shēnghuó	n	life; lifestyle
10.	表哥		biǎogē	n	older male cousin
11.	在线	在綫	zài xiàn	vo, adj	to be online; online
12.	方便		fāngbiàn	adj	convenient
13.	城市		chéngshì	n	city
14.	逛		guàng	v	to stroll
15.	胡同		hútong	n	hutong (old-fashioned alleys in Beijing); lane, alley
16.	不同		bùtóng	adj	different
17.	博物馆	博物館	bówùguǎn	n	museum

LESSON VOCABULARY 16.1 (continued)

	SIMPLIFIED	TRADITIONAL	PINYIN	WORD CATEGORY	DEFINITION
18.	逛街		guàng jiē	*vo*	to go shopping
19.	上网	上網	shàng wǎng	*vo*	to go online
20.	自己		zìjǐ	*pr*	oneself
21.	笔记本电脑	筆記本電腦	bǐjìběn diànnǎo	*n*	laptop computer
	笔记本	筆記本	bǐjìběn	*n*	laptop computer
22.	无线上网卡	無綫上網卡	wúxiàn shàng wǎng kǎ	*n*	wireless internet card
23.	网吧	網吧	wǎngbā	*n*	Internet café
24.	等		děng	*cj*	wait until; when

REQUIRED VOCABULARY 16.1

ACTIVITIES

25.	舞会	舞會	wǔhuì	*n*	dance party

OPTIONAL VOCABULARY 16.1

RELATED TO THE INTERNET

26.	网站	網站	wǎngzhàn	*n*	website
27.	网页	網頁	wǎngyè	*n*	webpage
28.	博客		bókè	*n*	blog

RELATED TO CELLPHONES

29.	发短信	發短信	fā duǎnxìn	*vo*	to send a text message

ACTIVITIES AND SIGHTS IN BEIJING

30.	卡拉OK		kǎlā OK	*n*	karaoke
31.	天安门	天安門	Tiān'ānmén	*n*	Tian'anmen (Gate of Heavenly Peace)

Terms for "Online"

This lesson covers the term 在线 (zài xiàn: "to be online; online"). There are, in fact, a number of words that convey this meaning. Both 线上 (xiàn shàng) and 网上 (wǎng shàng) can also be used to mean "online." Some common phrases involving these different terms are listed opposite. Remember also that, just as in English, there are separate terms for "to be online" (在线) and "to go online" (上网).

Terms	Pinyin	Meaning
在线音乐	zàixiàn yīnyuè	online music (streaming)
在线辞典	zàixiàn cídiǎn	online dictionary
线上游戏	xiànshàng yóuxì	online games
网上购物	wǎngshàng gòu wù	online shopping
网上银行	wǎngshàng yínháng	online banking

Review of Measure Words

This book has introduced a number of measure words that apply to different nouns. Presented below is a review of these measure words and some examples of what they can be paired with. It is worth remembering that other nouns in this book are partnered with measure words that may not be listed here.

Measure Word	Pinyin	Usage	Noun Examples
个	ge	most nouns	礼物，手机，人，地方
只	zhī	birds and some mammals	鸡，猫，狗，鸟
口	kǒu	people	人
条	tiáo	long, thin objects	项链，鱼，裤子
杯	bēi	cups of liquid	茶，咖啡，汽水，果汁
盘	pán	plates of food	青菜，饺子
份	fèn	portions of food	饺子，麻婆豆腐，米饭
碗	wǎn	bowls of food or liquid	米饭，酸辣汤，茶
家	jiā	businesses	饭馆，公司，商店
瓶	píng	bottles of liquid	水，汽水，茶
本	běn	books	书
张	zhāng	flat objects	书桌，床，卡，票，照片
间	jiān	rooms	卧室，厨房，客厅
块	kuài	money; a piece of something	钱，肉，蛋糕
门	mén	courses	课
件	jiàn	items; articles of clothing	事，毛衣，衬衫，外套
双	shuāng	pairs	鞋子，袜子，眼睛，手
顶	dǐng	hats	帽子
部	bù	films	电影
盒	hé	boxes of something	茶叶，糖果

Some measure words may also act as nouns in themselves. The words for "cup," "bottle," and "box" are the same as the measure words, with the addition of 子 (杯子, 瓶子, 盒子). Sometimes, a measure word and a noun may be reversed to form a new noun which carries a plural or generic connotation. For example, 一口人 (a person) becomes 人口 (population), and 一本书 (a book) becomes 书本 (books).

STRUCTURE NOTE 16.1
Use 除了...以外 *to say "besides"*

除了...以外 (chúle…yǐwài) *is a pattern that can be used to form a number of meanings with slightly different variations. When used on its own, the construction indicates "with the exception of" or "in addition to," depending on the context. The meaning can be clarified by adding an adverb to the following clause. This can either be* 还 / 也, *in which case the pattern means "in addition to" or "besides," or* 都, *in which case it means "with the exception of." In all cases,* 以外 *is optional.*

Subject + 除了 + Noun/Verb/Adjective (+ 以外) , + Verb Phrase

Subject + 除了 + Noun/Verb/Adjective (+ 以外) , + 还 / 也 + Verb Phrase

Subject + 除了 + Noun/Verb/Adjective (+ 以外) + 都 + Verb Phrase

From the Lesson Text:
除了了解中国的工作情况以外，你还可以参观北京有名的景点。

Chúle liǎojiě Zhōngguó de gōngzuò qíngkuàng yǐwài, nǐ hái kěyǐ cānguān Běijīng yǒumíng de jǐngdiǎn.

In addition to gaining an understanding of the employment situation in China, you'll also be able to visit famous sites in Beijing.

Other examples:
除了肉以外，我什么都可以吃。

Chúle ròu yǐwài, wǒ shénme dōu kěyǐ chī.

I can eat anything except for meat.

我很忙，除了明天以外，我没有时间去银行。

Wǒ hěn máng, chúle míngtiān yǐwài, wǒ méiyǒu shíjiān qù yínháng.

I'm really busy; apart from tomorrow, I don't have time to go to the bank.

Practice: Create complete sentences using 除了…以外 and the information provided below.

Example:　　　　我 / 安娜 / 也 / 喜欢打网球
　　　　　　　→ 除了我以外，安娜也喜欢打网球。

1.　　她 / 中文 / 也 / 会说法语

　　　_____

2.　　王老师 / 我们的老师 / 都 / 是男的

　　　_____

3.　　中国的节日 / 中国人 / 还 / 过西方的节日

　　　_____

4.　　大东 / 周末 / 每天 / 都 / 要上班

　　　_____

5.　　带笔记本电脑 / 你 / 也 / 可以去网吧上网

　　　_____

STRUCTURE NOTE 16.2
Use question words with 都 to express "any" or "every"

Chinese does not have special words for "everything/anything," "everywhere/anywhere," or "everyone/everything." These meanings are instead created by placing 都 after the question words 什么, 谁, and 哪儿/哪里. Because the 都 phrase must precede the verb, the object is placed before the verb when it is modified by 都.

> Subject + Question Word + 都 + Verb Phrase

> Subject + Question Word + Object + 都 + Verb Phrase

From the Lesson Text:　　有什么好玩儿的活动？
　　　　　　　　　　什么都有。
　　　　　　　　　　Yǒu shénme hǎowánr de huódòng?
　　　　　　　　　　Shénme dōu yǒu.
　　　　　　　　　　What fun things are there to do?
　　　　　　　　　　You can do anything! (literally: There is everything!)

Other examples:　　哪儿都有网吧。　　　　　　我们什么地方都可以去。
　　　　　　　　Nǎr dōu yǒu wǎngbā.　　　　Wǒmen shénme dìfang dōu kěyǐ qù.
　　　　　　　　There are Internet cafés every-　　We can go anywhere.
　　　　　　　　where.

Practice: Answer the following questions using the question word in brackets and 都, following the example given.

Example:　她在北京没有朋友吗？（谁）
→ 她刚来几天，谁都不认识。

1.　第十六课的练习容易吗？（谁）
_____

2.　这家商店卖什么东西？（什么）
_____

3.　你的课本找到了吗？（哪儿）
_____

4.　你今天晚上想去哪儿？（哪儿）
_____

5.　你去北京的时候想看哪些景点？（什么）
_____

STRUCTURE NOTE 16.3

Use 自己 to refer to oneself or another

自己 (zìjǐ) *usually corresponds to "my own," "your own," "his/her own," or "their own" in English. Watch out for the context to figure out who is being referred to.*

Pronoun + 自己

From the Lesson Text:　你可以带自己的笔记本电脑来，买无线上网卡，或者去网吧。
Nǐ kěyǐ dài zìjǐ de bǐjìběn diànnǎo lái, mǎi wúxiàn shàng wǎng kǎ, huòzhě qù wǎngbā.
You can bring your own laptop and buy a wireless card or go to an Internet café.

Other examples:　每个人都有自己的想法。　这个蛋糕是他自己做的。
Měi ge rén dōu yǒu zìjǐ de xiǎngfǎ.　Zhèi ge dàngāo shì tā zìjǐ zuò de.
Everyone has his or her own opinions.　He made this cake himself.

Practice: Change the following sentences into Chinese using 自己.

Example: I cleaned the living room myself. → 客厅是我自己打扫的。

1.   If you still don't believe me, go and look for yourself.

_____

2.   I don't have time to help you, you'll have to do your homework by yourself.

_____

3.   This isn't the school's textbook, it's the teacher's own copy.

_____

4.   He has a job now; he can pay for the sweater himself.

_____

5.   The kids made the dinner themselves.

_____

STRUCTURE NOTE 16.4

Use 等 to express "at the point when / by the time"

等 (děng) *generally means "to wait," but in some contexts it can preface a time expression in order to convey the meaning "by the time" or "when."*

等 + Time Expression + Sentence

From the Lesson Text:

等我到了北京以后，再麻烦你了！
Děng wǒ dào le Běijīng yǐhòu, zài máfan nǐ le!
When I get to Beijing, I will have to trouble you again!

Other examples:

等你买好了衣服天都黑了。
Děng nǐ mǎi hǎo le yīfu, tiān dōu hēi le.
By the time you finished buying clothes, it was dark.

等你长大了，我就带你去旅行。
Děng nǐ zhǎngdà le, wǒ jiù dài nǐ qù lǚxíng.
When you grow up, I'll take you traveling.

Practice: Complete the following sentences by matching the appropriate beginnings with the appropriate endings.

Example:　　等我们去中国旅行的时候，我就给你介绍我的中国朋友。

等我们去中国旅行的时候，	我们就可以吃年糕和饺子。
等你吃完饭，	我们可以去逛街。
等你长大了，	你就可以自己付钱买东西。
等元宵节的时候，	别的客人都走了。
等考完试以后，	我们会挂花灯。
等春节的时候，	我就给你介绍我的中国朋友。

PRACTICE 16.1

Working with a partner, answer the questions below by placing 都 after the question words 什么, 谁, or 哪儿 / 哪里, and provide an explanation for your answer. You may then practice the dialogues that you have created.

Example:
A: 这里的服务员你都认识吗？
B: 我在这里工作了两年了，所以谁都认识。

这里的服务员你都认识吗？

北京有名的景点你都去过吗？

你有没有可以联络的公司？

医生开了什么药给你？

找工作需要的东西你准备好了吗？

PRACTICE 16.2

Do a survey to find out what students would most want to do in Beijing. Record the most popular answer below.

Activity in Beijing	Number of Students

Sun Mali is chatting online with Wang Xiaomei's cousin. Working with a partner, fill in appropriate responses and questions in the spaces provided, then practice the dialogue that you have made.

嗨，我下个月要去北京。我有点紧张，因为我怕我会不习惯那儿的生活。

玛丽，你别担心，你来了以后我会好好地照顾你。

你可以问问你的公司有没有宿舍。要不然到时候我可以再帮你找找。

从车站到你的公司，走路只要十分钟。你最好不要坐出租车，因为会比较贵。

这里有中医也有西医。

长城和故宫是一定要去的。你也可以逛胡同、去博物馆。

这里的食物有辣的也有不辣的。你来到北京一定要吃北京烤鸭！如果这次来不吃的话，就像去北京不去故宫一样。

那我一定要吃！对了，在北京怎么能上网呢？

好，等我到了北京以后，再麻烦你了！

PRACTICE 16.4

Make an audio recording and send it to your teacher. In the recording, describe what you would do on a trip to Beijing. Include things such as what famous sights you would see and what you would eat.

PRACTICE 16.5

	Radical	Stroke Order
便	亻(人) rén person	丿 亻 亻 亻 仠 仠 佢 便 便
城	土 tǔ earth	一 十 土 圵 圵 坊 城 城 城
市	巾 jīn cloth	、 亠 产 方 市
街	行 xíng walk	丿 彳 彳 彳 彳 往 往 徉 徔 徔 街 街
除	阝 fù hill	阝 阝 阝 阼 阼 阼 除 除 除
况	冫(冰) bīng ice	、 冫 冫 沪 沪 沪 况
观	见 jiàn see	又 又 邓 邓 观 观
怕	忄(心) xīn heart	、 丷 忄 忄 忄 怕 怕 怕
无	无 wú negative	一 二 チ 无
线	纟(糸) sī silk	乚 纟 纟 纟 纟 线 线 线
卡	卜 bǔ divination	丨 卜 上 卡 卡
胡	肉 ròu meat	一 十 古 古 古 刮 胡 胡 胡
博	十 shí ten	一 十 十 忄 忄 忄 恒 博 博 博 博 博
自	自 zì self	丿 亻 白 白 自 自
己	己 jǐ self	丁 コ 己

PRACTICE 16.6

Type the following sentences on your computer.

1. 除了工作以外，你还可以参观有名的景点。
2. 我在北京找到了一份暑假实习的工作。
3. 我怕我会不习惯这儿的生活。
4. 北京是一个最现代化的大城市。
5. 我要带自己的笔记本电脑去。

PRACTICE 16.7

中平：

我快要去北京了。我问了小美的表哥关于在北京上网的问题，他说我可以带自己的笔记本电脑去，或者去网吧。我觉得带自己的笔记本去上网会比较方便，可是我不知道在哪里能买无线上网卡。你可以帮我找找看能在哪里买到吗？谢谢。

—玛丽

Read Sun Mali's note and answer the following questions.
1. What does Sun Mali think will be the most convenient way to go online in Beijing?
2. What does Sun Mali ask Li Zhongping to help her look for?

PRACTICE 16.8

陈大东：这次去北京你打算去哪儿玩儿？

孙玛丽：第一个地方当然是故宫！你听过吗？"没去故宫就像是没去北京一样。"

陈大东：我听过。故宫是北京最有名的景点，而且是了解中国历史的好地方。

孙玛丽：小美的表哥还建议我多逛北京的胡同和博物馆，了解一下中国的生活和文化。

陈大东：你打算去这么多地方，你知道在北京坐车方便吗？

孙玛丽：现在的北京可以说是一个最现代化的大城市，生活非常方便，所以不用担心坐车的问题。

Read the dialogue and answer the following questions.
1. What does Chen Dadong think about the Forbidden City?
2. Is Sun Mali worried about transportation in Beijing? Why?

Modern Architecture

With the construction frenzy surrounding the 2008 Beijing Olympics, the Chinese capital city emerged on the global stage as a modern metropolis and a budding architectural mecca. A number of contemporary masterpieces designed by famous architects from around the globe were erected in time for the opening ceremony of the games, and they now stand as memorable landmarks of the new-look Beijing. These are four of Beijing's most eye-catching works of modern architecture:

The Beijing National Stadium
(鸟巢 niǎocháo: "the bird's nest")
Originally designed with the practical use of concealing support beams in mind, the "nest" shape of the stadium brings to mind the Chinese culinary delicacy of a bird's nest.

The Beijing National Aquatics Center
(水立方 shuǐ lìfāng: "the water cube")
The National Aquatics center is a cube-like structure clad in plastic "bubbles," which express the purpose of the structure while cutting energy costs by allowing light and heat into the building.

The National Center for the Performing Arts
(巨蛋 jùdàn: "the giant egg")
Located near Tian'anmen Square, this giant glass-and-steel opera house sits in the center of a man-made lake, accessible only by an underwater tunnel. The curved dome makes it look like an enormous egg, hence its colloquial name.

China Central Television Headquarters
(大裤衩 dà kùchǎ: "big boxer shorts")
The CCTV headquarters is one of central Beijing's most iconic skyscrapers. Comprised of 44 stories enclosed in a complex loop, the building was designed with radical angles to appear almost as a visual puzzle. It is said that the unofficial name for this unusual structure was coined by a Beijing taxi driver.

The Internet in China

While the Internet is of course a sensation all around the world, there is no denying that it has achieved particular popularity in the People's Republic of China. As early as 2008, China had already surpassed the United States as the country with the most Internet users worldwide.

Homegrown websites have developed rapidly in China, and have on the whole proved more popular than their Western counterparts. Among other things, China has its own social networking websites, online encyclopedias, search engines, auction sites, photo sharing forums, and blog hosts. Online gaming is another popular Internet activity in China, and many games are created specifically for the Chinese market.

In order to get online, people will often go to a 网吧 (wǎngbā: "Internet café"). Another conspicuous feature of the Internet in China, these "cafés" are usually large spaces with rows and rows of terminals, like a college computer room. While personal computer ownership is on the rise, paying a small fee to go to an Internet café and chat with your friends or play online games remains a favorite pastime of many young Chinese.

孙玛丽：	小美，我在北京找到了一份暑假实习的工作！	Xiaomei, I found a summer internship in Beijing!
王小美：	恭喜你！除了了解中国的工作情况以外，你还可以参观北京有名的景点。	Congratulations! Not only will you get to learn about the work environment in China, you will also get to visit a lot of Beijing's famous attractions.
孙玛丽：	北京那么大，人口那么多，我怕我会不习惯那儿的生活。	Beijing is so big, and there are so many people, I'm worried that I won't be able to get used to life there.
王小美：	别担心，我的表哥住在北京。来，我们看看他在不在线上。	Don't worry. My cousin lives in Beijing. Let's see if he's online.

王小美：	嗨，表哥，这是我的好朋友孙玛丽，她今年暑假要去北京，你一定要照顾她喔！	Hi, cousin, this is my good friend Sun Mali. She's going to Beijing this summer. You better take care of her!
小美的表哥：	没问题！北京虽然人口多，但是生活很方便。可以说是一个最现代化的大城市。	Not a problem! Even though there are a lot of people in Beijing, life here is very convenient. It is a very modern city.
孙玛丽：	有什么好玩儿的活动？	What fun things are there to do in Beijing?
小美的表哥：	什么都有！可以逛胡同，吃很多不同的食物，去博物馆。你当然也可以去逛街、看电影。	Beijing has everything! You can walk around the old alleys, eat different types of foods, and visit museums. Of course, you can also go shopping and watch movies.
孙玛丽：	听起来真不错。在北京怎么能上网呢？	Sounds good. How can I get online in Beijing?

小美的表哥：	你可以带自己的笔记本电脑来，买无线上网卡，或者去网吧。	You can bring your own laptop and buy a wireless Internet card or go to an Internet café.
孙玛丽：	好，等我到了北京以后，再麻烦你了！	OK. When I get to Beijing, I will have to trouble you again!

What Can You Do?

INTERPRETIVE
- I can understand an article or a discussion that uses terms related to computing and the internet.

INTERPERSONAL
- I can engage in an online chat or phone call with someone.
- I can discuss tourism and city life.

PRESENTATIONAL
- I can give a presentation about a city or place which includes its size, population, and what one can do there.

一路顺风!
Have a Safe Trip!

玛丽，你一个人在那么远的地方，
bǎo zhòng　　　　　xiǎng niàn
要保重身体。我会很想念你的。

wǎng luò
现在网络这么方便，
diàn zǐ yóu jiàn
我们可以用电子邮件，
liáo tiān ruǎn jiàn
聊天软件，还是可以
天天联络。

可是，我们不能一起
liáo tiān
吃饭，见面聊天儿……

你这样说，玛丽
ān xīn　　　　la
就不能安心实习啦。

pāi　 zhào piàn
玛丽，记得多拍些照片，
放在网上给我们看。

LESSON TEXT 16.2

Have a Safe Trip! 一路顺风！

The group gathers at the airport to bid farewell to Sun Mali and talk about their respective plans for the summer break.

李中平： 玛丽，你一个人在那么远的地方，要保重身体。我会很想念你的。

Mǎlì, nǐ yí ge rén zài nàme yuǎn de dìfang, yào bǎozhòng shēntǐ. Wǒ huì hěn xiǎngniàn nǐ de.

孙玛丽： 现在网络这么方便，我们可以用电子邮件，聊天软件，还是可以天天联络。

Xiànzài wǎngluò zhème fāngbiàn, wǒmen kěyǐ yòng diànzǐ yóujiàn, liáo tiān ruǎnjiàn, háishì kěyǐ tiāntiān liánluò.

李中平： 可是，我们不能一起吃饭，见面聊天儿......

Kěshì, wǒmen bù néng yìqǐ chī fàn, jiàn miàn liáo tiānr...

张安娜： 你这样说，玛丽就不能安心实习啦。玛丽，记得多拍些照片，放在网上给我们看。

Nǐ zhèyàng shuō, Mǎlì jiù bù néng ānxīn shíxí la. Mǎlì, jìde duō pāi xiē zhàopiàn, fàng zài wǎng shàng gěi wǒmen kàn.

陈大东： 这个暑假，我和小美会去欧洲旅行，我会给你们买纪念品！

Zhèi gè shǔjià, wǒ hé Xiǎoměi huì qù Ōuzhōu lǚxíng, wǒ huì gěi nǐmen mǎi jìniànpǐn!

黄祥安： 真羡慕你们，我们要去南非乡下陪我外婆。现在那里是冬天，会冷死我的！

Zhēn xiànmù nǐmen, wǒmen yào qù Nánfēi xiāngxia péi wǒ wàipó. Xiànzài nàli shì dōngtiān, huì lěng sǐ wǒ de!

张安娜： 没关系，我们多带几件大衣就没事了！

Méi guānxi, wǒmen duō dài jǐ jiàn dàyī jiù méi shì le!

李中平： 玛丽，别忘了告诉我你的地址喔。我会寄包裹给你。

Mǎlì, biè wàng le gàosu wǒ nǐ de dìzhǐ o. Wǒ huì jì bāoguǒ gěi nǐ.

王小美： 时间到了，你应该登机了。

Shíjiān dào le, nǐ yīnggāi dēng jī le.

李中平：	到了那边，有人接你吗？	Dào le nà biān, yǒu rén jiē nǐ ma?
孙玛丽：	有。小美的表哥会来接我。	Yǒu. Xiǎoměi de biǎogē huì lái jiē wǒ.
大家：	祝你一路顺风！	Zhù nǐ yílùshùnfēng!

LESSON VOCABULARY 16.2

	SIMPLIFIED	TRADITIONAL	PINYIN	WORD CATEGORY	DEFINITION
1.	保重		bǎozhòng	v	to take care (of oneself)
2.	想念		xiǎngniàn	v	to miss (someone)
3.	网络	網絡	wǎngluò	n	the Internet
4.	电子邮件	電子郵件	diànzǐ yóujiàn	n	email
5.	聊天软件	聊天軟件	liáo tiān ruǎnjiàn	n	chat software
	聊天		liáo tiān	vo	to chat
	软件	軟件	ruǎnjiàn	n	software
6.	安心		ānxīn	adj, vo	relieved; at ease; to rest assured
7.	啦		la	p	(exclamation particle, a combination of 了 and 啊)
8.	拍		pāi	v	to shoot; to take (photos)
9.	照片		zhàopiàn	n	photograph
10.	欧洲	歐洲	Ōuzhōu	n	Europe
11.	纪念品	紀念品	jìniànpǐn	n	souvenir
12.	羡慕		xiànmù	v	to envy
13.	南非		Nánfēi	n	South Africa
14.	乡下	鄉下	xiāngxia	n	countryside
15.	陪		péi	v	to accompany; to keep sb. company
16.	外婆		wàipó	n	maternal grandmother
17.	冬天		dōngtiān	n	winter
18.	死		sǐ	v, adv	to die; extremely
19.	地址		dìzhǐ	n	address

LESSON VOCABULARY 16.2 (continued)

	SIMPLIFIED	TRADITIONAL	PINYIN	WORD CATEGORY	DEFINITION
20.	寄		jì	*v*	to send
21.	包裹		bāoguǒ	*n*	package
22.	登机	登機	dēng jī	*vo*	to board a plane
23.	接		jiē	*v*	to receive, to pick up, to meet (someone)
24.	一路顺风	一路順風	yílùshùnfēng	*ie*	have a safe flight!

REQUIRED VOCABULARY 16.2

OTHER

	SIMPLIFIED	TRADITIONAL	PINYIN	WORD CATEGORY	DEFINITION
25.	安全		ānquán	*adj*	safe
26.	发	發	fā	*v*	to send (email, text message)
27.	邮局	郵局	yóujú	*n*	post office

OPTIONAL VOCABULARY 16.2

TRAVEL AND THE AIRPORT

	SIMPLIFIED	TRADITIONAL	PINYIN	WORD CATEGORY	DEFINITION
28.	护照	護照	hùzhào	*n*	passport
29.	签证	簽證	qiānzhèng	*n*	visa
30.	大使馆	大使館	dàshǐguǎn	*n*	embassy
31.	海关	海關	hǎiguān	*n*	customs
32.	旅游	旅遊	lǚyóu	*v, n*	to travel; tour; tourism
33.	报纸	報紙	bàozhǐ	*n*	newspaper
34.	杂志	雜誌	zázhì	*n*	magazine

文化背景 LANGUAGE NOTES 语言注释

Sentence-Final Particle Review

"Sentence-final particle" is the commonly-used term for a particle that can go at the end of certain phrases in Chinese. While a few sentence-final particles have a definite grammatical function, such as 吗, which turns a sentence into a question, most sentence-final particles have a more vague function of adding a certain type of emphasis to a sentence. Often the rules about when to use particular particles are very subtle – some particles imply surprise, some imply agreement, etc.

Chinese speakers use sentence-final particles more frequently in casual speech, and particles differ considerably from region to region. Because of this, many particles do not have one standard representation in Chinese characters – for example, the sentence-final particle 喔 is also sometimes written as 哦. The particles introduced in this textbook are some of the more common particles used across different regions.

吗	ma	question	玛丽，你好吗?
吧	ba	suggestion, softening	我们点菜吧!
呢	ne	question (what about x?), marks progressive aspect	(我) 没什么活动。你呢? 玛丽他们呢?
啊	a	emphasis, surprise	我很高兴啊!
呀	ya	variant of 啊, most often following vowels	哇，她还是个音乐家呀!
啦	la	variant of 啊, combination of 了 plus 啊	你这样说，玛丽就不能安心实习啦。
喔/哦	o	surprise, emphatic reminder	玛丽，别忘了告诉我你的地址喔。
耶	ye	emphasis, surprise	吃年夜饭，最重要的是全家人在一起，跟圣诞节一样耶。

STRUCTURE NOTE 16.5

Use Verb Phrase 给 Someone 看/听 to express doing something to show someone else

In Structure Note 12.6, the pattern Subject + 帮 + Someone + Verb Phrase was introduced to express doing something for someone (帮他买东西). In the present pattern, 给 is used in a similar way. It comes after the main verb and is used to express the meaning "to do something for the purpose of showing someone," either through seeing or listening.

> Subject + Verb Phrase + 给 + Someone + 看/听

From the Lesson Text:
记得多拍些照片，放在网上给我们看。
Jìde duō pāi xiē zhàopiàn, fàng zài wǎng shàng gěi wǒmen kàn.
Remember to take some photos and put them on the Internet for us to see.

Other examples:
请说给我听。
Qǐng shuō gěi wǒ tīng.
Please say it for me.

他喜欢画画儿给妈妈看。
Tā xǐhuan huà huàr gěi māma kàn.
He likes to paint paintings to show his mother.

Practice: Match the phrases below to create complete sentences, following the example given.
Example: 饺子有点难做，来，我做给你看。

我最近开始学吉他，
你刚才说的那个字是什么字？
如果你有建议的话，
中国的国歌你没听过吗？
我今天买了一件毛衣，
饺子有点难做，来，

那我就唱给你听。
我做给你看。
可以写给我看吗？
你要我穿给你看吗？
我弹给你听好不好？
你就说给我听。

STRUCTURE NOTE 16.6

Use 陪 to express keeping someone company

Unlike 送, which means to transport or escort, 陪 (péi) specifically means to accompany someone somewhere, or stay with someone and keep them company.

> Subject + 陪 + Someone (+ Verb Phrase)

From the Lesson Text:
我们要去南非乡下陪我外婆。
Wǒmen yào qù Nánfēi xiāngxia péi wǒ wàipó.
We're going to the countryside in South Africa to visit my grandmother.

Other examples:
他陪我去参加比赛。
Tā péi wǒ qù cānjiā bǐsài.
He accompanied me to the match.

我希望你今天晚上可以陪我。
Wǒ xīwàng nǐ jīntiān wǎnshang kěyǐ péi wǒ.
I hope you can stay with me tonight.

Practice: Fill in the blanks in the following sentences by adding 送 or 陪, as appropriate.

Example: 我们下班以后，你想 ___ 我吃晚饭吗？

→ 我们下班以后，你想陪我吃晚饭吗？

1. 我也要往那边去，我 ___ 你回家吧。
2. 妈妈说我上班以前得 ___ 弟弟去学校。
3. 你可以帮我把这本书 ___ 到图书馆吗？
4. 爸爸生病了，我应该去医院 ___ 他。
5. 你今天晚上想 ___ 我去看电影吗？

STRUCTURE NOTE 16.7

Use 会…的 to stress that something will be the case

In Structure Note 3.1, it was noted that 会 *can be used to indicate the possibility of an action taking place in the future. Adding sentence-final* 的 *to this kind of expression gives the assertion a greater deal of certainty, equivalent to including the phrase* 一定 *in the sentence.*

> Subject + 会 + Verb Phrase + 的

From the Lesson Text:
我会很想念你的。
Wǒ huì hěn xiǎngniàn nǐ de.
I will miss you very much.

Other Examples:
我们会找到它的。
Wǒmen huì zhǎo dào tā de.
We're going to find it.

她会记住的。
Tā huì jì zhù de.
She will keep it in mind.

Practice: Change the following 会…的 sentences into English.

Example: 她的派对听起来很好玩，我一定会参加的。

→ Her party sounds like a lot of fun; I will definitely attend.

1. 回到家我会打电话给你的。

2. 到了中国以后我会寄照片给你看的。

3. 看这么让人难过的电影，我一定会哭的！

4. 你自己出门妈妈一定不会放心的。

5. 你要小心，你说这样的话别人会误会你的。

STRUCTURE NOTE 16.8
Use 死 to mean "extremely" or "to death"

Like the intensifier 极了 *(see Structure Note 13.8),* 死 *(sǐ) can be placed after certain adjectives as an adverb used to express a high degree. Its literal meaning is "so (adjective) that I'm going to die." Some common expressions using* 死 *are:* 冷死 *(lěng sǐ: "really cold"),* 气死 *(qì sǐ: "really angry"), and* 饿死 *(è sǐ: "really hungry").* 死 *is often followed by* 了.

Adjective + 死 (+ 了)

From the Lesson Text:　　会冷死我的!
Huì lěng sǐ wǒ de!
I'm going to freeze to death!

Other Examples:　　我饿死啦!　　　　　　　我真的气死了!
Wǒ è sǐ la!　　　　　　　Wǒ zhēnde qì sǐ le!
I'm starving!　　　　　　 I'm so angry!

Practice: Fill in the blanks in the following sentences with an appropriate adjective and the intensifier 死.

Example:　　你做了这么多菜, ___ 我了!
→ 你做了这么多菜, 饱死我了!

1.　　我今天没有时间吃早饭, ___ 我了!

2.　　北京的夏天 ___ 我了!

3.　　我下了课就得去上班, ___ 我了!

4.　　老师说儿子昨天又没有去上课, ___ 我了!

5.　　你妈妈做的酸辣汤 ___ 我了!

PRACTICE 16.9

Working with a partner, look at the information below and take it in turns to describe the problems indicated and potential solutions to those problems.

这里的手机很贵！

Example:
A: 这里的手机很贵！可是我得跟爸爸妈妈联络，怎么办？
B: 你可以用电子邮件，上网联络比较便宜。

这里的网吧很贵。

我没有他的地址。

写信很麻烦。

这里不能上网。

PRACTICE 16.10

Take a survey of the class to find out what mode of communication your classmates use most frequently to keep in touch with people. Record the most popular answer below.

Mode of Communication	Number of Students

PRACTICE 16.11

Working in groups of three or four, act out a scenario in which your friend is leaving for the summer vacation and you are seeing him/her off at the airport. Talk about how you are going to keep in touch with each other and what everyone's plans for the summer are.

↑	登机口 Gates ✈
→	海关申报 Customs Declaration
←	行李打包 Packaging
↑	洗手间 Toilets
↑	问讯、银行 Information,Banks ? ¥

PRACTICE 16.12

Imagine that you are Sun Mali. Write an email to Li Zhongping explaining to him that you have taken pictures and you have put them on the Internet. In addition, discuss life in Beijing. Describe the souvenirs you have bought and tell him that you have sent them to him. Read your email to the class after you have finished.

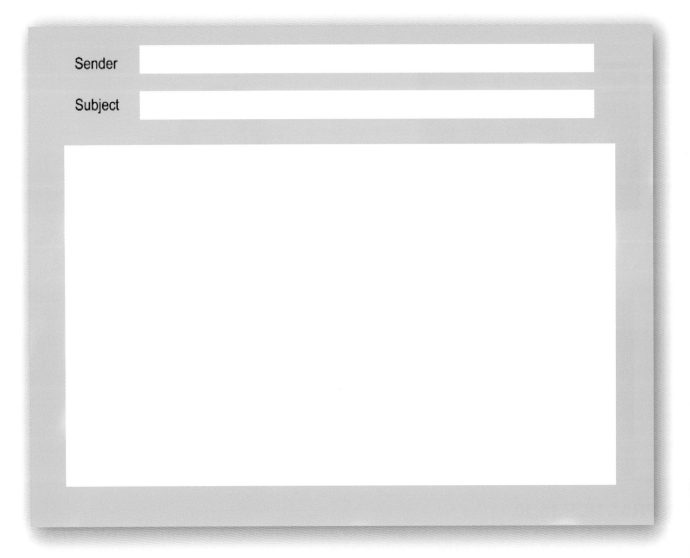

Sender

Subject

PRACTICE 16.13

Make an audio recording and send it to your teacher. In the recording, discuss what you plan to do during the summer vacation. Will you find a job or an internship? Will you go traveling? Explain the reasons for your decisions.

	Radical	Stroke Order
品	口 kǒu mouth	丶 丨 口 口 吊 吊 品 品 品
软	车 chē cart	一 �десь 车 车 轫 轫 软 软
片	片 piàn slice	丿 丿 ㄏ 片
纪	纟(糸) sī silk	乚 纟 纟 纟 纪 纪
留	田 tián field	丶 丿 ㄠ 丣 勹 勿 卯 留 留 留
继	纟(糸) sī silk	乚 纟 纟 纟 纟 纟 绊 绊 继 继
续	纟(糸) sī silk	乚 纟 纟 纟 纟 续 续 续 续 续
乡	乙 yǐ secon heav-enly stem	乚 纟 乡
婆	女 nǚ female	丶 丶 氵 氵 氵 泸 波 波 婆 婆
寄	宀 mián roof	丶 丶 宀 宀 宀 安 安 宀 宇 寄
登	癶 bò legs	乛 丆 丷 癶 癶 癶 癶 登 登 登 登 登
路	足 zú foot	丶 丨 口 口 丮 丮 丮 丮 趵 趵 政 政 路 路
顺	页 yè page	丿 丿 川 川 川 川 顺 顺 顺
风	风 fēng wind	丿 几 风 风
安	宀 mián roof	丶 丶 宀 宀 安 安

PRACTICE 16.15

Type the following sentences on your computer.

1. 我会很想念你的。
2. 我们可以用电子邮件和聊天软件联络。
3. 祝你一路顺风!
4. 你会寄包裹给我吗?
5. 南非的冬天冷死我了!

PRACTICE 16.16

Sender	中平
Subject	实习

玛丽：

我寄给你的包裹你收到了吗？那是我去西班牙玩的时候买的纪念品，是一条很特别的项链，希望你会喜欢。

最近你好像都不在线上，你不是说每天都会寄电子邮件给我吗？上个月你把两三张照片放在网上以后，你就没有再放了。你实习的工作很忙吗？听朋友说这个星期北京的天气冷了，你要记得多穿衣服才出门。我下个月也要去加拿大实习，以后可能会更忙，但是我们一定要继续联络喔！

Read the email and answer the following questions.
1. What did Li Zhongping buy for Sun Mali?
2. What does Li Zhongping hope that he and Sun Mali can continue to do in the future?

PRACTICE 16.17

Sender	祥安
Subject	南非

大东：

你好吗？我跟安娜都很想念你。我们快要从南非回来了！来了南非以后，我一直陪着安娜去逛街买东西，累死我了！因为这样，我外婆有点不高兴。

Read the email and answer the following questions.
1. Where was Huang Xiang'an when he wrote the email?
2. Why has he been so tired?

PRACTICE 16.18

陈大东：小美，你来看看祥安发给我的电子邮件，还有他们在南非拍的照片。

王小美：真羡慕他们，安娜看起来在南非玩得很开心。

陈大东：安娜怎么买了这么多东西啊？

王小美：我们也把在欧洲旅行的照片放在网上给他们看吧！告诉他我们在欧洲买了纪念品给他们，还有问问他们什么时候回来，要不要我们去机场接他们……

陈大东：好，好，好，说慢一点。

王小美：快一点吧！时间到了，你忘了我们八点要跟中平去看电影吗？

Read the dialogue and answer the following questions.
1. What does Chen Dadong show to Wang Xiaomei?
2. What does Wang Xiaomei ask Chen Dadong to write in the email?

Cell Phones in China

China has become the world's largest mobile phone market in recent years, with the total number of cellphone user accounts surpassing 900 million in 2011. That number seems even larger when one considers the number of accounts was just over 400 million in 2006. The market expansion has grown rapidly as the wealth of the average Chinese citizen steadily increases and luxuries like a smartphone, which are simultaneously dropping in price, become more readily available. Cellphone use is not restricted to the major metropolitan areas, either; all over the country, people are buying mobile phones and getting hooked on their ease and efficiency.

High-Speed Rail and the Maglev Train

The Maglev

The Maglev is a railway system that works by using magnets to suspend the train above the tracks, a method that makes the ride smoother and quicker. Shanghai's Maglev Train, or 上海磁浮示范运营线 (Shànghǎi Cífú Shìfàn Yùnyíng Xiàn: "Shanghai Magnetic Levitation Demonstration Operation Line") was the first commercial high-speed Maglev line in the world, with record speeds of over 400 km/h. The journey from Shanghai Pudong International Airport to the Longyang Road station in central Shanghai spans roughly 30 kilometers and takes only 7.5 minutes. The train's top speed is around 431 km/h, making it the world's fastest train in regular commercial service to date.

China's HSR Network

Following the launch of a number of joint projects between Chinese and foreign companies, China's 中国高速铁路 (Zhōngguó Gāosù Tiělù: "China High-Speed Rail") has expanded at astronomical rates. To date, this system already spans over 8,000 kilometers and is the longest high-speed rail network in the world. Certain lines have reached speeds of up to 350 km/h and it is projected that the network will span roughly 25,000 kilometers upon scheduled completion in 2020. These higher-speed trains are expected to allow more trains to share the tracks and improve overall rail transport capacity. As a result, the Chinese government not only expects an increase in job opportunities for rail laborers, but also anticipates elevated levels of transport efficiency and economic growth.

李中平： 玛丽，你一个人在那么远的地方，要保重身体。我会很想念你的。

Mali, you're going to be on your own in such a far-off place; you must take care of yourself. I will miss you very much.

孙玛丽： 现在网络这么方便，我们可以用电子邮件，聊天软件，还是可以天天联络。

The internet is so convenient these days; we can use email or chat services to talk to each other every day.

李中平： 可是，我们不能一起吃饭，见面聊天儿……

But we won't be able to have meals together or hang out.

张安娜： 你这样说，玛丽就不能安心实习啦。玛丽，记得多拍些照片，放在网上给我们看。

If you keep on like that Mali won't be able to keep her mind on her internship. Mali, remember to take some photos and put them on the Internet for us to see.

陈大东： 这个暑假，我和小美会去欧洲旅行，我会给你们买纪念品！

This summer, Xiaomei and I are going traveling in Europe. I'll buy souvenirs for all of you!

黄祥安： 真羡慕你们，我们要去南非乡下陪我外婆。现在那里是冬天，会冷死我的！

I'm so envious of you. We're going to the countryside in South Africa to visit my grandmother. It's winter there right now; I'm going to freeze to death!

张安娜： 没关系，我们多带几件大衣就没事了！

Don't worry, we'll bring a few extra jackets and we'll be fine!

李中平： 玛丽，别忘了告诉我你的地址喔。我会寄包裹给你。

Mali, don't forget to tell me your address. I will send you packages.

王小美： 时间到了，你应该登机了。

It's time. You should get on the plane.

李中平： 到了那边，有人接你吗？

Is someone picking you up when you get there?

孙玛丽：　有。小美的表哥会来接我。

Yeah. Xiaomei's cousin will come pick me up.

大家：　　祝你一路顺风！

Have a safe trip!

What Can You Do?

INTERPRETIVE
- I can understand the terms used for posting letters, packages, and emails.

INTERPERSONAL
- I can discuss and use different modes of communication such as email and chat software.
- I can exchange the appropriate leave-taking expressions when seeing someone off.

PRESENTATIONAL
- I can give a detailed presentation about a trip I have taken or plan to take.

ACT IT OUT

Working in groups, compose an original three-minute skit that utilizes the vocabulary and structures introduced in Unit 16. Each of you should assume a role and have a roughly equal number of lines in the skit. Be prepared to perform your skit in class. You can either come up with your own story or choose from one of the following situations:

A) Your cousins from out of town just flew in to visit you for the first time.

B) You and your friends look online to decide what to do when you visit China.

C) You and your friends are planning a vacation and need to compare various modes of transportation.

CHECK WHAT YOU CAN DO

RECOGNIZE				WRITE	
Adjectives	*Nouns*	□ 照片	□ 逛	□ 便	□ 品
□ 有名	□ 情况	□ 纪念品	□ 逛街	□ 城	□ 软
□ 方便	□ 景点	□ 乡下	□ 上网	□ 市	□ 片
□ 不同	□ 人口	□ 外婆	□ 保重	□ 街	□ 纪
□ 安心	□ 生活	□ 冬天	□ 想念	□ 除	□ 留
□ 安全	□ 表哥	□ 地址	□ 拍	□ 况	□ 继
	□ 城市	□ 包裹	□ 羡慕	□ 观	□ 续
Adverbs	□ 胡同		□ 陪	□ 怕	□ 乡
□ 死	□ 博物馆	*Particles*	□ 寄	□ 无	□ 婆
	□ 网吧	□ 啦	□ 登机	□ 线	□ 寄
Conjunctions	□ 笔记本电脑		□ 接	□ 卡	□ 登
□ 除了	□ 无线上网卡	*Pronouns*		□ 胡	□ 路
□ 以外	□ 舞会	□ 自己		□ 博	□ 顺
□ 等	□ 电子邮件			□ 自	□ 风
	□ 聊天软件	*Verbs*		□ 己	□ 安
Idiomatic Expressions		□ 参观			
□ 一路顺风		□ 怕			
		□ 在线			

USE	
□ 除了…以外 to say "besides"	□ Verb Phrase 给 Someone 看/听 to express doing something to show someone else
□ Question words with 都 to express "any" or "every"	□ 陪 to express keeping someone company
□ 自己 to refer to oneself or another	□ 会…的 to stress that something will be the case
□ 等 to express "at the point when / by the time"	□ 死 to mean "extremely" or "to death"

附录
APPENDIX

第九單元

第一課　買衣服

售貨員：　歡迎光臨！

王小美：　你今天想買甚麼衣服？

孫瑪麗：　我想買毛衣、襯衫，還有裙子。走吧，我們去看毛衣。

張安娜：　這件毛衣太大了，你應該穿中號的或者小號的。

————————

孫瑪麗：　這件很漂亮，你覺得呢？

張安娜　　我覺得這件看起來比那件更大！

孫瑪麗：　可是這件比那件便宜一點。

張安娜：　你看，這件紅色的毛衣是中號的，又漂亮又便宜。

孫瑪麗：　不錯啊！裙子呢？

張安娜：　這條裙子跟那件毛衣一樣便宜，也很配。

第二課　你喜歡甚麼顏色?

孫瑪麗：　嗨，祥安，進來吧！我看，你應該買新褲子了。

黃祥安：　不用啊，這條還可以穿。我很喜歡這條長褲 —

孫瑪麗：　安娜，我先走了，祥安需要幫忙，幫他找一找吧！

張安娜：　沒問題！祥安，你喜歡甚麼顏色?

————————————

黃祥安：　我最喜歡藍色。黑色，灰色或者黃色也可以。

張安娜：　明白了。這條黑黑的牛仔褲怎麼樣? 大小合適嗎? 試試看！

黃祥安：　這條有一點兒短......

張安娜：　不短！我覺得很合適，你看起來好酷。

黃祥安：　哦 — 真的嗎? 好！就這條。

第十單元

第一課　星期六的活動

張安娜：　大家都很忙，都沒空！看看祥安在不在。

黃祥安：　喂，安娜！你好！

張安娜：　嗨，祥安，你在做甚麼？

黃祥安：　我一邊吃飯一邊跟你說話啊！

張安娜：　哈哈，我是說，今天是星期六，你有甚麼活動嗎？

黃祥安：　沒甚麼活動。你呢？瑪麗他們呢？

張安娜：　他們有的去打球，有的去游泳，還有的去跑步，可是我對這些活動都沒有興趣。

────────────

黃祥安：　那你喜歡做甚麼？

張安娜：　我常常去跳舞 、唱歌、看電影…

黃祥安：　是嗎？我今天晚上八點要去看一部新的功夫電影。你想跟我一起去嗎？

張安娜：　哦！聽起來很有意思。

黃祥安：　好吧，你能不能七點五十分在電影院門口等我？

張安娜：　行，晚上見。

孫瑪麗：　大東，中平，你們下個周末有空嗎？

李中平：　有甚麼特別的事嗎？

孫瑪麗：　星期六小美會在音樂會表演，我們一起去看，好不好？

———————————————

陳大東：　哇，小美真是個天才！念書念得好，網球打得好，畫畫兒也畫得好，還是個音樂家呀！

李中平：　她今天表演甚麼呢？

孫瑪麗：　她要彈吉他。她最近每天都練習五六個小時，很認真！

李中平：　瑪麗，你不是會拉小提琴嗎？你也是個天才！

孫瑪麗：　哪裏，哪裏！大東拉得比我更好！

孫瑪麗：　小美出來了！你們看，她笑得這麼開心。

李中平：　喂，大東，爲甚麼小美只對你笑呢？

第一課　約會

陳大東：　小美，你的表演真棒！我可以請你去吃晚飯嗎？

王小美：　好啊！瑪麗、中平他們也一起去嗎？

陳大東：　我想就只有我和你……

王小美：　哦……好的！

陳大東：　我晚點兒跟你說在哪兒見面。

王小美：　好，你再打電話告訴我吧！

───────────

陳大東：　我真的緊張得不得了。這是我第一次跟小美約會。

黃祥安：　你喜歡小美的哪一點？

陳大東：　她很聰明、善良，也很可愛。

黃祥安：　女孩子都希望聽別人說她美。你不要忘記對她說喔。

陳大東：　甚麼？我會記不住！

黃祥安：　你還要讓她知道，你對她的感情是真的！

陳大東：　祥安！不要鬧了，你還有甚麼建議嗎？

黃祥安：　吃完飯，你可以跟她去公園散散步，再約她下次出去玩。

第二課　分手

孫瑪麗：　安娜，你怎麼了？發生了甚麼事？可以跟我説説嗎？

張安娜：　我……跟我的男朋友分手了。

孫瑪麗：　哦，別難過了！

張安娜：　我不是難過，我是非常生氣。

孫瑪麗：　他做甚麼了？

張安娜：　我被他騙了。他跟我交往的時候，還一直跟他在俄羅斯的女朋友有聯絡。

———————————

孫瑪麗：　真的嗎？怎麼會這樣？

張安娜：　我們還談過結婚的事，可是現在……

孫瑪麗：　唉，別哭了。就忘了他吧。

張安娜：　可是我做不到，我從來沒有這麼愛過一個人。

孫瑪麗：　你會找到一個更好的男朋友。

第一課　生病了

黃祥安：　安娜，你還好嗎？你看起來不舒服，你生病了嗎？

張安娜：　我想是吧。我跟男朋友分手了以後，天天睡不著。我肚子疼，頭也很疼。

黃祥安：　最近天氣冷得很，你要注意身體啊！你的眼睛和鼻子都紅了，你最好去看病。

張安娜：　可是現在下雨了，我不想出去⋯⋯

黃祥安：　我可以送你去啊！你在這兒等我，我馬上回來。

張安娜：　好吧，謝謝！

————————————

黃祥安：　我認識一個很好的中醫。我帶你去他那兒看看好不好？

張安娜：　中醫？爲甚麼不去看西醫？

黃祥安：　他真的很不錯。

張安娜：　好，試試吧。

第二課　　付現金還是刷卡?

醫生：　　　來，請坐。你哪兒不舒服?

張安娜：　我頭疼，肚子也不舒服。

醫生：　　　你的眼睛紅紅的，而且有點發燒了。請你張開嘴巴，讓我看看你的舌頭。

醫生：　　　你的感冒不是很嚴重。

張安娜：　需要打針嗎?

醫生：　　　中醫不用打針。 我幫你開一周的藥，吃完就沒事了。

張安娜：　中藥會很苦嗎?

醫生：　　　別擔心。 等一會兒，護士會告訴你怎麼吃。記住，你要多喝水，好好兒地休息。

張安娜：　謝謝醫生，我一定會記得。

————————————

黃祥安：　醫生說甚麼?

張安娜：　還好，他說我感冒了。

護士：　　　這是你的藥， 一天兩次，吃七天。

黃祥安：　大衣穿好，外面又下雨了。

護士：　　　你的男朋友對你真好。

張安娜：　他……只是好朋友!

第一課　打工

陳大東：　小美！沒想到你會來看我！

王小美：　我想看看你打工的地方。這裏環境真不錯，你每天在這兒工作幾小時？

陳大東：　我每天晚上從八點到十二點上班。

王小美：　你十二點才下班，難怪晚上很少見到你。

─────────────

王小美：　你在這兒都做些甚麼樣的事？

陳大東：　我要泡咖啡、做收銀、還要打掃厨房。

王小美：　聽起來很忙啊！

陳大東：　我以前只管打掃。老板看我很努力，慢慢地就讓我管更多的事了。

王小美：　你不但要上學，而且還要工作。這樣一天到晚都很忙，不會太累嗎？

陳大東：　雖然累一點，但是我想賺錢，這樣的話，今年暑假可以出國旅行。

王小美：　大東，你一定做得到！加油！

第二課　去中國實習

孫瑪麗：　劉老師，我打算今年夏天去中國，在中國公司裏實習。
　　　　　您有甚麼建議嗎？
　　　　　我已經準備了一份簡歷，介紹我的背景和工作經驗。
劉老師：　好極了！你想找甚麼樣的工作？在中國有很多機會。
孫瑪麗：　我畢業後想要做跟商務有關的事。

————————————

劉老師：　首先，在中國關係很重要。你可以先問問你的中國朋
　　　　　友。他們可以幫你跟他們認識的公司聯絡。
　　　　　我也可以幫你問一下我的朋友。在那裏有很多外國公司
　　　　　和中國公司都需要你這樣的人才。
孫瑪麗：　謝謝老師！
劉老師：　祝你今年夏天實習成功！

第一課　新年快樂！

孫瑪麗：　小美，你家真漂亮，有這麼多紅色的裝飾。

王小美：　中國人過春節喜歡用紅色來裝飾，這是傳統習慣。

張安娜：　難怪你要我們今天穿紅色的衣服。你看，我戴了紅帽子。那，祥安，你呢？

黃祥安：　我穿著紅襪子！

王小美：　你們見到我的爸媽的時候，要説"恭喜發財"！

————————

大家：　　伯父伯母，恭喜發財！

小美媽：　新年快樂！

小美爸：　來來來，每個人都有一個紅包，祝你們學業進步，萬事如意。

孫瑪麗：　謝謝！祝伯父伯母身體健康。

小美媽：　請坐，先吃些糖果，我去拿年糕和瓜子。

李中平：　伯父，您這兒有那麼多的花燈啊！

小美爸：　是啊，元宵節快要到了，我們會挂花燈，放烟火，會非常熱鬧。到時候歡迎你們再來玩兒！

王小美：　今天我們吃年夜飯。過年，我們習慣吃魚。因爲"魚"聽起來像"多餘"的"餘"，所以吃魚就是希望"年年有餘"。

李中平：　吃年夜飯，最重要的是全家人在一起，跟聖誕節一樣耶。

小美爸：　我們過節都有傳統的食物。中秋節要吃月餅，春節吃魚、吃年糕。你們呢？

孫瑪麗：　我們家感恩節一定會吃火鷄。

————————————————

黃祥安：　我們家好像每天都在過節，每天都吃大餐！

孫瑪麗：　我記得有一個中國節日是吃粽子的 ……

王小美：　那是端午節。端午節的時候還會有划龍舟比賽。

張安娜：　哇，中國的節日那麼多，中國人還過西方節日嗎？

王小美：　現在有一些西方節日在中國越來越流行。

小美爸：　比方説，在中國有的年輕人會參加萬聖節派對。

陳大東：　沒想到中國人連萬聖節都會過啊！

第十五單元

第一課　　有禮貌

小美爸：　服務員，麻煩您，買單。

陳大東：　小美，今天晚上應該是我請客，讓我來買單吧。

王小美：　今天晚飯是我父母請你。

陳大東：　爲甚麼？

王小美：　因爲中國傳統是長輩要照顧晚輩，所以你讓他們請客
　　　　　是尊敬他們。

──────────

陳大東：　可是我真的很想請他們。

王小美：　下次吧。今天，你應該給他們一點兒面子，要不然他
　　　　　們會不高興。

陳大東：　給他們面子是甚麼意思？

王小美：　就是說，今天讓他們請你吃飯。

陳大東：　好吧，我應該對你的父母表示尊敬。

王小美：　第一次見面，你可以送他們一份禮物。我正好買了一
　　　　　盒茶葉，給你送他們吧。

陳大東：　小美，你太好了！

陳大東：　謝謝伯父伯母。

小美爸：　哪裏哪裏。

陳大東：　這是我送你們的小禮物，很希望下次可以請你們吃
　　　　　飯。

小美媽：　別客氣！你們還是學生，我們是長輩，應該照顧你
　　　　　們。

第二課　了解中國文化

孫瑪麗：　中平，快來看看這些書，我剛剛在中文書店買的。

李中平：　武術、京劇、書法……怎麼都是中國傳統文化的東西？

孫瑪麗：　我暑假要去中國實習，所以想先了解一下中國的文化。

李中平：　甚麼？那些都太古老了，現代的中國很不一樣吧。

孫瑪麗：　雖然中國已經現代化了，可是傳統文化還很重要。比方說，孔子的想法還是很被重視的。

———————————

孫瑪麗：　中國人的禮節很複雜，如果你做得不對，很容易發生誤會。

黃祥安：　沒錯，比如，一個人把東西交給你，你該怎麼樣？

孫瑪麗：　我要用雙手接受。用一隻手接是不禮貌的。

黃祥安：　這樣我就放心了，你已經學了很多了。你可以去中國交很多新朋友！

李中平：　有了新朋友，不要忘記老朋友喔！

第十六單元

第一課　綫上聊天

孫瑪麗：　小美，我在北京找到了一份暑假實習的工作！

王小美：　恭喜你！除了了解中國的工作情況以外，你還可以參觀北京有名的景點。

孫瑪麗：　北京那麼大，人口那麼多，我怕我會不習慣那兒的生活。

王小美：　別擔心，我的表哥住在北京。來，我們看看他在不在綫上。

王小美：　嗨，表哥，這是我的好朋友孫瑪麗，她今年暑假要去北京，你一定要照顧她喔！

小美的
表哥：　沒問題！北京雖然人口多，但是生活很方便。可以説是一個最現代化的大城市。

孫瑪麗：　有甚麼好玩兒的活動？

小美的
表哥：　甚麼都有！可以逛胡同、吃很多不同的食物、去博物館。你當然也可以去逛街、看電影。

孫瑪麗：　聽起來真不錯。在北京怎麼能上網呢？

小美的
表哥：　你可以帶自己的筆記本電腦來，買無綫上網卡，或者去網吧。

孫瑪麗：　好，等我到了北京以後，再麻煩你了！

李中平：　瑪麗，你一個人在那麼遠的地方，要保重身體。我會很想念你的。

孫瑪麗：　現在網絡這麼方便，我們可以用電子郵件，聊天軟件，還是可以天天聯絡。

李中平：　可是，我們不能一起吃飯，見面聊天兒……

張安娜：　你這樣說，瑪麗就不能安心實習啦。瑪麗，記得多拍些照片，放在網上給我們看。

———————————

陳大東：　這個暑假，我和小美會去歐洲旅行，我會給你們買紀念品！

黃祥安：　真羨慕你們，我們要去南非鄉下陪我外婆。現在那裏是冬天，會冷死我的！

張安娜：　沒關係，我們多帶幾件大衣就沒事了！

李中平：　瑪麗，別忘了告訴我你的地址喔。我會寄包裹給你。

王小美：　時間到了，你應該登機了。

李中平：　到了那邊，有人接你嗎？

孫瑪麗：　有。小美的表哥會來接我。

大家：　　祝你一路順風！

Vocabulary Index (Chinese-English)

The Chinese-English index is alphabetized according to pinyin. Required Vocabulary is shown in purple. Optional Vocabulary is shown in green.

Characters	Pinyin	Word Category	Definition	Lesson
A				
唉	ài	interj	(expresses sadness, sympathy, disappointment etc.)	11.2
爱	ài	v	to love	11.2
安全	ānquán	adj	safe	16.2
安心	ānxīn	adj, vo	relieved; at ease; to rest assured	16.2
B				
白色	báisè	n	white	9.2
办法	bànfǎ	n	way; means	15.2
帮忙	bāng máng	vo	to help	9.2
棒	bàng	adj	great; wonderful	11.1
包裹	bāoguǒ	n	package	16.2
保重	bǎozhòng	v	to take care (of oneself)	16.2
报纸	bàozhǐ	n	newspaper	16.2
悲剧	bēijù	n	tragedy	10.1
被	bèi	prep	by (passive)	11.2
背景	bèijǐng	n	background	13.2
鼻子	bízi	n	nose	12.1
比	bǐ	prep	compared to	9.1
比方说	bǐ fāngshuō	ie	for example	14.2
笔记本	bǐjìběn	n	laptop computer	16.1
笔记本电脑	bǐjìběn diànnǎo	n	laptop computer	16.1
比如	bǐ rú	cj	for instance	15.2
毕业	bì yè	vo	to graduate	13.2
表哥	biǎogē	n	older male cousin	16.1
表示	biǎoshì	v	to express	15.1
表演	biǎoyǎn	v, n	to perform; performance	10.2
别人	biérén	n	other people	11.1

Characters	Pinyin	Word Category	Definition	Lesson
伯父	bófù	n	uncle (polite term of address for a man of one's parents' generation)	14.1
博客	bókè	n	blog	16.1
伯母	bómǔ	n	aunt (polite term of address for a woman of one's parents' generation)	14.1
博物馆	bówùguǎn	n	museum	16.1
不但	búdàn	cj	not only	13.1
不要	bú yào	adv	don't	11.1
不要闹了	bú yào nào le	ie	stop it! (used when others are not being serious, poking fun at someone)	11.1
部	bù	mw	(used for movies)	10.1
不常	bùcháng	adv	not often; seldom	10.1
不得了	bùdeliǎo	adv	(to a degree)	11.1
不同	bùtóng	adj	different	16.1

C

Characters	Pinyin	Word Category	Definition	Lesson
猜谜	cāi mí	vo	to guess a riddle	14.1
参观	cānguān	v	to tour; to visit	16.1
参加	cānjiā	v	to take part in, to participate in	14.2
茶叶	cháyè	n	tea leaves	15.1
常常	chángcháng	adv	often	10.1
唱歌	chàng gē	vo	to sing	10.1
吵架	chǎo jià	vo	to quarrel; to fight	11.2
长裤	chángkù	adj	pants, trousers (lit. "long pants")	9.2
衬衫	chènshān	n	shirt	9.1
成功	chénggōng	v, n	to succeed; success	13.2
橙色	chéngsè	n	orange	9.2
城市	chéngshì	n	city	16.1
吃药	chī yào	vo	to take medicine	12.2
出国	chū guó	vo	to leave the country	13.1
出来	chūlai	dc	to emerge; come out	10.2
出去	chūqu	dc	to go outside	11.1
出去玩(儿)	chūqu wánr	ie	to go out and play, have a good time	11.1
厨房	chúfáng	n	kitchen	13.1
除了	chúle	cj	in addition to; apart from; besides	16.1
厨师	chúshī	n	cook, chef	13.1

Characters	Pinyin	Word Category	Definition	Lesson
除夕	Chúxī	n	(Chinese) New Year's Eve	14.1
穿	chuān	v	to wear	9.1
传统	chuántǒng	adj, n	traditional; tradition	14.1
春节	Chūnjié	n	Spring Festival	14.1
春天	chūntiān	n	spring	12.1
次	cì	mw	(used to describe the frequency of an action)	11.1
聪明	cōngmíng	adj	smart, intelligent	11.1
从来	cónglái	adv	always, all along; never (when used in the negative)	11.2

D

Characters	Pinyin	Word Category	Definition	Lesson
打工	dǎ gōng	vo	to work part-time; to temp	13.1
打鼓	dǎ gǔ	vo	to play the drums	10.2
打球	dǎ qiú	vo	to play ball	10.1
打扫	dǎsǎo	v	to clean up; to sweep	13.1
打针	dǎ zhēn	vo	to give or have an injection	12.2
大餐	dàcān	n	a large feast	14.2
大人	dàrén	n	adults	15.1
大使馆	dàshǐguǎn	n	embassy	16.2
大提琴	dàtíqín	n	cello	10.2
大小	dàxiǎo	n	size	9.2
大衣	dàyī	n	overcoat	12.2
带	dài	v	to bring	12.1
戴	dài	v	to wear (for glasses and hats)	14.1
担心	dānxīn	v	to worry	12.2
当	dāng	v	to serve as, to be (a profession)	13.2
得罪	dézuì	v	to offend; to displease	15.1
地	de	p	(used to express the manner in which an action is performed)	12.2
登机	dēng jī	vo	to board a plane	16.2
等	děng	v	to wait	10.1
等	děng	cj	wait until; when	16.2
地址	dìzhǐ	n	address	16.2
点	diǎn	n	point, characteristic	11.1
电影	diànyǐng	n	movie	10.1
电影院	diànyǐngyuàn	n	cinema, movie theater	10.1

Characters	Pinyin	Word Category	Definition	Lesson
电子邮件	diànzǐ yóujiàn	n	email	16.2
顶	dǐng	mw	(used for hats)	9.1
冬天	dōngtiān	n	winter	16.2
肚子	dùzi	n	stomach	12.1
端午节	Duānwǔjié	n	Dragon-Boat Festival	14.2
短	duǎn	adj	short	9.2
对	duì	prep	at; toward	10.1
多余	duōyú	n, adj	surplus; superfluous	14.2

E

Characters	Pinyin	Word Category	Definition	Lesson
而且	érqiě	cj	furthermore; and also	12.2

F

Characters	Pinyin	Word Category	Definition	Lesson
发	fā	v	to send (email, text message)	16.2
发短信	fā duǎnxìn	vo	to send a text message	16.1
发烧	fā shāo	vo	to have a fever	12.2
发生	fāshēng	v	to happen	11.2
翻译	fānyì	v, n	to translate; translation; translator	13.2
方便	fāngbiàn	adj	convenient	16.1
放	fàng	v	to put; to set off	14.1
放心	fàngxīn	v	to put one's mind at ease	15.2
非常	fēicháng	adv	very, extremely	11.2
分手	fēn shǒu	vo	to break up	11.2
复活节	Fùhuójié	n	Easter	14.2
父母	fùmǔ	n	parents (formal)	15.1
父亲节	Fùqīnjié	n	Father's Day	14.2
复杂	fùzá	adj	complex, complicated	15.2

G

Characters	Pinyin	Word Category	Definition	Lesson
干净	gānjìng	adj	clean	13.1
感恩节	Gǎn'ēnjié	n	Thanksgiving	14.2
感冒	gǎnmào	v	to catch/have a cold; a cold	12.2
感情	gǎnqíng	n	feeling, emotion	11.1
刚刚	gānggāng	adv	just	15.2
钢琴	gāngqín	n	piano	10.2
高傲	gāo'ào	adj	arrogant	15.1

Characters	Pinyin	Word Category	Definition	Lesson
高尔夫球	gāo'ěrfūqiú	n	golf	10.1
告诉	gàosu	v	to tell	11.1
更	gèng	adv	even more	9.1
工程师	gōngchéngshī	n	engineer	13.2
功夫	gōngfu	n	Kung Fu	10.1
公司	gōngsī	n	company	13.2
恭喜	gōngxǐ	v	to congratulate	14.1
恭喜发财	gōngxǐ fācái	ie	wishing you happiness and prosperity (greeting used during the New Year)	14.1
公园	gōngyuán	n	park	11.1
古代	gǔdài	adj, n	ancient; ancient times	15.2
古典音乐	gǔdiǎn yīnyuè	n	classical music	10.2
古老	gǔlǎo	adj	ancient; old-fashioned	15.2
瓜子	guāzǐ	n	melon seeds	14.1
挂	guà	v	to hang	14.1
关系	guānxi	n	relation; relationship; connections	13.2
官员	guānyuán	n	official	13.2
管	guǎn	v	to be in charge of	13.1
光明节	Guāngmíngjié	n	Hanukkah	14.2
逛	guàng	v	to stroll	16.1
逛街	guàng jiē	vo	to go shopping	16.1
过	guò	v	to spend (the holiday, an occasion)	14.1
过节	guò jié	vo	to celebrate a festival	14.2
过年	guò nián	vo	to celebrate the New Year	14.2
过	guo	p	(used after a verb to indicate a past experience)	11.2

H

Characters	Pinyin	Word Category	Definition	Lesson
嗨	hāi	ie	hi	9.2
还好	háihǎo	adj	not bad; OK; so-so	12.1
海关	hǎiguān	n	customs	16.2
好看	hǎokàn	adj	pretty; good-looking	11.1
好听	hǎo tīng	adj	lovely; pleasant (to the ear)	10.2
好像	hǎoxiàng	adv	apparently; it appears; it seems like	14.2
号	hào	n	size	9.1
盒	hé	n, mw	box; a box of	15.1
合适	héshì	adj	suitable	9.2

Characters	Pinyin	Word Category	Definition	Lesson
黑色	hēisè	n	black	9.2
很少	hěnshǎo	adv	very infrequently; rarely	13.1
红包	hóngbāo	n	red envelope	14.1
红色	hóngsè	n	red	9.1
胡同	hútong	n	hutong (old-fashioned alleys in Beijing); lane, alley	16.1
护士	hùshi	n	nurse	12.2
护照	hùzhào	n	passport	16.2
花灯	huādēng	n	festive/decorative lantern	14.1
划	huá	v	to row	14.2
画儿	huàr	n	painting; drawing	10.2
画画(儿)	huà huà(r)	vo	to paint; to draw	10.2
画家	huàjiā	n	artist	13.2
坏	huài	adj	bad	11.2
环境	huánjìng	n	environment	13.1
黄色	huángsè	n	yellow	9.2
灰色	huīsè	n	gray	9.2
活动	huódòng	n	activity	10.1
火鸡	huǒjī	n	turkey	14.2
或者	huòzhě	cj	or	9.1

J

Characters	Pinyin	Word Category	Definition	Lesson
机会	jīhuì	n	opportunity	13.2
极了	jíle	adv	extremely	13.2
吉他	jítā	n	guitar	10.2
寄	jì	v	to send	16.2
记不住	jì bu zhù	rv	to be unable to remember	11.1
记得	jìde	v	to remember	12.2
纪念品	jìniànpǐn	n	souvenir	16.2
家教	jiājiào	n	tutor	13.1
家庭主妇	jiātíng zhǔfù	n	homemaker	13.2
加油	jiāyóu	ie	you can do it! (literally "add oil"; used when offering words of encouragement)	13.1
简历	jiǎnlì	n	résumé, curriculum vitae	13.2
件	jiàn	mw	(used for articles of clothing such as shirts, dresses, jackets, coats)	9.1

Characters	Pinyin	Word Category	Definition	Lesson
健康	jiànkāng	adj, n	healthy; health	14.1
见面	jiàn miàn	vo	to meet	11.1
建议	jiànyì	v, n	to suggest; suggestion, advice	11.1
交给	jiāogěi	v	to hand/give to	15.2
交朋友	jiāo péngyou	vo	to make friends	15.2
交往	jiāowǎng	v	to be in a relationship; to associate (with); to contact	11.2
脚	jiǎo	n	foot	12.1
接	jiē	v	to receive; to pick up; to meet (someone)	16.2
接待	jiēdài	v	to receive (guests)	13.1
接受	jiēshòu	v	to accept	15.2
结婚	jié hūn	vo	to get married	11.2
节日	jiérì	n	holiday; festival	14.2
今年	jīnnián	n	this year	13.1
紧张	jǐnzhāng	adj	nervous	11.1
进来	jìnlai	dc	to come in	9.2
京剧	Jīngjù	n	Peking opera	15.2
经验	jīngyàn	n	experience	13.2
景点	jǐngdiǎn	n	scenic spot	16.1
就是说	jiùshìshuō	ie	that is to say; in other words	15.1

K

Characters	Pinyin	Word Category	Definition	Lesson
咖啡色	kāfēisè	n	coffee color; brown	9.2
卡拉OK	kǎlā OK	n	kareoke	16.1
开刀	kāi dāo	v	to perform/have an operation	12.2
开心	kāixīn	adj	happy	10.2
开药	kāi yào	vo	to prescribe medicine	12.2
看	kàn	v	(after a reduplicated verb) try and see, do something and see	9.2
看病	kàn bìng	vo	to see a doctor	12.1
看法	kànfǎ	n	opinion; perspective	15.2
看起来	kànqilai	ie	it appears, it seems	9.1
可爱	kě'ài	adj	cute	11.1
客气	kèqi	adj, v	polite; to be polite	15.1
客人	kèrén	n	guests; customers	13.1
恐怖片	kǒngbù piàn	n	horror movie	10.1

Characters	Pinyin	Word Category	Definition	Lesson
孔子	Kǒngzǐ	name	Confucius	15.2
哭	kū	v	to cry	11.2
苦	kǔ	adj	bitter	12.2
酷	kù	adj	cool	9.2
裤子	kùzi	n	pants, trousers	9.2
快	kuài	adj	fast; quick	15.2

L

Characters	Pinyin	Word Category	Definition	Lesson
拉	lā	v	to play (an instrument with a bow); to pull	10.2
啦	la	p	(exclamation particle, a combination of 了 and 啊)	16.2
蓝色	lánsè	n	blue	9.2
老板	lǎobǎn	n	boss	13.1
老人	lǎorén	n	elders	15.1
冷	lěng	adj	cold	12.1
离婚	lí hūn	vo	to divorce	11.2
礼节	lǐ jié	n	etiquette; courtesy	15.2
礼貌	lǐ mào	n	manners	15.2
连	lián	prep	even	14.2
联络	liánluò	v	to contact; to have contact	11.2
聊天	liáo tiān	vo	to chat	16.2
聊天软件	liáo tiān ruǎnjiàn	n	chat software	16.2
了解	liǎojiě	v	to understand	15.2
刘	liú	surname	Liu	13.2
流行	liúxíng	adj	popular	14.2
流行音乐	liúxíng yīnyuè	n	pop music	10.2
龙舟	lóngzhōu	n	dragon boat	14.2
旅行	lǚxíng	v, n	to travel; travel	13.1
旅游	lǚyóu	v, n	to travel; tour; tourism	16.2
绿色	lǜsè	n	green	9.2
锣鼓	luó gǔ	n	gong and drum	14.1

M

Characters	Pinyin	Word Category	Definition	Lesson
麻烦	máfan	v, n, adj	to trouble someone to do something; trouble; troublesome	15.1
买单	mǎi dān	vo, n	trouble; troublesome	15.1

Characters	Pinyin	Word Category	Definition	Lesson
慢	màn	adj	to pay the bill; bill	10.2
慢慢	mànmàn	adv	slow	13.1
忙	máng	adj	slowly; gradually	10.1
毛衣	máoyī	n	busy	9.1
帽子	màozi	n	hat	14.1
没错	méi cuò	adj	hat	15.2
玫瑰花	méiguīhuā	n	not wrong; (that's) right	11.1
没事	méi shì	vo	rose	12.2
没想到	méi xiǎng dào	ie	it doesn't matter; it's not a problem	13.1
每	měi	pr	to not have expected or thought of	10.2
			every, each	
美	měi	adj	beautiful	11.1
门口	ménkǒu	n	entrance	10.1
孟子	Mèngzǐ	name	Mencius	15.2
面子	miànzi	n	reputation, face; feelings	15.1
明白	míngbai	v	to understand	9.2
墨镜	mòjìng	n	sunglasses	9.1
母亲节	Mǔqīnjié	n	Mother's Day	14.2

N

Characters	Pinyin	Word Category	Definition	Lesson
拿	ná	v	to hold; to get; to take	14.1
哪里哪里	nǎlǐ nǎlǐ	ie	not at all, (a polite reply to a compliment)	10.2
南非	Nánfēi	n	South Africa	16.2
难怪	nánguài	adv	no wonder	13.1
难过	nánguò	adj	sad	11.2
男朋友	nánpéngyou	n	boyfriend	11.2
闹	nào	v	to stir up trouble; to make noise	11.1
能	néng	av	can; be able to	10.1
年糕	niángāo	n	New Year's rice cake	14.1
年年有余	niánnián yǒu yú	ie	may you have abundance every year (greeting used at New Year)	14.2
年轻	niánqīng	adj	young	14.2
年轻人	niánqīng rén	n	young people	14.2
年夜饭	niányèfàn	n	a reunion dinner for the whole family on Chinese New Year's Eve	14.2
念书	niàn shū	vo	to study; to read	10.2

Characters	Pinyin	Word Category	Definition	Lesson
牛仔裤	niúzǎikù	n	jeans (lit. "cowboy pants")	9.2
努力	nǔlì	adj, v	diligent; to work hard	13.1
女朋友	nǚpéngyou	n	girlfriend	11.2

O

喔	o	interj	(used to indicate a reminder, admonition, or warning)	11.1
欧洲	Ōuzhōu	n	Europe	16.2

P

怕	pà	v	to fear, to be afraid of	16.1
拍	pāi	v	to shoot; to take (photos)	16.2
排球	páiqiú	n	volleyball	10.1
跑步	pǎo bù	vo	to jog	10.1
泡	pào	v	to make (coffee or tea); to steep	13.1
陪	péi	v	to accompany; to keep sb. Company	16.2
配	pèi	v, adj	to match, suit	9.1
骗	piàn	v	to trick, to fool, to cheat	11.2
漂亮	piàoliang	adj	pretty, beautiful	9.1
乒乓球	pīngpāngqiú	n	ping pong	10.1

Q

骑马	qí mǎ	vo	to ride a horse	10.1
谦虚	qiānxū	adj	modest	15.1
签证	qiānzhèng	n	visa	16.2
清明节	Qīngmíngjié	n	Tomb Sweeping Day	14.2
情况	qíngkuàng	n	situation	16.1
情人	qíngrén	n	lover; sweetheart	11.2
情人节	Qíngrénjié	n	Valentine's Day	14.2
晴天	qíngtiān	n	clear day, sunny day	12.1
秋天	qiūtiān	n	autumn	12.1
全	quán	adj, adv	complete, whole; completely	14.2
裙子	qúnzi	n	skirt; dress	9.1

Characters	Pinyin	Word Category	Definition	Lesson
R				
让	ràng	v	to allow or cause (somebody to do something)	11.1
热	rè	adj	hot (as in temperature)	12.1
热闹	rènao	adj	lively	14.1
人才	réncái	n	a person of ability/talent	13.2
人口	rénkǒu	n	population	16.1
认真	rènzhēn	adj	serious; conscientious; diligent	10.2
软件	ruǎnjiàn	n	software	16.2
S				
散步	sàn bù	vo	to go for a stroll	11.1
善良	shànliáng	adj	nice, kind, kind-hearted	11.1
商务	shāngwù	n	business	13.2
上班	shàng bān	vo	to go to work	13.1
上次	shàngcì	n	last time	11.1
上网	shàng wǎng	vo	to go online	16.1
上学	shàng xué	vo	to attend school	13.1
舌头	shétou	n	tongue	12.2
身体	shēntǐ	n	body	12.1
什么样	shénme yàng	pr	what kind/sort	13.1
生病	shēng bìng	vo	to get sick	12.1
生活	shēnghuó	n	life; lifestyle	16.1
生气	shēngqì	adj	mad, angry	11.2
圣诞节	Shèngdànjié	n	Christmas	14.2
食物	shíwù	n	food	14.2
实习	shíxí	v	to intern; to have an internship	13.2
收银	shōu yín	vo	to collect money	13.1
手	shǒu	n	hand	12.1
首先	shǒuxiān	prep	first	13.2
书法	shūfǎ	n	calligraphy	15.2
舒服	shūfu	adj	comfortable; feeling well	12.1
暑假	shǔjià	n	summer vacation	13.1
帅	shuài	adj	handsome	11.1
双	shuāng	adj, mw	double, two; a pair	9.1

Characters	Pinyin	Word Category	Definition	Lesson
双手	shuāngshǒu	n	both hands	15.2
水	shuǐ	n	water	12.2
睡不着	shuì bu zháo	rv	to be unable to sleep	12.1
说话	shuō huà	vo	to talk	10.1
思想	sīxiǎng	n	thought, idea	15.2
死	sǐ	v, adv	to die; extremely	16.2
送花	sòng huā	vo	to give flowers	11.1
虽然	suīrán	cj	even though	13.1

T

Characters	Pinyin	Word Category	Definition	Lesson
太极拳	tàijíquán	n	Taichi	15.2
弹	tán	v	to play (a musical instrument); to pluck	10.2
谈	tán	v	to talk, discuss	11.2
糖果	tángguǒ	n	candy	14.1
特别	tèbié	adj	special	10.2
疼	téng	adj	painful; sore	12.1
踢	tī	v	to kick	10.1
天安门	Tiān'ānmén	n	Tian'anmen (Gate of Heavenly Peace)	16.1
天才	tiāncái	n	genius; talent	10.2
天气	tiānqì	n	weather	12.1
天天	tiāntiān	adv	every day	12.1
跳舞	tiào wǔ	vo	to dance	10.1
听起来	tīngqilai	ie	to sound like	10.1
痛	tòng	adj	painful	12.1
头	tóu	n	head	12.1
头疼	tóuténg	adj, n	to have a headache; headache	12.2
T-恤衫	T-xùshān	n	T-shirt	9.1

W

Characters	Pinyin	Word Category	Definition	Lesson
袜子	wàzi	n	socks	14.1
外国	wàiguó	adj, n	foreign; foreign country	13.2
外面	wàimian	n	outside	12.2
外婆	wàipó	n	maternal grandmother	16.2
外套	wàitào	n	coat, jacket	9.1
玩	wán	v	to play	10.1
晚辈	wǎnbèi	n	younger generation	15.1

Characters	Pinyin	Word Category	Definition	Lesson
晚点	wǎndiǎn	adv	(a bit) later	11.1
万圣节	Wànshèngjié	n	Halloween	14.2
万事如意	wànshì rúyì	ie	(wishing you) all the best (greeting used during the New Year)	14.1
网吧	wǎngbā	n	Internet café	16.1
网络	wǎngluò	n	the Internet	16.2
网球	wǎngqiú	n	tennis	10.2
网页	wǎngyè	n	webpage	16.1
网站	wǎngzhàn	n	website	16.1
忘记	wàngjì	rv	to forget	11.1
文化	wénhuà	n	culture	15.2
吻	wěn	v, n	to kiss; kiss	11.1
无线上网卡	wúxiàn shàng wǎng kǎ	n	wireless internet card	16.1
舞会	wǔhuì	n	dance party	16.1
舞龙舞狮	wǔlóngwǔshī	n	dragon and lion dance	14.1
侮辱	wǔrǔ	n, v	insult; to insult; to humiliate	15.1
武术	wǔshù	n	martial arts	15.2
误会	wùhuì	v	to misunderstand	15.2

X

Characters	Pinyin	Word Category	Definition	Lesson
西方	Xīfāng	n	the West	14.2
希望	xīwàng	v, n	to hope; hope	11.1
西医	xīyī	n	(doctor of) Western medicine	12.1
西装	xīzhuāng	n	suit	9.1
习惯	xíguàn	n, v	habit; to be used to	14.1
喜剧	xǐ jù	n	comedy	10.1
下班	xià bān	vo	to get off work	13.1
下次	xiàcì	n	next time	11.1
夏天	xiàtiān	n	summer	13.2
下雪	xià xuě	vo	to snow	12.1
下雨	xià yǔ	vo	to rain	12.1
现代	xiàndài	adj, n	modern; modern times	15.2
现代化	xiàndàihuà	adj, v, n	modernized; modernize; modernization	15.2
羡慕	xiànmù	v	to envy	16.2
乡下	xiāngxia	n	countryside	16.2
相信	xiāngxìn	v	to believe	11.2

Characters	Pinyin	Word Category	Definition	Lesson
想	xiǎng	v	to think	11.1
想法	xiǎngfǎ	n	idea; opinion; way of thinking	15.2
想念	xiǎngniàn	v	to miss (someone)	16.2
想要	xiǎngyào	av	want; wish; would like	13.2
像	xiàng	v, adv	to resemble; like; similar	14.2
小	xiǎo	adj	small; little	9.1
小时	xiǎoshí	n	hour	10.2
小提琴	xiǎotíqín	n	violin	10.2
笑	xiào	v	to smile; to laugh	10.2
孝	xiào	n, v	filial piety; to be filial	15.1
孝顺	xiàoshùn	v, adj	to show filial obedience; filial	15.1
些	xiē	mw	some	10.1
鞋(子)	xié(zi)	n	shoes	9.1
血	xiě, xuè	n	blood	12.2
心	xīn	n	heart	11.2
新年	xīnnián	n	new year	14.1
行	xíng	adj	OK, all right	10.1
兴趣	xìngqu	n	interest	10.1
休息	xiūxi	v	to rest	12.2
需要	xūyào	v	to need; to want	9.2
学业	xuéyè	n	studies; academics	14.1

Y

Characters	Pinyin	Word Category	Definition	Lesson
呀	ya	p	(used to express surprise like 啊 but follows vowels)	10.2
烟火	yānhuǒ	n	firework	14.1
颜色	yánsè	n	color	9.2
严重	yánzhòng	adj	serious	12.2
眼镜	yǎnjìng	n	glasses	9.1
眼睛	yǎnjing	n	eyes	12.1
眼泪	yǎnlèi	n	tears	11.2
摇滚乐	yáogǔnyuè	n	rock music	10.2
要不然	yàoburán	cj	otherwise	15.1
耶	ye	p	(particle used at end of sentence)	14.2
一会儿	yíhuìr	adv	in a while, in a moment	12.2
一路顺风	yílùshùnfēng	ie	have a safe flight!	16.2

Characters	Pinyin	Word Category	Definition	Lesson
医生	yīshēng	n	doctor	12.2
医院	yīyuàn	n	hospital	12.2
一定	yídìng	adv	certain(ly), definite(ly)	12.2
一样	yíyàng	adj	same	9.1
以前	yǐ qián	prep	before	13.1
以外	yǐ wài	cj	other than; except	16.1
一边	yìbiān	conj	on the one hand; at the same time	10.1
一天到晚	yì tiān dào wǎn	adv	from morning till night; all day long	13.1
一直	yìzhí	adv	straight; continuously, all along	11.2
阴天	yīntiān	n	cloudy day	12.1
音乐家	yīnyuè jiā	n	musician	10.2
邮局	yóujú	n	post office	16.2
游戏	yóuxì	n	game	10.1
游泳	yóu yǒng	vo	to swim	10.1
有关	yǒu guān	vo	to be relevant; to be about; to do with	13.2
有空	yǒu kòng	vo	to have free time	10.1
有名	yǒumíng	adj	famous	16.1
又...又...	yòu...yòu...	adv	both...and	9.1
又	yòu	adv	again; moreover	12.2
鱼	yú	n	fish	14.2
羽毛球	yǔmáoqiú	n	badminton	10.1
元旦	Yuándàn	n	New Year's Day	14.2
元宵节	Yuánxiāojié	n	Lantern Festival	14.1
约	yuē	v	to arrange; to make an appointment	11.1
约会	yuē huì	vo, n	to go on a date; date	11.1
月饼	yuèbǐng	n	mooncake	14.2
越来越	yuèláiyuè	adv	more and more	14.2
乐器	yuèqì	n	musical instrument	10.2

Z

Characters	Pinyin	Word Category	Definition	Lesson
杂志	zázhì	n	magazine	16.2
在线	zài xiàn	vo, adj	to be online; online	16.1
怎么了	zěnme le	qph	what's wrong; what's the matter	11.2
张开	zhāngkāi	rv	to open	12.2
长辈	zhǎngbèi	n	elder generation	15.1
照顾	zhàogù	v	to take care of	15.1

Characters	Pinyin	Word Category	Definition	Lesson
照片	zhàopiàn	n	photograph	16.2
哲学家	zhéxuéjiā	n	philosopher	15.2
这些	zhèxiē	n	these	10.1
着	zhe	p	(added to verb or adjective to indicate a continued action or state)	14.1
真的	zhēnde	adv, ie	really	9.2
正月	zhēngyuè	n	first month of the lunar year	14.1
整理	zhěnglǐ	v	to sort out; to put in order; to arrange	13.1
正好	zhènghǎo	adv	happen to, as it happens	15.1
中	zhōng	adj	middle	9.1
中号	zhōnghào	adj	medium size	9.1
中秋节	Zhōngqiūjié	n	Mid-Autumn Festival	14.2
中药	zhōngyào	n	Chinese herbal medicine	12.2
中医	zhōngyī	n	(doctor of) Traditional Chinese Medicine	12.1
重视	zhòngshì	v	think highly of; attach importance to	15.2
周	zhōu	n	week	12.2
助教	zhùjiào	n	teaching assistant	13.1
注意	zhùyì	v	to be careful; to pay attention to	12.1
赚钱	zhuàn qián	vo	to earn money	13.1
装饰	zhuāngshì	v, n	to decorate; decoration	14.1
庄子	Zhuāngzǐ	name	Zhuangzi	15.2
紫色	zǐ sè	n	purple	9.2
自己	zìjǐ	pr	oneself	16.1
粽子	zòngzi	n	pyramid-shaped dumpling made of glutinous rice wrapped in bamboo leaves	14.2
嘴巴	zuǐ ba	n	mouth	12.2
最	zuì	adv	most (used to describe superlative degree)	9.2
最好	zuìhǎo	adv	had better	12.1
最近	zuìjìn	adv	recently	10.2
尊敬	zūnjìng	v	to pay respect to (used for people)	15.1
作家	zuòjiā	n	writer, author	13.2
做生意	zuò shēngyì	vo	to do business	13.2
做事	zuò shì	vo	to work; to handle matters	13.1

Vocabulary Index (English-Chinese)

The measure words and particles index is arranged according to the lesson. The Chinese-English index is alphabetized according to English. Required Vocabulary is shown in purple. Optional Vocabulary is shown in green.

Definition	Characters	Pinyin	Word Category	Lesson
Measure Words				
(used for articles of clothing such as shirts, dresses, jackets, coats)	件	jiàn	mw	9.1
double, two; a pair	双	shuāng	adj, mw	9.1
(used for hats)	顶	dǐng	mw	9.1
some	些	xiē	mw	10.1
(used for movies)	部	bù	mw	10.1
(used to describe the frequency of an action)	次	cì	mw	11.1
box; a box of	盒	hé	n, mw	15.1
Particles				
hi	嗨	hāi	ie	9.2
(used to express surprise like 啊 but follows vowels)	呀	ya	p	10.2
(used to indicate a reminder, admonition, or warning)	喔	o	interj	11.1
(expresses sadness, sympathy, disappointment etc.)	唉	ài	interj	11.2
(particle used at end of sentence)	耶	ye	p	14.2
(exclamation particle, a combination of 了 and 啊)	啦	la	p	16.2

Definition	Characters	Pinyin	Word Category	Lesson
A				
(a bit) later	晚点	wǎndiǎn	adv	11.1
a large feast	大餐	dàcān	n	14.2
a person of ability/talent	人才	réncái	n	13.2
a reunion dinner for the whole family on Chinese New Year's Eve	年夜饭	niányèfàn	n	14.2
to accept	接受	jiēshòu	v	15.2
to accompany; to keep sb. Company	陪	péi	v	16.2
activity	活动	huódòng	n	10.1
(added to verb or adjective to indicate a continued action or state)	着	zhe	p	14.1
address	地址	dìzhǐ	n	16.2
adults	大人	dàrén	n	15.1
(after a reduplicated verb) try and see, do something and see	看	kàn	v	9.2
again; moreover	又	yòu	adv	12.2
to allow or cause (somebody to do something)	让	ràng	v	11.1
always, all along; never (when used in the negative)	从来	cónglái	adv	11.2
ancient; ancient times	古代	gǔdài	adj, n	15.2
ancient; old-fashioned	古老	gǔlǎo	adj	15.2
apparently; it appears; it seems like	好像	hǎoxiàng	adv	14.2
to arrange; to make an appointment	约	yuē	v	11.1
arrogant	高傲	gāo'ào	adj	15.1
artist	画家	huàjiā	n	13.2
at; toward	对	duì	prep	10.1
to attend school	上学	shàng xué	vo	13.1
aunt (polite term of address for a woman of one's parents' generation)	伯母	bómǔ	n	14.1
autumn	秋天	qiūtiān	n	12.1
B				
background	背景	bèijǐng	n	13.2
bad	坏	huài	adj	11.2

Definition	Characters	Pinyin	Word Category	Lesson
badminton	羽毛球	yǔmáoqiú	n	10.1
beautiful	美	měi	adj	11.1
before	以前	yǐ qián	prep	13.1
to believe	相信	xiāngxìn	v	11.2
bitter	苦	kǔ	adj	12.2
black	黑色	hēisè	n	9.2
blog	博客	bókè	n	16.1
blood	血	xiě, xuè	n	12.2
blue	蓝色	lánsè	n	9.2
to board a plane	登机	dēng jī	vo	16.2
body	身体	shēntǐ	n	12.1
boss	老板	lǎobǎn	n	13.1
both hands	双手	shuāngshǒu	n	15.2
both…and	又…又…	yòu...yòu...	adv	9.1
box; a box of	盒	hé	n, mw	15.1
boyfriend	男朋友	nánpéngyou	n	11.2
to break up	分手	fēn shǒu	vo	11.2
to bring	带	dài	v	12.1
business	商务	shāngwù	n	13.2
busy	忙	máng	adj	10.1
by (passive)	被	bèi	prep	11.2

C

Definition	Characters	Pinyin	Word Category	Lesson
calligraphy	书法	shūfǎ	n	15.2
can; be able to	能	néng	av	10.1
candy	糖果	tángguǒ	n	14.1
to be careful; to pay attention to	注意	zhùyì	v	12.1
to catch/have a cold; a cold	感冒	gǎnmào	v	12.2
to celebrate a festival	过节	guò jié	vo	14.2
to celebrate the New Year	过年	guò nián	vo	14.2
cello	大提琴	dàtíqín	n	10.2
certain(ly), definite(ly)	一定	yídìng	adv	12.2
to chat	聊天	liáo tiān	vo	16.2
chat software	聊天软件	liáo tiān ruǎnjiàn	n	16.2
Chinese herbal medicine	中药	zhōngyào	n	12.2
(Chinese) New Year's Eve	除夕	Chúxī	n	14.1

Definition	Characters	Pinyin	Word Category	Lesson
Christmas	圣诞节	Shèngdànjié	n	14.2
cinema, movie theater	电影院	diànyǐngyuàn	n	10.1
city	城市	chéngshì	n	16.1
classical music	古典音乐	gǔdiǎn yīnyuè	n	10.2
clean	干净	gānjìng	adj	13.1
to clean up; to sweep	打扫	dǎsǎo	v	13.1
clear day, sunny day	晴天	qíngtiān	n	12.1
cloudy day	阴天	yīntiān	n	12.1
coat, jacket	外套	wàitào	n	9.1
coffee color; brown	咖啡色	kāfēisè	n	9.2
cold	冷	lěng	adj	12.1
to collect money	收银	shōu yín	vo	13.1
color	颜色	yánsè	n	9.2
to come in	进来	jìnlai	dc	9.2
comedy	喜剧	xǐ jù	n	10.1
comfortable; feeling well	舒服	shūfu	adj	12.1
company	公司	gōngsī	n	13.2
compared to	比	bǐ	prep	9.1
complete, whole; completely	全	quán	adj, adv	14.2
complex, complicated	复杂	fùzá	adj	15.2
Confucius	孔子	Kǒngzǐ	name	15.2
to congratulate	恭喜	gōngxǐ	v	14.1
to contact; to have contact	联络	liánluò	v	11.2
convenient	方便	fāngbiàn	adj	16.1
cook, chef	厨师	chúshī	n	13.1
cool	酷	kù	adj	9.2
countryside	乡下	xiāngxia	n	16.2
to cry	哭	kū	v	11.2
culture	文化	wénhuà	n	15.2
customs	海关	hǎiguān	n	16.2
cute	可爱	kě'ài	adj	11.1

D

Definition	Characters	Pinyin	Word Category	Lesson
to dance	跳舞	tiào wǔ	vo	10.1
dance party	舞会	wǔhuì	n	16.1
to decorate; decoration	装饰	zhuāngshì	v, n	14.1

Definition	Characters	Pinyin	Word Category	Lesson
to die; extremely	死	sǐ	v, adv	16.2
different	不同	bùtóng	adj	16.1
diligent; to work hard	努力	nǔlì	adj, v	13.1
to divorce	离婚	lí hūn	vo	11.2
to do business	做生意	zuò shēngyì	vo	13.2
doctor	医生	yīshēng	n	12.2
(doctor of) Traditional Chinese Medicine	中医	zhōngyī	n	12.1
(doctor of) Western medicine	西医	xīyī	n	12.1
don't	不要	bú yào	adv	11.1
double, two; a pair	双	shuāng	adj, mw	9.1
dragon and lion dance	舞龙舞狮	wǔlóngwǔshī	n	14.1
dragon boat	龙舟	lóngzhōu	n	14.2
Dragon-Boat Festival	端午节	Duānwǔjié	n	14.2

E

Definition	Characters	Pinyin	Word Category	Lesson
to earn money	赚钱	zhuàn qián	vo	13.1
Easter	复活节	Fùhuójié	n	14.2
elder generation	长辈	zhǎngbèi	n	15.1
elders	老人	lǎorén	n	15.1
email	电子邮件	diànzǐ yóujiàn	n	16.2
embassy	大使馆	dàshǐguǎn	n	16.2
to emerge; come out	出来	chūlai	dc	10.2
engineer	工程师	gōngchéngshī	n	13.2
entrance	门口	ménkǒu	n	10.1
environment	环境	huánjìng	n	13.1
to envy	羡慕	xiànmù	v	16.2
etiquette; courtesy	礼节	lǐ jié	n	15.2
Europe	欧洲	Ōuzhōu	n	16.2
even	连	lián	prep	14.2
even more	更	gèng	adv	9.1
even though	虽然	suīrán	cj	13.1
every day	天天	tiāntiān	adv	12.1
every, each	每	měi	pr	10.2
experience	经验	jīngyàn	n	13.2
to express	表示	biǎoshì	v	15.1
extremely	极了	jíle	adv	13.2

Definition	Characters	Pinyin	Word Category	Lesson
eyes	眼睛	yǎnjing	n	12.1

F

Definition	Characters	Pinyin	Word Category	Lesson
famous	有名	yǒumíng	adj	16.1
fast; quick	快	kuài	adj	15.2
Father's Day	父亲节	Fùqīnjié	n	14.2
to fear, to be afraid of	怕	pà	v	16.1
feeling, emotion	感情	gǎnqíng	n	11.1
festive/decorative lantern	花灯	huādēng	n	14.1
filial piety; to be filial	孝	xiào	n, v	15.1
firework	烟火	yānhuǒ	n	14.1
first	首先	shǒuxiān	prep	13.2
first month of the lunar year	正月	zhēngyuè	n	14.1
fish	鱼	yú	n	14.2
food	食物	shíwù	n	14.2
foot	脚	jiǎo	n	12.1
for example	比方说	bǐ fāngshuō	ie	14.2
for instance	比如	bǐ rú	cj	15.2
foreign; foreign country	外国	wàiguó	adj, n	13.2
to forget	忘记	wàngjì	rv	11.1
from morning till night; all day long	一天到晚	yì tiān dào wǎn	adv	13.1
furthermore; and also	而且	érqiě	cj	12.2

G

Definition	Characters	Pinyin	Word Category	Lesson
game	游戏	yóuxì	n	10.1
genius; talent	天才	tiāncái	n	10.2
to get married	结婚	jié hūn	vo	11.2
to get off work	下班	xià bān	vo	13.1
to get sick	生病	shēng bìng	vo	12.1
girlfriend	女朋友	nǚpéngyou	n	11.2
to give flowers	送花	sòng huā	vo	11.1
to give or have an injection	打针	dǎ zhēn	vo	12.2
glasses	眼镜	yǎnjìng	n	9.1
to go for a stroll	散步	sàn bù	vo	11.1
to go on a date; date	约会	yuē huì	vo, n	11.1

Definition	Characters	Pinyin	Word Category	Lesson
to go online	上网	shàng wǎng	vo	16.1
to go out and play, have a good time	出去玩(儿)	chūqu wánr	ie	11.1
to go outside	出去	chūqu	dc	11.1
to go shopping	逛街	guàng jiē	vo	16.1
to go to work	上班	shàng bān	vo	13.1
golf	高尔夫球	gāo'ěrfūqiú	n	10.1
gong and drum	锣鼓	luó gǔ	n	14.1
to graduate	毕业	bì yè	vo	13.2
gray	灰色	huīsè	n	9.2
great; wonderful	棒	bàng	adj	11.1
green	绿色	lǜsè	n	9.2
to guess a riddle	猜谜	cāi mí	vo	14.1
guests; customers	客人	kèrén	n	13.1
guitar	吉他	jítā	n	10.2

H

Definition	Characters	Pinyin	Word Category	Lesson
habit; to be used to	习惯	xíguàn	n, v	14.1
had better	最好	zuìhǎo	adv	12.1
Halloween	万圣节	Wànshèngjié	n	14.2
hand	手	shǒu	n	12.1
to hand/give to	交给	jiāogěi	v	15.2
handsome	帅	shuài	adj	11.1
to hang	挂	guà	v	14.1
Hanukkah	光明节	Guāngmíngjié	n	14.2
to happen	发生	fāshēng	v	11.2
happen to, as it happens	正好	zhènghǎo	adv	15.1
happy	开心	kāixīn	adj	10.2
hat	帽子	màozi	n	14.1
to have a fever	发烧	fā shāo	vo	12.2
to have a headache; headache	头疼	tóuténg	adj, n	12.2
have a safe flight!	一路顺风	yílùshùnfēng	ie	16.2
to have free time	有空	yǒu kòng	vo	10.1
head	头	tóu	n	12.1
healthy; health	健康	jiànkāng	adj, n	14.1
heart	心	xīn	n	11.2
to help	帮忙	bāng máng	vo	9.2

Definition	Characters	Pinyin	Word Category	Lesson
to hold; to get; to take	拿	ná	v	14.1
holiday; festival	节日	jiérì	n	14.2
homemaker	家庭主妇	jiātíng zhǔfù	n	13.2
to hope; hope	希望	xīwàng	v, n	11.1
horror movie	恐怖片	kǒngbù piàn	n	10.1
hospital	医院	yīyuàn	n	12.2
hot (as in temperature)	热	rè	adj	12.1
hour	小时	xiǎoshí	n	10.2
hutong (old-fashioned alleys in Beijing); lane, alley	胡同	hútong	n	16.1

I

Definition	Characters	Pinyin	Word Category	Lesson
idea; opinion; way of thinking	想法	xiǎngfǎ	n	15.2
to be in a relationship; to associate (with); to contact	交往	jiāowǎng	v	11.2
in a while, in a moment	一会儿	yíhuìr	adv	12.2
in addition to; apart from; besides	除了	chúle	cj	16.1
to be in charge of	管	guǎn	v	13.1
insult; to insult; to humiliate	侮辱	wǔrǔ	n, v	15.1
interest	兴趣	xìngqu	n	10.1
to intern; to have an internship	实习	shíxí	v	13.2
Internet café	网吧	wǎngbā	n	16.1
it appears, it seems	看起来	kànqilai	ie	9.1
it doesn't matter; it's not a problem	没事	méi shì	vo	12.2

J

Definition	Characters	Pinyin	Word Category	Lesson
jeans (lit. "cowboy pants")	牛仔裤	niúzǎikù	n	9.2
to jog	跑步	pǎo bù	vo	10.1
just	刚刚	gānggāng	adv	15.2

K

Definition	Characters	Pinyin	Word Category	Lesson
karaoke	卡拉OK	kǎlā OK	n	16.1
to kick	踢	tī	v	10.1
to kiss; kiss	吻	wěn	v, n	11.1
kitchen	厨房	chúfáng	n	13.1
Kung Fu	功夫	gōngfu	n	10.1

Definition	Characters	Pinyin	Word Category	Lesson

L

Definition	Characters	Pinyin	Word Category	Lesson
Lantern Festival	元宵节	Yuánxiāojié	n	14.1
laptop computer	笔记本电脑	bǐjìběn diànnǎo	n	16.1
laptop computer	笔记本	bǐjìběn	n	16.1
last time	上次	shàngcì	n	11.1
to leave the country	出国	chū guó	vo	13.1
life; lifestyle	生活	shēnghuó	n	16.1
lively	热闹	rènao	adj	14.1
to love	爱	ài	v	11.2
lovely; pleasant (to the ear)	好听	hǎo tīng	adj	10.2
lover; sweetheart	情人	qíngrén	n	11.2

M

Definition	Characters	Pinyin	Word Category	Lesson
mad, angry	生气	shēngqì	adj	11.2
magazine	杂志	zázhì	n	16.2
to make (coffee or tea); to steep	泡	pào	v	13.1
to make friends	交朋友	jiāo péngyou	vo	15.2
manners; politeness	礼貌	lǐ mào	n	15.2
martial arts	武术	wǔshù	n	15.2
to match, suit	配	pèi	v, adj	9.1
maternal grandmother	外婆	wàipó	n	16.2
may you have abundance every year (greeting used at New Year)	年年有余	niánnián yǒu yú	ie	14.2
medium size	中号	zhōnghào	adj	9.1
to meet	见面	jiàn miàn	vo	11.1
melon seeds	瓜子	guāzǐ	n	14.1
Mencius	孟子	Mèngzǐ	name	15.2
Mid-Autumn Festival	中秋节	Zhōngqiūjié	n	14.2
middle	中	zhōng	adj	9.1
to miss (someone)	想念	xiǎngniàn	v	16.2
to misunderstand	误会	wùhuì	v	15.2
modern; modern times	现代	xiàndài	adj, n	15.2
modernized; modernize; modernization	现代化	xiàndàihuà	adj, v, n	15.2
modest	谦虚	qiānxū	adj	15.1

Definition	Characters	Pinyin	Word Category	Lesson
mooncake	月饼	yuèbǐng	n	14.2
more and more	越来越	yuèláiyuè	adv	14.2
most (used to describe superlative degree)	最	zuì	adv	9.2
Mother's Day	母亲节	Mǔqīnjié	n	14.2
mouth	嘴巴	zuǐ ba	n	12.2
movie	电影	diànyǐng	n	10.1
museum	博物馆	bówùguǎn	n	16.1
musical instrument	乐器	yuèqì	n	10.2
musician	音乐家	yīnyuè jiā	n	10.2

N

Definition	Characters	Pinyin	Word Category	Lesson
to need; to want	需要	xūyào	v	9.2
nervous	紧张	jǐnzhāng	adj	11.1
new year	新年	xīnnián	n	14.1
New Year's Day	元旦	Yuándàn	n	14.2
New Year's rice cake	年糕	niángāo	n	14.1
newspaper	报纸	bàozhǐ	n	16.2
next time	下次	xiàcì	n	11.1
nice, kind, kind-hearted	善良	shànliáng	adj	11.1
no wonder	难怪	nánguài	adv	13.1
nose	鼻子	bízi	n	12.1
not at all, (a polite reply to a compliment)	哪里哪里	nǎlǐ nǎlǐ	ie	10.2
not bad; OK; so-so	还好	háihǎo	adj	12.1
to not have expected or thought of	没想到	méi xiǎng dào	ie	13.1
not often; seldom	不常	bùcháng	adv	10.1
not only	不但	búdàn	cj	13.1
not wrong; (that's) right	没错	méi cuò	adj	15.2
nurse	护士	hùshi	n	12.2

O

Definition	Characters	Pinyin	Word Category	Lesson
to offend; to displease	得罪	dézuì	v	15.1
official	官员	guānyuán	n	13.2
often	常常	chángcháng	adv	10.1
OK, all right	行	xíng	adj	10.1
older male cousin	表哥	biǎogē	n	16.1

Definition	Characters	Pinyin	Word Category	Lesson
on the one hand; at the same time	一边	yìbiān	conj	10.1
oneself	自己	zìjǐ	pr	16.1
to be online; online	在线	zài xiàn	vo, adj	16.1
to open	张开	zhāngkāi	rv	12.2
opinion; perspective	看法	kànfǎ	n	15.2
opportunity	机会	jīhuì	n	13.2
or	或者	huòzhě	cj	9.1
orange	橙色	chéngsè	n	9.2
other people	别人	biérén	n	11.1
other than; except	以外	yǐ wài	cj	16.1
otherwise	要不然	yàoburán	cj	15.1
outside	外面	wàimian	n	12.2
overcoat	大衣	dàyī	n	12.2

P

Definition	Characters	Pinyin	Word Category	Lesson
package	包裹	bāoguǒ	n	16.2
painful	痛	tòng	adj	12.1
painful; sore	疼	téng	adj	12.1
to paint; to draw	画画(儿)	huà huà(r)	vo	10.2
painting; drawing	画儿	huàr	n	10.2
pants, trousers	裤子	kùzi	n	9.2
pants, trousers (lit. "long pants")	长裤	chángkù	adj	9.2
parents (formal)	父母	fùmǔ	n	15.1
park	公园	gōngyuán	n	11.1
passport	护照	hùzhào	n	16.2
to pay respect to (used for people)	尊敬	zūnjìng	v	15.1
to pay the bill; bill	买单	mǎi dān	vo, n	15.1
Peking opera	京剧	Jīngjù	n	15.2
to perform; performance	表演	biǎoyǎn	v, n	10.2
to perform/have an operation	开刀	kāi dāo	v	12.2
philosopher	哲学家	zhéxuéjiā	n	15.2
photograph	照片	zhàopiàn	n	16.2
piano	钢琴	gāngqín	n	10.2
ping pong	乒乓球	pīngpāngqiú	n	10.1
to play	玩	wán	v	10.1
to play (a musical instrument); to pluck	弹	tán	v	10.2

Definition	Characters	Pinyin	Word Category	Lesson
to play (an instrument with a bow); to pull	拉	lā	v	10.2
to play ball	打球	dǎ qiú	vo	10.1
to play the drums	打鼓	dǎ gǔ	vo	10.2
point, characteristic	点	diǎn	n	11.1
polite; to be polite	客气	kèqi	adj, v	15.1
pop music	流行音乐	liúxíng yīnyuè	n	10.2
popular	流行	liúxíng	adj	14.2
population	人口	rénkǒu	n	16.1
post office	邮局	yóujú	n	16.2
to prescribe medicine	开药	kāi yào	vo	12.2
pretty, beautiful	漂亮	piàoliang	adj	9.1
pretty; good-looking	好看	hǎokàn	adj	11.1
purple	紫色	zǐ sè	n	9.2
to put one's mind at ease	放心	fàngxīn	v	15.2
to put; to set off	放	fàng	v	14.1
pyramid-shaped dumpling made of glutinous rice wrapped in bamboo leaves	粽子	zòngzi	n	14.2

Q

Definition	Characters	Pinyin	Word Category	Lesson
to quarrel; to fight	吵架	chǎo jià	vo	11.2

R

Definition	Characters	Pinyin	Word Category	Lesson
to rain	下雨	xià yǔ	vo	12.1
really	真的	zhēnde	adv, ie	9.2
to receive (guests)	接待	jiēdài	v	13.1
to receive; to pick up; to meet (someone)	接	jiē	v	16.2
recently	最近	zuìjìn	adv	10.2
red	红色	hóngsè	n	9.1
red envelope	红包	hóngbāo	n	14.1
relation; relationship; connections	关系	guānxi	n	13.2
to be relevant; to be about; to do with	有关	yǒu guān	vo	13.2
relieved; at ease; to rest assured	安心	ānxīn	adj, vo	16.2
to remember	记得	jìde	v	12.2
reputation, face; feelings	面子	miànzi	n	15.1
to resemble; like; similar	像	xiàng	v, adv	14.2
to rest	休息	xiūxi	v	12.2

Definition	Characters	Pinyin	Word Category	Lesson
résumé, curriculum vitae	简历	jiǎnlì	n	13.2
to ride a horse	骑马	qí mǎ	vo	10.1
rock music	摇滚乐	yáogǔnyuè	n	10.2
rose	玫瑰花	méiguīhuā	n	11.1
to row	划	huá	v	14.2

S

Definition	Characters	Pinyin	Word Category	Lesson
sad	难过	nánguò	adj	11.2
safe	安全	ānquán	adj	16.2
same	一样	yíyàng	adj	9.1
scenic spot	景点	jǐngdiǎn	n	16.1
to see a doctor	看病	kàn bìng	vo	12.1
to send	寄	jì	v	16.2
to send (email, text message)	发	fā	v	16.2
to send a text message	发短信	fā duǎnxìn	vo	16.1
serious	严重	yánzhòng	adj	12.2
serious; conscientious; diligent	认真	rènzhēn	adj	10.2
to serve as, to be (a profession)	当	dāng	v	13.2
shirt	衬衫	chènshān	n	9.1
shoes	鞋(子)	xié(zi)	n	9.1
to shoot; to take (photos)	拍	pāi	v	16.2
short	短	duǎn	adj	9.2
to show filial obedience; filial	孝顺	xiàoshùn	v, adj	15.1
to sing	唱歌	chàng gē	vo	10.1
situation	情况	qíngkuàng	n	16.1
size	号	hào	n	9.1
size	大小	dàxiǎo	n	9.2
skirt; dress	裙子	qúnzi	n	9.1
slow	慢	màn	adj	10.2
slowly; gradually	慢慢	mànmàn	adv	13.1
small; little	小	xiǎo	adj	9.1
smart, intelligent	聪明	cōngmíng	adj	11.1
to smile; to laugh	笑	xiào	v	10.2
to snow	下雪	xià xuě	vo	12.1
socks	袜子	wàzi	n	14.1
software	软件	ruǎnjiàn	n	16.2

Definition	Characters	Pinyin	Word Category	Lesson
to sort out; to put in order; to arrange	整理	zhěnglǐ	v	13.1
to sound like	听起来	tīngqilai	ie	10.1
South Africa	南非	Nánfēi	n	16.2
souvenir	纪念品	jìniànpǐn	n	16.2
special	特别	tèbié	adj	10.2
to spend (the holiday, an occasion)	过	guò	v	14.1
spring	春天	chūntiān	n	12.1
Spring Festival	春节	Chūnjié	n	14.1
to stir up trouble; to make noise	闹	nào	v	11.1
stomach	肚子	dùzi	n	12.1
stop it! (used when others are not being serious, poking fun at someone)	不要闹了	bú yào nào le	ie	11.1
straight; continuously, all along	一直	yìzhí	adv	11.2
to stroll	逛	guàng	v	16.1
studies; academics	学业	xuéyè	n	14.1
to study; to read	念书	niàn shū	vo	10.2
to succeed; success	成功	chénggōng	v, n	13.2
to suggest; suggestion, advice	建议	jiànyì	v, n	11.1
suit	西装	xīzhuāng	n	9.1
suitable	合适	héshì	adj	9.2
summer	夏天	xiàtiān	n	13.2
summer vacation	暑假	shǔjià	n	13.1
sunglasses	墨镜	mòjìng	n	9.1
surplus; superfluous	多余	duōyú	n, adj	14.2
sweater	毛衣	máoyī	n	9.1
to swim	游泳	yóu yǒng	vo	10.1

T

Definition	Characters	Pinyin	Word Category	Lesson
T-shirt	T-恤衫	T-xùshān	n	9.1
Taichi	太极拳	tàijíquán	n	15.2
to take care (of oneself)	保重	bǎozhòng	v	16.2
to take care of	照顾	zhàogù	v	15.1
to take medicine	吃药	chī yào	vo	12.2
to take part in, to participate in	参加	cānjiā	v	14.2
to talk	说话	shuō huà	vo	10.1
to talk, discuss	谈	tán	v	11.2

Definition	Characters	Pinyin	Word Category	Lesson
tea leaves	茶叶	cháyè	n	15.1
teaching assistant	助教	zhùjiào	n	13.1
tears	眼泪	yǎnlèi	n	11.2
to tell	告诉	gàosu	v	11.1
tennis	网球	wǎngqiú	n	10.2
Thanksgiving	感恩节	Gǎn'ēnjié	n	14.2
that is to say; in other words	就是说	jiùshìshuō	ie	15.1
the Internet	网络	wǎngluò	n	16.2
the West	西方	Xīfāng	n	14.2
these	这些	zhèxiē	n	10.1
to think	想	xiǎng	v	11.1
think highly of; attach importance to	重视	zhòngshì	v	15.2
this year	今年	jīnnián	n	13.1
thought, idea	思想	sīxiǎng	n	15.2
Tian'anmen (Gate of Heavenly Peace)	天安门	Tiān'ānmén	n	16.1
(to a degree)	不得了	bùdeliǎo	adv	11.1
Tomb Sweeping Day	清明节	Qīngmíngjié	n	14.2
tongue	舌头	shétou	n	12.2
to tour; to visit	参观	cānguān	v	16.1
traditional; tradition	传统	chuántǒng	adj, n	14.1
tragedy	悲剧	bēijù	n	10.1
to translate; translation; translator	翻译	fānyì	v, n	13.2
to travel; tour; tourism	旅游	lǚyóu	v, n	16.2
to travel; travel	旅行	lǚxíng	v, n	13.1
to trick, to fool, to cheat	骗	piàn	v	11.2
to trouble someone to do something; trouble; troublesome	麻烦	máfan	v, n, adj	15.1
turkey	火鸡	huǒjī	n	14.2
tutor	家教	jiājiào	n	13.1

U

Definition	Characters	Pinyin	Word Category	Lesson
to be unable to remember	记不住	jì bu zhù	rv	11.1
to be unable to sleep	睡不着	shuì bu zháo	rv	12.1
uncle (polite term of address for a man of one's parents' generation)	伯父	bófù	n	14.1
to understand	明白	míngbai	v	9.2

Definition	Characters	Pinyin	Word Category	Lesson
to understand	了解	liǎojiě	v	15.2
(used after a verb to indicate a past experience)	过	guo	p	11.2
(used to express the manner in which an action is performed)	地	de	p	12.2

V

Definition	Characters	Pinyin	Word Category	Lesson
Valentine's Day	情人节	Qíngrénjié	n	14.2
very infrequently; rarely	很少	hěnshǎo	adv	13.1
very, extremely	非常	fēicháng	adv	11.2
violin	小提琴	xiǎotíqín	n	10.2
visa	签证	qiānzhèng	n	16.2
volleyball	排球	páiqiú	n	10.1

W

Definition	Characters	Pinyin	Word Category	Lesson
to wait	等	děng	v	10.1
wait until; when	等	děng	cj	16.1
want; wish; would like	想要	xiǎngyào	av	13.2
water	水	shuǐ	n	12.2
way; means	办法	bànfǎ	n	15.2
to wear	穿	chuān	v	9.1
to wear (for glasses and hats)	戴	dài	v	14.1
weather	天气	tiānqì	n	12.1
webpage	网页	wǎngyè	n	16.1
website	网站	wǎngzhàn	n	16.1
week	周	zhōu	n	12.2
what kind/sort	什么样	shénme yàng	pr	13.1
what's wrong; what's the matter	怎么了	zěnme le	qph	11.2
white	白色	báisè	n	9.2
winter	冬天	dōngtiān	n	16.2
wireless internet card	无线上网卡	wúxiàn shàng wǎng kǎ	n	16.1
wishing you happiness and prosperity (greeting used during the New Year)	恭喜发财	gōngxǐ fācái	ie	14.1
(wishing you) all the best (greeting used during the New Year)	万事如意	wànshì rúyì	ie	14.1

Definition 附录 • 英中索引	Characters	Pinyin	Word Category	Lesson
to work part-time; to temp	打工	dǎ gōng	vo	13.1
to work; to handle matters	做事	zuò shì	vo	13.1
to worry	担心	dānxīn	v	12.2
writer, author	作家	zuòjiā	n	13.2

Y

yellow	黄色	huángsè	n	9.2
you can do it! (literally "add oil"; used when offering words of encouragement)	加油	jiāyóu	ie	13.1
young	年轻	niánqīng	adj	14.2
young people	年轻人	niánqīng rén	n	14.2
younger generation	晚辈	wǎnbèi	n	15.1

Z

Zhuangzi	庄子	Zhuāngzǐ	name	15.2